HELEN TAYLOR AND HER FIGHT FOR THE PEOPLE

'She fought for the people.'

HELEN TAYLOR

AND HER FIGHT FOR THE PEOPLE

EDUCATION REFORMER, FEMINIST AND PIONEER OF THE LABOUR MOVEMENT

JANET SMITH

PEN & SWORD HISTORY

AN IMPRINT OF PEN & SWORD BOOKS LTD.
YORKSHIRE – PHILADELPHIA

First published in Great Britain in 2025 by
PEN AND SWORD HISTORY
An imprint of
Pen & Sword Books Ltd
Yorkshire – Philadelphia

ISBN 978 1 03612 571 4

A CIP catalogue record for this book is available from the British Library.

Typeset in Times New Roman 11/14 by
SJmagic DESIGN SERVICES, India.
Printed and bound in the UK by CPI Group (UK) Ltd.

The Publisher's authorised representative in the EU for product safety is Authorised Rep Compliance Ltd., Ground Floor, 71 Lower Baggot Street, Dublin D02 P593, Ireland.
www.arccompliance.com

For a complete list of Pen & Sword titles please contact
PEN & SWORD BOOKS LIMITED
George House, Units 12 & 13, Beevor Street, Off Pontefract Road,
Barnsley, South Yorkshire, S71 1HN, England
E-mail: enquiries@pen-and-sword.co.uk
Website: www.pen-and-sword.co.uk

or

PEN AND SWORD BOOKS
1950 Lawrence Rd, Havertown, PA 19083, USA
E-mail: uspen-and-sword@casematepublishers.com
Website: www.penandswordbooks.com

MIX
Paper | Supporting responsible forestry
FSC® C013604

CONTENTS

INTRODUCTION[1]

In late October 1885, in the South London borough of Camberwell, an extraordinary public meeting took place organised by the Camberwell Radical Club. On the platform, in a packed-out Oakley Hall, on the Old Kent Road, stood a genteel lady of 53. She had been chosen by Camberwell Radical Club to stand in the Camberwell North constituency as the Independent Radical candidate in the forthcoming general election. As she tried to start her speech, pandemonium broke out. There were loud cheers from her supporters and jeers from those who had come to oppose her. The noise was so great, as the two sides tried to drown each other out, that the woman could not continue for several minutes. After some protesters were ejected from the hall, the room quietened enough for her to proclaim her message. In a strong firm voice, a legacy of her time as an apprentice actress, she declared that she was 'determined to go to the poll.'[2] This was a direct challenge to the 1832 Reform Act which had legally restricted the suffrage and election candidature to men rather than women being denied merely through social custom. Despite growing disorder in the room, a resolution supporting her candidature was passed. This resulted in the hall erupting into violence. Supporters and opponents of her candidature fought a physical battle as chairs were hurled at the platform by those who had come to disrupt the proceedings. The prospective parliamentary candidate and her election agent, the suffragist and Great Yarmouth School Board member, Ethel Leach, were hurried off stage to the safety of an ante-room. This was guarded by half a dozen men, using chairs as weapons against those who might try to gain entry and attack the women inside. The women remained thus protected until the fight had subsided and the pugilists had departed the hall. Only then could they leave and return home.[3]

The woman at the centre of this unrest was Helen Taylor. How she came to be on the platform that night and why she generated such strong feelings of both support and opposition to her is the subject of this book. The episode encapsulates the divided opinion her contemporaries had of this extraordinary woman. Helen espoused many causes during her life, women's suffrage, socialism, education reform, land reform, Irish Home Rule and moral reform. Her work on the London School Board, administrating the new state elementary schools, made her incredibly popular amongst the working-class voters of Southwark in Camberwell. In this impoverished borough of South London, the voters returned her three times as their Member of the London School Board and she topped the poll in 1879 and 1882. She commanded huge support amongst the working-class Irish immigrants living there as a result of her work in the Irish Land League, supporting the Irish in their campaign to end the system of landlordism in Ireland and for her advocacy of an Irish parliament in Dublin. Leading Irish nationalists, Anna Parnell and Michael Davitt, supported her parliamentary aspirations as did some women suffragists including Ethel Leach and Jessie Craigen. Leading land reformers also gave their support including the renowned American political economist, Henry George. Taylor also received assistance from her former Social Democratic Federation colleagues, the first Marxist party in Britain. On the other hand, Helen's opponents were legion. Anti-women suffragists regarded her as one of the unsexed monstrous legion of women. During her time on the London School Board she had received hate mail for daring to be an opinionated political woman in the public eye:

> HT
> Disgusting creature
> Man in Petticoats
> Satan's masterpiece
> Her end
> Destruction[4]

Even within the women's suffrage movement she divided opinion as a result of conflict between Helen and her fellow suffragists in the 1860s within the London National Suffrage Committee. This antagonism had increased over the subsequent decades as Helen involved herself in causes which many believed would bring the suffrage movement into disrepute, socialism, land nationalisation, support for Irish Home Rule and this attempt to stand for Parliament before women's suffrage had been granted. Many Liberals abhorred her for her opposition to some of their educational policies on the London School Board on which Helen championed free, secular education and also for her opposition to Gladstone's 1881 Coercion Act in Ireland and her membership of the nationalist Irish Land League. Landowners reviled her for her campaigning to have all land, both urban and rural, nationalised. Finally, some disliked her on a personal level for her strident prickly nature. Yet her nieces and the children of Henry George adored her and found her fun to be with. Ernest Belfort Bax of the Social Democratic Federation, abhorred her:

> Of a thin, spare figure, her self-conceit was unabounded. She had a lofty smugness about her which had to be seen to be appreciated… a preposterous creature with her airs and pseudo dignity.[5]

Henry George, however, regarded her as 'one of the most intelligent women I have ever met, if not the most intelligent.'[6] The *Lancashire Evening Post* classed her, on her visit to Preston to speak on land nationalisation, as 'a lady who may without exaggeration be described as one of the foremost women of her time.'[7]

Who was the real Helen Taylor and which of her contemporaries was closest to the truth in their estimation of her? How had this middle-aged, upper middle-class woman managed to be in the position of being the first woman to attempt to become a member of parliament, and how was it that she faded so quickly from historical memory after her death? To discover this, we have to go back in time, to the year 1831, and chart the course of her incredible life.

PART 1
AN APPRENTICESHIP FOR A CAMPAIGNING LIFE

(i) Childhood 1831–1856

Helen Taylor was born on 27 July 1831 at 4 Christopher Street, Finsbury Square in the Parish of Shoreditch, London, to a non-conformist Unitarian family. Her mother, 24-year-old Harriet Taylor, already had two sons, Herbert, 4 years old, and Algernon, a toddler of 18 months. Harriet had been born in 1807 in Walworth, South London and was the daughter of Harriet and Thomas Hardy. Her father was a surgeon. She had married John Taylor, a wholesale druggist, in 1826 before her 20th birthday. John, a much older man, was 39 when he married Harriet. Harriet and John attended the Unitarian Chapel in nearby South Place where the radical Unitarian William Fox was the minister, and reform politics, including women's suffrage, were widely discussed.[1] From her birth, Helen Taylor was surrounded by people who were working for women's rights, improved democracy in Great Britain, and the extension of voting rights to the working-man and woman.

Today Christopher Street is a busy thoroughfare of modern offices and number 4 is a block of serviced offices on the edge of the City of London, the financial centre of the capital. The row of surviving early nineteenth century four-storey town houses further down this street stand as a reminder of the way it looked when Helen first opened her eyes on the world. Finsbury Square was then a middle-class area in a rapidly expanding capital city; situated on the north bank of the River Thames, not far from the Tower of London and St Paul's Cathedral. Forty years later, in 1885, when many of the surrounding areas were socially and economically deprived, with high levels of poverty, Christopher Street remained affluent and middle-class.[2]

And what of the world which greeted this baby? King William IV, the last Hanoverian king, was on the throne. Earlier that year, Whig prime minister, John Russell, had introduced a bill in the House of Commons which would become the Great Reform Act of 1832. This would grant parliamentary representation to previously disenfranchised growing urban areas and increase the male suffrage to one in five men. It would, however, disenfranchise women by legal statute rather than, as previously, social custom by explicitly defining a voter as male. *The Times* of 27 July 1831, reporting on the bill's passage through Parliament, noted 'the growing impatience in the country at the slowness of its progress.' Hansard recorded the parliamentary business of that day as debating the Reform Bill and listening to petitions received. The Cotton Factories Apprentice Bill, which would restrict the hours worked by children, was debated in the House of Commons on the day of Helen's birth. Also, MPs discussed the Poor Law (Ireland) Bill which aimed to alleviate the appalling poverty of the majority of the Irish.[3] The clamour for social and political reform, influenced by the egalitarian ideals of the French Revolution of the previous century, was gathering pace. Helen would live, in old age, to see a world utterly changed and, in many aspects, unrecognisable from that of the London in which she drew her first breath.

The seemingly middle-class respectable household of chapel-attending Mr and Mrs Taylor held a dark, though gossiped about, secret even before Helen's birth. Harriet had, while pregnant with Helen, met her soul mate, the economic philosopher John Stuart Mill.[4] Harriet and Mill's active interest in social and political reform stood in direct contrast to her amiable, but intellectually incurious husband, who had no philosophical interests or pretensions. Mill and Harriet both attended William Fox's meetings, which discussed social and political reform. They fell in love while sharing their ideas and writings; philosophic studies on how the world could be a better place, especially for women who were excluded from politics and employment opportunities. Respectability had to be maintained to avoid a scandal and social ostracism. The two years following Helen's birth were fraught for Mill and Harriet as they fought to maintain social respectability whilst emotionally drawing ever closer. They both feared that any scandal would destroy Mill's growing reputation as the foremost economic philosopher of the day.

In 1832 Harriet and John Taylor, with their three children, moved to Kent Terrace, a row of elegant townhouses, designed by John Nash and Decimus Burton, near Hyde Park. Mill was a frequent visitor and, during his visits, John Taylor made himself conveniently absent. It is believed the relationship was chaste but acquaintances gossiped and speculated about the Taylor-Mill ménage-a-trois. What made Harriet turn from the husband she loved and to whom she had written a passionate love letter in 1828? It has been suggested that John gave Harriet syphilis, which he had contracted through relationships with prostitutes before his marriage, and which she discovered she suffered from during her pregnancy with Helen. This is very plausible, although there is no definitive proof. Harriet's symptoms and her documented attempt to procure mercury, then a treatment for syphilis, from John Roebuck, a friend of Mill's, is compelling evidence. Harriet later contacted a Dr Tuson, known for his syphilis treatment. Harriet and Mill always insisted that they did not have sex in these years and it has been suggested that the reason may have been that Harriet knew she was infected with venereal disease.[5] Whatever the truth of the estrangement, Harriet and John Taylor amicably separated in 1833 and he leased a house for her in Keston Heath near Bromley, south of London. Was this him making reparation for infecting her with a deadly disease?

Propriety was respected, after the marital separation, to ensure there would be no scandal. Mill was a frequent visitor at Keston but the relationship remained hidden from society as far as possible. Herbert and Algernon continued to live with their father in Kent Terrace while Helen went to Keston with her mother. There were, however, frequent visits to Harriet and Helen from her sons, and mother and daughter regularly visited John Taylor in London. Helen was devoted to her natural father but forged a strong bond with John Stuart Mill who, along with her intellectual mother, had the greatest influence on her childhood years. Mary Taylor, Helen's niece, who looked after her aunt in her final years, recalled Helen talking of her natural father with great affection. As a child she would sit chatting with him while he ate 'his solitary dinner.'[6] It was Helen's father who instilled in her a love of history. Mary believed that John gave Helen unconditional love in contrast to Harriet, who, suffering constant ill health, used Helen as a carer. As a young girl, Helen slept with her mother and administered to her needs, including being in charge of the money purse when they were travelling.[7] Helen, who loved her mother dearly, remembered her as a harsh critic, particularly of her writings, in great contrast with the gentleness of both her father and John Stuart Mill.[8] In 1839, John Taylor rented a house in Walton, Surrey, for Harriet and Helen and it is here where we can discover Helen Taylor as a teenage girl in the 1840s and hear her voice for the first time. She wrote a diary, during her adolescent years, which gives us our first insight into the child who would become such a renowned figure in middle-age as a political and social campaigner.[9] Herbert and Algernon stayed in the care of their father in Kent Terrace. The census of 1841 records the brothers residing in nearby Manchester Street, in Marylebone, at a small private school with the tutor, his wife, a third pupil George Skelton and two servants.

Walton-on-Thames, just 15 miles from central London, was a sleepy village until the coming of the railway in 1838 which made travel to London relatively quick and easy. Today it is a pleasant commuter market town of 23,000 people. In 1839 when Helen and her mother went to live there it would have provided a discreet home which John Stuart Mill could regularly visit without tongues wagging. It was its accessibility which delighted Harriet, both for the ease with which Mill could visit and it being connected by rail to London and Brighton.[10] Mill, at 33, lived with his mother and sisters at 18 Kensington Square, London. His own first house would be in Blackheath, Kent, where he moved in 1851 after his marriage to Harriet, following the death of her husband two years' previously.[11] Life for Helen was isolated in Walton, in the company of intellectual adults, Harriet and Mill, but with regular visits from her father, grandparents and two brothers. Algernon, or Hadji as he was affectionately called within the family, and Helen were inseparable and maintained a close bond throughout their lives. In contrast, Herbert, or Herby as he was called by family, never seems to have been close to his sister and his behaviour towards their mother, and later to his own wife and family, would increase the animosity she felt towards him. Helen, in 1888, wrote that his behaviour towards Harriet had been unforgivable.[12]

Helen was not sent to school. Although this appears strange to modern eyes, Helen's self-schooling at home was by no means unique. At this time, middle-class girls were most often taught at home, either by parents or a governess, though sometimes they attended small private schools.[13] Harriet did not employ a governess for Helen – perhaps to guard against a stranger witnessing Mill's visits. From the 1840s there was a growing campaign for better education for girls. North London Collegiate School opened in 1850 and Cheltenham Ladies' College in 1853, but not until after the First

World War did it become usual to send upper middle-class girls to school. Helen regretted all her life that she had not gone to school and frequently mentioned it, in old age, to her niece, Mary:

> She often complained that in her childhood she had been too much tied to her mother's side. She had wished to go to school, that she might be prepared for taking an active part in life, but her wishes were not granted. Her mother was somewhat strict, and this made her sometimes say that she had been hard, yet most of her recollections were full of affectionate admiration.[14]

Mary believed that Helen was kept at home, as a child, as a chaperone. This lent a level of respectability to Mill's frequent visits to a married woman; protecting both Mill's and Harriet's reputation. Harriet has been accused by historians of being a selfish, controlling mother who put her own needs before her children.[15] Helen recalled later in life, in a letter to her friend Lady Amberley, the lasting effects of an isolated childhood, spent mostly in the company of close family and Harriet's unofficial partner, John Stuart Mill:

> What a long habit of solitary life has given me is a great dislike to be brought close to fellow creatures with whom I cannot feel in harmony, hence my dislike of various or numerous society. It is painful to me owing to the habit of living chiefly with my own family not to be able to either love or respect those with whom I associate, for this reason I never really enjoy the society of anyone with whom I am not willing to be intimate, but children one can always love and the more one sees of them the more one is sure to be with them.[16]

Certainly, Helen and Harriet had a close and often suffocating bond, as seen in letters when they were apart, but Harriet was ill throughout Helen's childhood at a time when early death was a common occurrence within families. That and the society gossip surrounding the exact nature of her mother's relationship with Mill exacted an understandably emotional toll and vulnerability on both mother and daughter. Harriet encouraged Helen's intellectual development and, as stated previously, there were the frequent visits to and from her grandparents, brothers and her father.

A regular pastime of Hadji and Helen, or Lily as she was known by close family throughout her life, was staging Catholic mass at Walton. Helen had a lifelong attraction to Catholicism, although she fought all her campaigning life for a secular society, especially in her work for state education. Her mother and father, though Unitarian, never discouraged this exploration of religion, believing that children should be free to explore the world without censorship. Her future step-father, Mill, would write in his famous work, *On Liberty*, that individuals should be allowed to express their views without censor and act freely, unless harm would be done to others by their actions. Freedom of speech and expression was necessary in a civilised democracy no matter how distasteful one individual might find the actions and speech of another. The basis of Mill's utilitarian philosophy was a morality based on the greatest happiness for the greatest number of people and the morality of an action depended on whether it caused no harm to others.[17] In January 1842, during the Christmas holiday, 10-year-old Helen recorded in her journal that Nicholas, a school friend of Hadji's, came to stay. The company of other children gave the lonely young girl great pleasure and they all built an altar and said mass twice.

The holidays over, Helen returned to her solitary existence, recording in her journal that she had begun to write a play and translate *Cinderella* into Italian. Helen adored the theatre and would, in adulthood, spend a few years as an apprentice actress. Her staging of mass and enjoyment of Catholic church services may be seen as an interest in performance art as well as in spirituality. She records, in her diary of 1841, attending mass in nearby Weybridge and putting on amateur dramatic performances for her mother and visiting family. Her father and paternal grandmother provided a regular audience though her maternal grandmother, Grandmama Taylor, died in August 1841. John Stuart Mill, despite being a constant presence, is never mentioned in her diary. Most likely this is self-censorship or her intimate diaries were expunged, after her death, by her niece, Mary, who would have been mindful to avoid any whiff of scandal to the family name. The probability is that, schooled by her mother, Helen knew that Harriet and John Stuart Mill's clandestine relationship, gossiped over by all who knew them, was not to be written about. In his *Autobiography* Mill commented on how he used to visit Harriet and her daughter 'in a quiet part of the country' and also in London when she was staying at the family home in Kent Terrace. He also wrote of how they travelled together. Mill insisted the relationship was chaste and expressed his gratitude to Harriet for ignoring the untrue rumours of her marital sexual infidelity:

> For though we did not consider the ordinances of society binding on a subject so entirely personal, we did feel bound that our conduct should be such as in no degree to bring discredit on her husband, nor therefore on herself. [18]

The locations from which Mill wrote letters during these years, prove that he and Harriet travelled together. However, Mill's presence went unrecorded by Helen when she was writing about these trips in her diary. Mill has been identified, as accompanying Harriet and Helen on a trip to Normandy, France, in 1844.[19] This trip is detailed in the diary minus Mill. Helen visited the Museum of Natural History in Rouen which she described as a 'momenti mouri' and went to mass at the cathedral, thrilled with the music and spectacle. Her family in England remained in her thoughts and she sent her love to Hadji, Herbert and her father in a letter describing her continental adventure with great enthusiasm.[20] She celebrated her thirteenth birthday on this trip whilst developing an aesthetic appreciation of the world around her. The cathedral at St Ouen gave her goose bumps of delight. 'When I entered the Cathedral, I felt that solitary feeling which anything fine always gives...One wants only it and feels oneself nothing.'

Attendance at Catholic mass continued once back in England. Christmas 1844 found Helen decorating her self-made altar at home with 'green and holly' and on Christmas Day she attended a local catholic service with her mother. She appreciated the music and beauty of the liturgy and would have been encouraged by Mill, who whilst disliking Catholicism on philosophical grounds as stifling freedom of thought in society, greatly appreciated the beauty of all church music.[21] Although Helen also enjoyed the music and the beauty of Church of England vespers, Anglican churches disappointed this young girl, searching for beauty in the world around her. Visiting Westminster Abbey, in late December of 1844, she expressed her disappointment with a seriousness beyond her years:

> If it was put into the hands of a rich Catholic chapter who would put *(in)* stained windows, statues, crucifixes I think it would be the finest church in the world. Protestantism does

> not suit churches. To make it effective, to make one feel it, their services should be celebrated in a sunny forest or on a mountain, then its simplicity would be fine.

The education of middle-class girls in the 1840s would usually have concentrated on preparing them to be the refined drawing-room companions of a future husband. The focus would have exclusively been on acquiring accomplishments such as music and languages.[22] Helen, in contrast, had total freedom to explore the world, and form her own opinions, through uncensored reading. She self-educated by reading all the books on her mother's shelves, often not fully understanding what she was reading but absorbing the ideas and philosophy.[23] Her mother and Mill were constantly engaged in philosophical writing. Harriet had been publishing articles since Helen was a baby; at first in the monthly repository, *The Unitarian*. In 1851 Harriet would publish her most well-known work on women's political and social oppression, *The Enfranchisement of Women*, upon which Mill would base his later work, *The Subjection of Women*. Harriet was as much a philosopher as Mill, a fact that has only been recently acknowledged.[24] Much of his work was in collaboration with Harriet, and later Helen. This he admitted in his *Autobiography.* On his essay, *The Subjection of Women,* he wrote:

> … all that is most striking and profound belongs to my wife, coming from the fund of thought which had been made common to us both, by our innumerable conversations and discussions on a topic which filled so large a place in our minds.'[25]

Such was the intellectual hothouse of Helen's youth and one can imagine her sitting in the room listening to her mother and Mill discussing how society was ordered and how it should be improved, especially for women. And so, a 13-year-old Helen discovered, no doubt on her mother's bookshelf, Mary Wollstonecraft's *A Vindication of the Rights of Women* (1792), and devoured it with delight. 'Why do not people write now? Why is there neither man nor woman who dares to say his or her opinion openly and so that all may know?'[26] What had thrilled Helen was Wollstonecraft's feminist philosophy and her argument that women were only inferior to men as a result of a lack of education. There was nothing natural nor biological to explain their inferior status in society. Harriet, in *The Enfranchisement of Women* argued in similar vein; that women's inferiority was not biological, rather it was a result of environmental factors. It was a social construction.[27]

However, many upper and middle-class parents would have been aghast at Helen's parents allowing her access to such reading matter. Wollstonecraft was 'her who cannot be named' in polite society. This was as a result of her devoted husband, William Godwin, having written a biography of his wife following her death. The book shocked middle-class respectability when he revealed her scandalous life during the French Revolution. Wollstonecraft had had two lovers before she married Godwin and an illegitimate daughter. Supporters of women's rights in the nineteenth century found her too scandalous to openly reference, due to her immoral lifestyle, and she remained undiscussed openly by feminists until the end of the century. And here was young, middle-class Helen Taylor being allowed to read such a fallen woman in middle-class respectable Surrey. It is hard to believe any of the local residents of Walton would have found Helen a suitable friend for their teenage daughters. All that mass going, amateur theatricals and racy reading matter and those visits from a man who was not her mother's husband. How the servants must have gossiped. How isolated she must have felt from her contemporaries.

The New Year of 1845 dawned and Helen continued her routine of reading, her visits to papa and her mass attendance. During Catholic services Helen was not content to be a mere observer. On Good Friday 1845, attending the Catholic service in Weybridge, she went up to the altar and kissed the cross. She read Willaim Ward's *Ideal of a Christian Church* that Easter and opined;

> …and I think it would be difficult to refute his attacks on Protestantism which it seems to me can only be a religion of extremely unthinking or intensely conceited people … It seems to me that Ward ought to profess himself Catholic as I am sure he is in his heart.

Ward, an Anglican priest, attacked the Thirty-nine Articles of the Church of England and did indeed convert to Catholicism that same year of 1845.[28] This was only sixteen years after the proscription on Catholics holding public office and sitting as MPs had been lifted by the Catholic Emancipation Act of 1829. On Corpus Christi day, 24 May 1845, Helen went to both mass and vespers at the local Catholic church, and recorded the happiness it gave her. 'The mass was most splendid…The sermon too was good. Vespers was as usual most beautiful.' Catholicism remained aesthetically pleasing for Helen throughout her life. She admired the beauty and spirituality she found in its churches and services and she examined the dichotomy between her political views and her admiration for the Catholic faith in a letter to Lady Amberley over twenty years later:

> Politically one cannot too much detest Catholicism but socially and personally I must admit that many of the nicest people I have known have been Catholics. There is so much that is exquisitely beautiful and touching in Catholicism that I never think anyone quite safe from becoming a Catholic.[29]

There were unsubstantiated claims that Helen converted to Catholicism at the end of her life.[30] Her niece's diaries make no mention of this and rather show that Helen was too mentally confused in her last years to make such a decision. Her mind cleared from time to time and during one lucid period she was able to rewrite her will.[31] There is no evidence for such claims but, whatever the truth of the matter, the religious philosophy of Thomas à Kempis, first recorded as a child in her personal diary, remained a lifelong favourite and source of spiritual comfort. Indeed both her mother and Mill enjoyed attending Catholic services to hear the music as did many Protestants, according to Algernon in his memoirs. Algernon's great uncle on his father's side, David and his own brother, Herbert, even sang the High Mass in the choir at St George's, Southwark as Protestants, having no 'bias whatsoever towards Romanism.'[32]

Amateur dramatics were a passion for Helen. She longed to become an actress.[33] This was not a respectable ambition for any mid-century young lady who wished to make an advantageous marriage and be accepted in polite society. Actresses had a reputation for being prostitutes.[34] Helen was an avid reader of plays and even wrote her own. She regularly went up to London to the theatre and opera, and made a little theatre at Walton where she and Hadji acted for the grown-ups; her mother, her father, her grandparents and the unseen, but ever present (though not at the same time as her father), John Stuart Mill. At first, she dismissed Shakespeare as 'being more praised than he deserves' but by 1846, aged 15, she admitted a strong liking for his *King John.* New Year 1846, found her reading Philip Massinger, the seventeenth century playwright. Reading his tragicomedy of 1637, *The Bashful Lover*, was a difficult task. She found the sentence structure so complicated. That winter, spending time alone without Hadji who had returned to his father and school in London after the Christmas break, Helen lost herself in books. She read Weber's *Life of Marie Antoinette.* She recorded her critique of the study, identifying the bias and propaganda of the biography. Weber, she analysed, portrayed all revolutionaries as 'fanatics or cruel ruffians' whilst 'instances of sincerity *(are)* all on the royalist side.' The republican fervour, which would mark her life, had its genesis in her reading by the fire in Walton on the cold winter days of her childhood. This was, without doubt, enhanced by the conversations she was allowed to witness between her mother, Mill and the infrequent visits of intellectuals who called on them despite their morally suspect life style. The writer and thinker, John Carlyle, visited them in Walton and Helen liked him 'very much.' Carlyle's wife, Jane, however, refused to befriend Harriet because of her extra marital relationship with Mill which she thought 'a dangerous passion.'[35] Jane worried that a friendship with Harriet would contravene social respectability and would not be 'safe.' It is inconceivable that Helen was not fully aware that they were subject to the approbation of many in the Mill-Taylor social and intellectual circle, including Mill's family.[36]

Helen's pastimes during the winter of 1846 continued to be staging plays, attending mass, reading and public lectures. She read the aforementioned Thomas à Kempis for the first time, whose recommendation of monastic solitude, as a way to spirituality, struck a chord with the solitary girl. She enjoyed Emerson's *Essays* with their explorations of feelings and moods. She also appreciated the beauty and spirituality to be found in the natural world around her. She would sit in the garden at Walton and enjoy living in the moment. Today we would call it 'mindfulness.' On a winter's night, 25 February 1846, which she recorded as being Ash Wednesday, she sat out in the Surrey garden from 5 pm until 8 pm and watched 'a most splendid' sunset which coloured every cloud. She gazed at the moon and stars and concluded that 'nothing in the world seems to me so beautiful as stars.' This meditation followed a day of serious philosophical reading. She had been studying the recently published, Johann Gottlieb Fichte's *The Destination of Man*, an exploration of faith and human consciousness. The following night saw her out in the garden again as the weather was unusually mild for February with a 'soft wind.' The Walton house looked out over the Surrey meadows and the garden would have been pitch black except for the light of the moon and stars. Star gazing would have been a different experience in the 1840s. In Surrey today the heavens are not as clear, being obscured by urban light pollution. Nights, which were too inclement for outside contemplation, were spent listening to her beloved mama play the piano. Her brother, Algernon, in his memoirs, detailed the delight of these musical evenings. Such evenings continued throughout Harriet's life, and Algernon wrote of how much John Stuart Mill enjoyed listening to Harriet play.[37]

The unusually mild weather continued into March 1846 and the early spring saw Helen continuing her self-education by studying a wide range of European writers on history and philosophy. She dismissed the *Memoirs* of Madame du Barry as fake and as 'much too silly' as to have been written by a woman. She disliked Dryden's plays intensely and found Countess Hahn's *Faustina* ridiculous. She was annoyed that the heroine 'talks the most intense nonsense.' The actress, Fanny Kemble's *Journal*, an account of her theatrical tour in America, Helen dismissed as 'silly' but 'amusing.' Helen found it hard to believe that Kemble, on this evidence, could be a good actress. 'Nothing happens without her crying.' What a serious solitary 14-year-old Lily was. With no contemporaries at home, with only the company of adults deep in their own philosophical studies and writings, Helen dwelt in the world she created in her mind through her reading. In March, Hadji came for a short visit which must have been greatly welcomed by his socially isolated sister. Herbert she rarely mentioned in her diaries though she did record that he visited that same month as he was leaving for a trip to America.

Sibling visits meant dramatic performances could be staged. The three siblings put on a play that month in their home-made theatre in front of their mother. They all then returned to London, with Herbert, to visit her father. As ever Helen sought out the natural world around her even in the metropolis. She went out into Regent's Park in the evening and found it very pretty. A trip to London enabled her to experience real theatre. She attended an English opera, called *Crusaders,* and saw a 'splendid actress,' Miss Rainforth. Even during this short trip to the capital, she managed to read *Henry VI Part 2* and *Richard III*. The short visit over and their goodbyes made to papa, Harriet and Herby, and Helen returned to Walton, where her paternal grandpa made a visit and they spent the evening playing whist. The next day, 2 April, Herbert, aged 18, left for Liverpool. The reason for his trip to America was not explained in her diary, Helen merely recorded that the boat journey would take two weeks and he was expected to be away for six months. It was most likely to further his career. Later censuses record him as a merchant. Her rustic solitude, after the departure of Hadji for school, was broken by another visit to her father up in Kent Terrace towards the end of the month. This included a visit to her paternal grandparents and an Italian Opera, *Don Giovanni.* She managed two further trips to the theatre during this short visit, going to Drury Lane on one occasion and two nights later seeing the famous actor William Macready in *Richelieu.* This serious 14-year-old was treated as an adult. Her grandparents came for dinner in Kent Terrace and the family, Helen included, 'did nothing but talk all evening.' All the adults encouraged young Helen in her serious reading. Her grandfather bought her, on this occasion, a small edition of Shakespeare which she could carry about with her.

A few days after returning to Surrey they travelled by train to Worthing on the South coast which Helen found 'a pretty little place' despite the sea not being 'so deep or blue' as in Brighton. They drove out by carriage to Arundel which remains today a delightful Sussex town nestled at the foot of the South Downs. It is the seat of the Duke of Norfolk, a family of recusant Catholics who retained their faith through the Reformation and whose castle dominates the hill above the town. Today there is a French-gothic style Catholic cathedral which is the seat of the Bishop of Brighton and Arundel. This was not completed until 1873 as the catholic parish church of Arundel and it became the cathedral of the diocese of Arundel and Brighton in 1965. When Helen visited in 1846, she came across, while wandering the town, a Catholic chapel and resolved to go to mass there the next day. Arundel delighted Helen as it still delights tourists today, with its hilly streets and old-world charm. She declared it the most beautiful place she had ever seen, nestled in the South Downs, overlooked and dominated by a magnificent stone medieval castle which had been restored in the seventeenth century by Charles Howard, the 11th Duke of Norfolk. During the visit she travelled to Littlehampton, a small seaside town, which she declared, with all her adolescent finality, 'a very ugly, poor and mean village.' Harriet and Helen also travelled on to Brighton, twelve miles east along the coast. The growth of the railway network made all these places easily accessible during Helen's youth. Brighton, located by the sea at the foot of the South Downs, had been a small fishing village. It was now a rapidly growing town due to being made fashionable by George IV at the turn of the century and its rail connection to London which had been completed in 1841. King George IV, when Prince Regent, had built himself a palace, the Brighton Pavilion, a distinctive oriental style building with minarets and domes.

After a pleasant stay, Helen settled back, for the next month, into the solitary world of private reading at home in Walton.

Many middle-class girls were forbidden by their parents to read the growing number of contemporary novels being published. Novel reading was discouraged in many middle-class households at the time. Protestant dissenters and Church of England evangelists, in particular, regarded them as morally bankrupt. The journalist whose investigation exposing the extent of child prostitution in London in 1885 shocked the nation, W.T. Stead, was brought up to regard the novel as 'a kind of Devil's bible.' The parents of the novelist, Edward Gosse, who were Plymouth Brethren, refused to have novels in the house during his childhood in the 1850s.[38] The women suffragist and educational campaigner, Emily Davies, born in 1831, was also not allowed to read novels as a child. She was taught at home by a governess and had an education restricted to singing, languages and drawing.[39] Some in the medical profession recommended that girls should not read novels for their mental wellbeing and went so far as to link hysteria in women with the reading of such books.[40] Helen growing up in the Unitarian tradition of rational thought was given the freedom to read contemporary novels as she wished, most of which she recorded utter contempt for. These included the novels of Catherine Gore, born in 1798. Gore's books dealt with gentility and etiquette and included *Maid of Honour*, written in 1824. Helen dismissed Gore as a writer of 'stupid vulgar novels.' Likewise, she was scathing on the Irish novelist, Lady Blessington, recording the book she was reading of hers, as 'a thing' and 'real trash.'[41] Catherine Crowe's *The Adventures of Susan Hopley*, written in 1841, was, in contrast, greatly enjoyed. This was a best seller and dealt with the mistreatment of women by men. The contemporary social commentary of the novel would have greatly interested Helen's nascent feminist mind. All in all, Helen preferred other forms of writing to reading novels, concluding that 'I find Novels *(sic)* very dull and tiresome after plays and memoirs.' Helen's mother was a subscriber to the London Library and parcels of books for Helen would arrive by post.[42] Her diary records the excitement of their arrival and the disappointment on the days when the expected parcel of library books did not arrive. 'No books from the London Library to my great indignation,' she recorded two days before Christmas 1846.

Respite from the solitary life at Walton came in June 1846 when Harriet and Helen travelled again to Europe. They took the steamboat to Ostend from

Ramsgate. Mill accompanied them on this trip though the diary, as usual, makes no reference to this unmentionable fact. Discretion was everything. The days of the aristocracy taking the Grand Tour of Europe were over but their place had been taken by the growing middle-classes who toured the cultural sites of Europe whilst maintaining a sense of Anglo-Saxon cultural superiority.[43] A Mary Wilson recorded such a trip in a diary of 1847, just a year after this trip of Helen's.[44] Mary describes an eight-month trip to Germany, Italy and Switzerland with her sister and brother. Nowhere in Helen's diary is the cultural superiority expressed by Mary Wilson. Mary recoiled with horror at the peasants and urchins of Europe. In 1842 Helen had visited Normandy in France and Germany. During the trip of 1846 she revisited Germany staying in Wiesbaden, Frankfurt, Nassau and Aix. In adulthood Helen always took a great interest in international politics, both European and American, and had her main home, until a few years before her death, in France. As a London School Board member in the 1880s she kept abreast of European education and best practice which she campaigned for the Board to adopt in its schools. For instance, she travelled to Paris to see the crèches set up in schools as she wanted to set up crèches in London's elementary schools. Helen's sense of a shared European culture from which nations could learn from each other was no doubt instilled in her by Harriet and Mill during visits abroad in her teenage years.

Helen was reunited with her father and two brothers (Herbert having safely returned from America) when they all visited her and her mother during a trip to the Isle of Wight, off the South coast of England, on her return to England in August. Relations between Harriet and her estranged husband were always civil and there was great respect between the two. They were honest that they could not live together. Helen was very excited when her father and brothers arrived by ferry in Ventour. The Isle of Wight became a favourite residence of Queen Victoria in later years who, at the time of Helen's visit, was having Osborne House on the island built as a summer residence for herself and Prince Albert. It would be completed in 1851 and Queen Victoria would die there in 1901. Returning to 1846, after a few glorious days bathing in the sea and visiting the surrounding area, the Taylor family took the ferry back to Portsmouth, travelled on to Chichester and took the train along the coast to Brighton. Helen was extremely pleased to find herself there once again. However, on travelling on to Hastings, she found it 'a most dismal place, poor mean and wretched looking.'

(ii) Treading the Boards as Miss Trevor, actress, 1856–1858

The end of Helen's childhood coincided with the death of her father when she was 18. By the spring of 1849, John Taylor was in poor health. Harriet received a letter from her husband whilst on a trip to Italy and the South of France with Mill and Helen, in which he wrote he was very ill.[45] Helen and Harriet returned to England immediately. To add to the distress, Harriet's own father died while they were travelling back, and on their return to Kent Terrace, they found John Taylor seriously ill. Harriet and Helen stayed by John's side in London to care for him over the next few months as bowel cancer rapidly consumed his body. Harriet's letters to Mill show how tenderly she nursed her husband during his final illness.[46] Herbert arrived from a trip to the United States, cutting short his stay abroad to be with his dying father. John Taylor died in July 1849 having been attended day and night since March by Harriet and Helen. The only glimpse of Helen's life we have during this time is a later letter to Lady Amberley. She describes the long hours she spent at the bedside of her dying father and how she would sit and reread all Berkeley's works quietly whilst he slept. She had first read his philosophical works between the ages of eleven and eighteen and believed she 'owed more to him than any other author.' The tenets of Berkeley's idealism are that reality is a state of sensual perception, it exists only through the perception of the mind.[47] Helen loved 'papa' and her parents had succeeded in enabling their dear 'Lily' to have a close relationship with both parents despite their separation. As she sat by her dying father she searched for philosophical comfort.

After a respectable two years in mourning, Harriet and Mill married at the Registry Office at Melcombe Regis, Dorset on 21 April 1851. Helen and Algernon signed the register as witnesses.[48] The census of 30 March 1851 records Harriet, Helen and Algernon as living in the area and also John Stuart Mill close by at another address. Presumably they had travelled to the West Country in order to be able to marry quietly and got lodgings while they applied for a licence and satisfied residence requirements. Herbert was notably absent. Herbert was now in his early twenties and living, according to the same census, in Furnival's Inn, a lodging house for professional men in Holborn, central London. His occupation is given on the 1851 census as 'merchant.' Relations with him were already strained, as Helen recorded in later life when she wrote that she believed that he had behaved intolerably towards her mother. Herbert, who had had a closer bond to his father than his mother, had been very angry, according to family letters, when John Taylor left everything to Harriet in his will. Herbert and his mother had also quarrelled, after the death of his father, when Harriet attempted to have her brother-in-law, Arthur Ley, removed as a trustee of her own marriage settlement. Ley, a heavy drinker, had been physically abusing his wife, Harriet's sister Caroline. Herbert took his uncle's side in the dispute.[49] Mill's marriage to Harriet also caused estrangement within his own family, who had disproved of his twenty-year relationship with a married woman. Two of his sisters, Jane and Wilhelmina, sent their congratulations but their mother and two other sisters, Clara and Harriet, snubbed the newly married couple by not making the required and expected, in polite society, social call to the newlyweds on their return to London.[50]

Harriet, Mill, Helen and Algernon went to live in Blackheath, in a house which still stands. It is a large detached Victorian villa now very much part of South East London, seven miles from central London. However, when Helen and her family moved to 113 Blackheath Park, the area was still quite separate from the capital with a village feel. Blackheath had been expanding as a wealthy suburb of villas for upper middle-class families since the 1790s. Further development of more modest worker houses had taken place, during the first half of the nineteenth century, as a result of the demand for servants and tradesmen among the prosperous villa dwellers.[51] The Chatham and North Kent Railway had connected Blackheath with Waterloo station, London in 1849.[52] This made it ideal for Mill's commute to his job at the East India Company in the capital where he dealt with Indian correspondence. Algernon, who lived at the house in Blackheath for nine years until his marriage in 1860, described it as 'one of the most distant suburbs of the metropolis, with green fields opposite, farmland on the left and the gardens of Morden College behind.'[53] He, too, was devoted to his step-father of whom he spoke fondly in his memoirs. He recalled the happy evenings he spent, with Mill and his sister, listening to his mother play the piano or reading quietly from Mill's extensive library.

In Blackheath the newly-married Mills settled down to working together on their campaigning and writing on women's rights, though Harriet's frequent bouts of ill health clouded their happiness. Both John Stuart Mill and Harriet suffered from reoccurring lung infections. It has been suggested that Harriet caught the consumption, which it is thought ultimately killed her (if it was not indeed the syphilis), from Mill.[54] The year after their marriage, in September 1852, they travelled to the south of France to find relief in a better climate. Presumably Helen travelled with them. Harriet was taken ill in Nice and was taken to Hyères where they remained until Spring 1853.[55] On their return the couple continued with their writing and Mill travelled up to London daily to India House to fulfil his job in the Examiner's Office of the British East India Company, the leading global trading company which now controlled much of India. The job was not exacting and allowed a great deal of time for his political and philosophical pursuits. Harriet and Mill had been collaborating in their writing since the late 1840s. They had published, in newspapers, co-written articles and letters on documented cases of violence of men on women and children. In 1846, the *Morning Chronicle* had published their account of the suicide of Sarah Brown who had been seduced and made pregnant by a man who then had physically beaten her. Further articles by Harriet and Mill, dealing with domestic abuse and child cruelty, appeared in papers and periodicals in the years up to 1854, highlighting the lack of legal protection for women and children.[56] Harriet had first-hand knowledge of the horrors of domestic abuse from the experience of her own sister, Caroline, at the hands of her husband, Arthur.

It was during the first year of her marriage to Mill that Harriet's most well-known essay, *The Enfranchisement of Women* was disseminated in the *Westminster Review*. The article was published anonymously which was not unusual at the time, though it was republished posthumously as a pamphlet in 1868 in her own name.[57] In the essay Harriet argued for full citizenship rights for women. She called for women to have equality in work, educational opportunities and within the law. She believed that women's inferiority was a social construct. There was nothing inherently inferior about women other than that their biology, as the bearers of children, had been used by a male-controlled society to create female dependency and exclusion. It suited men that women should be dependent with no interests of their own. Harriet would instil this philosophy of the wrong done to women in denying them opportunities on account of their sex in her daughter. Helen's campaigning life would have the need for equality between the sexes at its core.

Helen was now in her early 20s and determined, during these years in Blackheath, to win her mother's approval for her life ambition – to become an actress. Helen's childhood fascination and passion for the theatre had not dimmed as she entered adulthood.[58] Harriet was horrified at her daughter's desire to work in the theatre. Although attitudes were changing by the mid-nineteenth century, actresses were still regarded in middle-class polite society as no better than prostitutes. Harriet had spent much of her adult life avoiding the gossip of acquaintances about her unconventional living arrangements and now her daughter wanted to join a profession which might see the family at the receiving end of further disapproval from friends and family. Helen, however, proved tenacious. She wore down her mother's objections and succeeded in being allowed to take acting lessons from the renowned actress, Mary Anne (Fanny) Stirling. Mrs Sterling, in her early forties, was married to the playwright Edward Lambert and they both went by their professional name, Stirling. She would be active professionally until the late 1880s and had the contacts to launch Helen in the theatre. Fanny became a friend both to Helen and her mother and letters show Harriet's fondness and regard for her. Harriet allowed her daughter to stay with the actress when she travelled abroad with Mill during the latter part of the 1850s, such was her trust in her. With such an ally as Fanny Stirling, Helen succeeded in getting her mother's reluctant agreement to her theatrical ambitions. Mrs Stirling began the search for a theatrical apprenticeship for her pupil. Opportunities were increasing for young actresses. Until the Theatre Regulation Act of 1843, the only establishments allowed to put on plays had been Drury Lane, Covent Garden and the provincial Theatre Royals. The Theatre Royals had been created by government license. The lifting of restrictions on where performances of the spoken word could be held in 1843, led to the building of new theatres in provincial towns up and down the length of Great Britain. These catered for the leisure time of a rapidly increasing population and were facilitated by the growth of the railways which allowed easy travel to the new theatres both for audiences and travelling theatre troupes.

In 1856 Helen's mother finally agreed to pay for theatrical training, her lodgings, and a needlewoman for her costumes, but stipulated that Algernon must accompany her. He had just returned from his travels in Italy, about which he would publish a book in 1862, dedicated to his wife, entitled *Convent Life in Italy*.[59] Harriet stipulated that Helen was not to use her own name but hide her identity under the pseudonym of Miss Trevor. With twenty pounds in her purse and the good wishes of Mill, Harriet and Mrs Sterling, Helen and Algernon set off for Helen's first theatrical position, which Mrs Stirling had obtained for her. She was to serve as an apprentice actress in the northern city of Newcastle upon Tyne, some three hundred miles from home. Helen wrote to her mother that they had found lodgings at 34 Blackett Street, very close to the Theatre Royal. Tellingly

Helen did not address her letters to Blackheath, no doubt to avoid the prying eyes of servants, but sent them to Mill's office in India House. Helen was disappointed on arriving at the theatre to be told that the only part on offer was in a melodrama called *Dred*. She wrote to her mother that she had declined the role, presumably because melodramas were regarded as a low form of entertainment. Harriet had advised her to hold out for parts in Shakespeare. Helen, once away from her mother, soon found the confidence to decide for herself. Within a couple of weeks, she was writing home that it was the experience, not the play, which was important and that any part which allowed her to gain stagecraft and experience in front of an audience would be beneficial. Mrs Stirling had written to the theatre manager, Mr Davis, to arrange Helen's position but he had been ill on her arrival in Newcastle and his daughter had been dealing with the new arrival. On his return to the theatre, he auditioned Helen for the role of Lady Macbeth but warned her that, as he already had two apprentice actresses, he really did not need another. Following the audition, it was clear to Davis that she was too inexperienced to play such a leading figure and, instead, he offered her the part of Mariana, in Sheridan Knowles' play, *The Wrecker's Daughter*. Impatient that this would involve a delay of two weeks, Helen contacted Mr Davis's son, Alfred, who was managing the Lyceum Theatre in nearby Sunderland. Harriet, on hearing that Helen was to play the lead in the *Tragedy of Jane Shaw*, declared it unsuitable. The drama was a popular play, by the eighteenth-century playwright Nicholas Rowe, which tells of the tragic life of a mistress of King Edward IV. Harriet wrote that it was 'a very bad part for a debut because it is wearisome and monotonous and the interest too personal. Lady Macbeth is far more suitable because the interest is in <u>facts</u> not in mere personal sorrow.' Ignoring her mother's concerns, Helen and Hadji moved to Sunderland to lodge with a Mrs Christian Milne and Miss Trevor made her stage debut on 15 December, 1856, aged 25. Writing to her dear mama, she declared that her first night had gone well and she had not suffered from nerves. Hadji gave mama a more nuanced view – his sister had delivered her lines with great feeling and her 'fainting and dying' in the last act had been 'excellent.' However, he felt she needed to work on her speech delivery and her theatrical gestures. He assured his mother, however, that the performance showed 'great promise.' Hadji was soon bored with hanging round a strange northern town all day with nothing to occupy him, whilst his sister was at the theatre, and a few days later he returned to London breaking his promise to his mother to stay with

Helen. Alfred Davis, despite praising her lack of nerves at her debut, only offered Helen a part in one further play. She was to play Bianca in a drama which Helen did not identify in her letters. She was bitterly disappointed. Alfred Davis's father had promised Mrs Sterling that she would be given plenty of acting opportunities but no salary. Helen now found herself with too much spare time, frustrated at the lack of acting experience and the fact that her beloved brother had returned home to Blackheath. She wrote to Mrs Stirling asking her to find another engagement for her after the fast-approaching Christmas holidays.

Christmas 1856 was spent in Brighton with Harriet, Mill and Algernon. Festivities over, Helen travelled north again and New Year's Day 1857 found her in Doncaster. Mrs Sterling had used her contacts to secure her a position at the theatre there. Helen took French books and her favourite periodicals with her to while away the solitary hours she would face in her new lodgings. Hadji did not travel with her. As soon as she was settled into her lodgings at 8 Scot Lane, she went to see the manager of the Theatre Royal, Mr Chester, and his assistant, Mr Courtenay, who was also an actor. They offered her a role in a melodrama, *Memoirs of the Devil* by James Barber. This time, she took it thankfully, despite it being a melodrama. Helen wrote home describing the chaotic rehearsals. There was only one copy of the play which had to be cut up and the parts distributed between the cast. On the opening night the actors were ill-prepared and were reduced to ad-libbing. They talked over each other and this resulted in Helen's tragic speeches being inaudible. However, the following week Helen at last got to play the serious role she so desired. She was to fulfil a childhood ambition and take a leading role in a Shakespeare play as Juliet in *Romeo and Juliet*. Mrs Courtenay was to play Romeo. Helen wrote to her mother that she had worked on her lines one day from 8.30 am until 6 pm, only breaking for half an hour to eat. Helen was disappointed in her performance as her voice was weak after an infection and a number of disasters had befallen her on stage. Mrs Courtney was shorter than Helen and during the final death scene Helen had had to move herself after her supposed death in order to be in line with her dead amour. This had caused howls of laughter from the audience. Helen blamed the error on a lack of good theatre management. Other actors in the troupe were complaining that stage problems at the theatre were worse than usually experienced.

Mrs Stirling again stepped in and got Helen an offer from Mr Glover, a theatre manager in Glasgow. She left Doncaster for Scotland with a light heart, tired of the jealousy displayed by Mrs Courtenay if anyone but herself was given a leading part. So Helen arrived at the Theatre Royal Glasgow thrilled that she was now a professional actress for Mrs Stirling had negotiated that she would receive a wage of a guinea a week, whether or not a part was available. Helen lodged with the manager and his wife at 437 Parliamentary Road. The rent was eight shillings a week which included gas and fire. She found the Glovers, both actors, very amenable. The theatre was attractive and well managed. She hoped that this might be the turning point, and the opportunity she had been longing for. She was given the part of Helena in Shakespeare's *A Midsummer Night's Dream* and due to illness of another actress, Lady Capulet in *Romeo and Juliet*. She was now fulfilling her dream of being a serious actress. Helen knew she had a great deal to learn and watched the more experienced actors carefully to learn stagecraft. This was to be her happiest time as an apprentice actress. She was far from home but she had pleasant lodgings, congenial colleagues and money that she had earned, herself, in her purse. She liked both the theatre and the city. She went to the city's department stores in her free time in search of the perfect gift for her mother, either a shawl or Glasgow worked muslin. She was 25 and fully independent. Her mother's recurring bouts of ill-health were the only worry and she was thrilled when her mother decided to visit her. Mill accompanied Harriet to Edinburgh before returning to his job in London. Harriet then travelled the short distance alone by train to Glasgow, arriving on 17 February 1858. Unfortunately, mother and daughter became very ill, shortly after Harriet's arrival, and both had to return home to Blackheath a few weeks later. Precarious health had dealt Helen's ambitions a bitter blow. She had been doing so well in her new position.

Helen would not return to the theatre until a year and a half later, in October 1858. This was due to her mother's rapidly deteriorating health. Harriet was, in fact, dying and would not live another two years. On 4 May 1857 Helen wrote from Blackheath to Hadji, who was again travelling in Italy. She told him that their mother had 'bleeding of the lungs' and that she had decided to defer her theatrical plans 'for this year.'[60] Helen looked after the ailing Harriet and renewed her friendship with Mrs Stirling's daughter, Fanny. A young girl of 15, Fanny had recently returned from voice training in Italy. She too would become an actress and a portrait of her, from the 1860s, hangs in the National Gallery, London. Helen and Fanny went to the theatre together and gathered clothes which would make suitable costumes when Helen resumed her actress career. A solitary child and adolescent it must have been very pleasing to have the company, in her mid-twenties, of another young woman, despite the age difference.

Mill's retirement from India House, in 1858, gave Helen the opportunity to make plans to resume her theatrical ambitions. The Government of India Act 1858 had passed the administration of India from the East India Company to the British Government, thus making Mill redundant. He could now take a greater share in looking after Harriet, relieving Helen of her caring role, and his pension gave the couple the money to travel somewhere warmer in Europe to ease Harriet's lung problems. This would leave Helen free of family obligations. Mrs Stirling invited Helen to stay with her and her family and assured Harriet that she would look after her until a position in a theatre was found. The Mills set off for Europe in early October 1858 and Helen was very soon able to write to them that Mrs Stirling had secured her a position at a theatre in Aberdeen, Scotland. She would, however, not be paid. Helen's thrill at having her actress dreams renewed was tempered with worry for her now seriously ill mother's health. Her letters to mama were full of concerns for her health. She wrote to Harriet that, if her mama needed her, she must write and she would immediately come to her.

So, Helen, arriving in Aberdeen on 10 October, after a long journey north involving an overnight stay in Carlisle, was filled with emotional conflict. Excitement at the new found opportunity, tempered with constant worry about her mother. She took lodgings with a Mrs King at 36 Union Street who she found friendly: 'They are all so kind and helpful here I am quite comfortable alone,' she wrote to Harriet in a letter of 25 October 1858. Her landlady's son walked her home from the theatre at night and her rooms were light and airy. Her mother had no reason to worry she assured her. Helen found the Aberdeen accent hard to understand but liked the city because she felt it had a French atmosphere. Jessie Pollock, the theatre manager, was very supportive and by mid-October she was playing the Queen in *The Heart of Midlothian*, a melodrama in three acts adapted from a Walter Scott novel. She wrote to mama that she felt that she had performed well but she was worried that her voice was not strong enough. After this success she was chosen to play Sevia in *Virginius* by Sheridan Knowles, followed by Lady Macbeth, in the Shakespeare play. This was Helen's happiest time as an actress. Her fellow actors were supportive with none of the jealousy which had been displayed by colleagues in earlier engagements. The news from France was not good, however. Harriet's journey to the south of

France was slow because she was often just too ill to travel. The Mills had had to break their journey in Lyon because Harriet was too weak to travel further. Helen began to fear the worst. She told her mother that she had researched the train timetables in case she suddenly had to travel to be with her. She assured her mother that coming to France would not damage her prospects at the theatre. She could return to Aberdeen after her mother's health improved. Harriet and Mill left Lyon but were forced to stop again in Avignon as Harriet fell too ill to continue further south. Mill wrote to Helen to reassure her on 21 October:

> Mama is decidedly better today, and has no doubt that she shall be quite well with two or three days more rest. Her head is a great deal better than yesterday, but still it aches with the least exertion, and therefore she asks me to write for her. It has been one of the usual attacks of fever. She has taken the fever mixture and some pills, and it is now over. She is very weak, and does not mean to get up till tomorrow, when she has ordered a warm bath in the bedroom which she says will quite set her up. This is the exact state of the case, therefore be sure there is nothing to be uneasy about. As it is doubtful if they deliver letters on Sunday she will not write again till Saturday. If this reaches you in time to write a word to Avignon on Saturday, it will be sure to be in time, we shall go so slowly: or you might even write on Sunday with scarcely a chance of not being in time: besides that at the worst it would be sent on. And now, Mama says, adieu dear.[61]

He wrote again on the 27 October. He told her not to travel to Avignon and that mama wanted her continue her engagement in Aberdeen. Harriet knew how much the chance to break through as an actress meant to Helen and obviously was trying to avoid her daughter once again having to give up an opportunity because of her health. Academic studies of John Stuart Mill and Harriet have often judged her harshly as a woman who selfishly controlled her children and Mill but, in her dying days, Harriet tried to protect Helen's fledgling career in her chosen profession. [62] She refused to ask her to leave Aberdeen and come to her side. Both Mill and Harriet would have believed it to be yet another health crisis that would pass. Unknown to Helen, on 28 October, Mill wrote to an English doctor,

Dr Gurney, in Nice (the brother of Algernon's future wife Ellen) begging him to come and try to save Harriet's life for she had 'incessant coughing' which stopped her sleeping.[63] Dr Gurney came but Harriet did not improve. It became obvious to all that she was dying and Mill telegraphed Helen urging her to come immediately as her mother had taken a turn for the worse. How wretched Helen must have felt travelling the long distance through Scotland and England and on to France we can only surmise. Not knowing if her mother was alive or dead or what would greet her on her arrival in Avignon must have been heart breaking. Her brother Hadji was still travelling in Italy, gathering material for his book on the convents of the country. Herbert, we have seen, had long been estranged from his mother. Helen arrived in Avignon to the awful news that her mother had died on 3 November in the Hotel d'Europe while she was en route to the south of France. She wrote immediately to Hadji: 'My dear Hadji. I was stupefied by the blow; it is all over… I was too late too late.'[64] Mill was numb with grief. Helen found him, sitting by Harriet's bed gazing at his dead wife. At that moment Helen resolved to give up her independence and ambition to become an actress and be his support. She wrote to Hadji 'I must take care of him now.'[65] Harriet was buried in the cemetery of St Véran. Mill, supported by Helen, bought a small house near the cemetery. He also bought the contents of the hotel room in which his wife had died and installed them in the new house. Mill had a marble tomb erected over the grave, the inscription on which shows his, and undoubtedly Helen's, utter grief at their loss.

> To the beloved Memory
> Of Harriet Mill
> The deeply beloved and deeply regretted
> Wife of John Stuart Mill
> Her great and loving heart
> Her noble soul
> Her clear powerful and original
> Comprehensive Intellect
> Made her the Guide and Support
> The Instructor in Wisdom
> And the Example in Goodness
> As she was the sole Earthly Delight
> Of Those who had the Happiness to Belong to Her

As Earnest for the Public Good
As She was Generous and Devoted
To All who Surrounded Her
Her Influence has been felt
In Many of the Greatest
Improvements of the Age
And will be in those still to Come
Were there but a few Hearts and Intellects
Like Hers
The earth would already Become
The Hoped for Heaven
She Died
To the Irreparable Loss of those who Survive her
At Avignon
Nov 3, 1858.[66]

For the next fifteen years, Helen, or his 'dear Lily,' as he often referred to her in letters, would be her step-father's constant companion as she took the place of her mother.

The house, in sight of the Saint-Véran cemetery, was 'a low, detached house, far from comfortable.'[67] Mill had been too distraught with grief to make any decisions. It was Helen who had persuaded him to stay in Avignon and who found the house and organized its purchase. She was instrumental in restoring him to health with her care and love for him.[68] They began to make acquaintances and became friendly with the newly arrived pasteur of the Protestant church in Avignon, Pasteur Louis Rey and his wife. Rey later recalled the discussions he had with the philosopher on Mill's religious scepticism. Rey felt Mill had 'a sort of Christianity with a feminine Christ. His wife took the place which a believer gives to his saviour.'[69] This deification of his wife was regarded by some of his contemporaries, including Jane and Thomas Carlyle and Mill's own family, as detrimental to his intellect and well-being. A number of his biographers have also found his dependence on his wife a sign of Harriet's overbearing and negative influence. Certainly, she dominated both Helen and Mill in an exacting manner, both desperate to please her and win her affection.[70] However, she faced the displeasure of her contemporaries and possible ostracism for thirty years because of her relationship with Mill. She left a husband, who had possibly infected her with syphilis and who did not share her intellectual passions, but she cared for him tenderly in his dying days and ensured that her children grew up loving their father and spending time with him. She cannot be judged by modern standards which would have left her free to choose her course in life. She had married young and society of the time did not give women a second chance in life. She belonged to her husband. She was brave to risk a relationship with the man she loved and John Taylor is to be commended for helping her live independently apart from him. Perhaps it was guilt at infecting her with a sexually transmitted disease? Harriet's illness made her dependent on those who loved her and they became her nurses and carers.

Mill, despite having siblings, had had no childhood at all. He had been put to the task of philosophy, Greek and Latin, by his philosopher father, James, from the age of 3. Helen had had a childhood of limited contact with other children and adults outside a small tight family circle. Both Helen and Mill had been left by their upbringings emotionally needy. They took solace by clinging to each other after the death of the woman they both looked to for all their emotional needs. They were both psychologically scarred by their early life and Helen admitted throughout her life that her isolated childhood made it difficult to make friends. She believed 'it took ten years to make a friend of a person' which shows her wariness of social relationships. [71] Florence Fenwick Miller, Helen's colleague, in the early 1880s, on the London School Board, wrote, in her unpublished memoirs, that Helen was difficult to get to know.[72] Helen's childhood and early adulthood dependency on her mother for all her emotional needs, resulted in emotional isolation. Helen was lonely throughout much of her adult life. An indication of her yearning for intimacy may be surmised from the fact that two copies of the following poem survive in her papers. One is taken from the *American Spectator* and is dated 17 August 1878 and the other is in a notebook in her own hand:

> Sparrows when they choose to pair,
> Find their match everywhere.
> But the phoenix sadly great
> Cannot find an equal mate.
> Earth, though dark enjoys the honour
> Of a moon to wait upon her.
> Venus though divinely bright
> Cannot boast a satellite.[73]

Helen would have been a middle-aged woman of 47 when she snipped the poem out of the newspaper. There is only evidence of one suitor throughout her life. In 1862 Mill and Helen visited Theodor Gomperz, the German translator of Mill's work, in Vienna on their way back from travelling in Greece. Later that year he visited them in London and afterwards asked if he could come to Avignon, having the intention of asking Helen to marry him He had visited them previously in Blackheath when Harriet was alive. Mill dissuaded him from the visit in a letter that asserted that if he, Mill, 'rightly understood the wishes you speak of' he was unlikely to be successful.[74] There is no account that he actually did visit Avignon. Mill had stressed that they were too preoccupied with work and enjoying the solitude for visitors, nor is there documentation of Helen's thoughts and feelings on the matter. We can be certain, as Mill relied on Helen in all things, that Mill's assertion that Gomperz's proposal of marriage would be refused, was no doubt at Helen's behest. Gomperz had a nervous breakdown after Helen's rejection and correspondence between the two men ceased, although in 1869, Mill wrote to him congratulating him on his marriage.[75] Helen was 27 when her mother died and 42 on the death of Mill. The years were lost when she could have married and had children and a family life of her own. Her life with her beloved step-father, however, provided love (he referred to her always in letters as his daughter), companionship and shared intellectual pursuits which would prove an invaluable experience when sixteen years later she would commence her highly public life as a social and political campaigner. Mill, however, had worried about the effect on his dear Lily, of him being her only support. During an absence from Avignon, a few months after her mother's death, he wrote to her:

> It is a great happiness to me to be a support to you under depression, but it would be very painful to me to think that I should always continue to be the one, as I must necessarily fail you some day and I can never be at ease unless, either by means of persons or of pursuits, you have some other resource besides me, and I am sure my own darling *(Harriet)* would feel as I do.[76]

Mill and Helen settled down to life in Avignon, interspersed with visits to their house in Blackheath, London. William Thornton, a work colleague of Mill's at East India House and subsequently Professor of Political Economy at Cambridge, wrote to the Liberal politician and political economist, Henry Fawcett, describing the domestic life of Mill and Helen in Avignon. Thornton visited Avignon in October 1862 and recorded his visit to 'our friend Mill' who had, by this time, enlarged the house which stood about a mile from the centre of Avignon. It was reached by a walk, through meadows and vineyards, along the bank of the river Rhône and the canal:

> In front of the house is an oblong garden with an avenue of sycamores and mulberry trees down the middle, and at the end a trellis-work supporting a vine which serves as a veranda to the dwelling. This is a small square building, whitewashed, with a tiled roof and green Venetian blinds without, and within, three small rooms on the ground floor and two on the floor above all fitted up very simply, but with English comfort and neatness and a mixture of French and English taste. Two of the lower rooms are the drawing room and sitting room and the third is my bedroom .... Above are the bedrooms of Mill and Miss Taylor, opening upon the terrace, from which there is a view of green fields backed by ranges of mountains.[77]

They breakfasted at 8 am and then, if no excursions were planned, Mill read or wrote until 12 or 1 pm, when lunch was served. No doubt Helen did the same. Afterwards they went for a long walk until dinner-time. The evenings were spent listening to Mill reading a book out loud. Thornton believed this to be how they passed their days when guests were not there. Mill took his friend by coach to see the local sights, including the Pont du Gard, the first century AD Roman aqueduct, and the Roman monuments at St Remy. Thornton wrote that Mill and Miss Taylor went on whole day excursions, in this manner, once a week when alone. He saw how happy Mill was, 'living cheerfully and contentedly' and that 'in his step-daughter he has a companion in all respects worthy of him.'[78] Helen encouraged Mill to return to writing and publishing his work, and took on much of his correspondence. She edited, wrote or dictated this, not as a secretary, but as an intellectual equal. Helen was an accomplished editor and Mill often complimented her on her ability to improve his writing.[79] He admitted, in a letter to Duncan McLaren MP, that the last sentence had been dictated by Helen for '...we also agree in sentiments but she sometimes can find better words to put them in than I can myself.'[80] When they were not working

Helen and Mill went on their long walking excursions, noted by Thornton, collecting plants for they were both keen amateur botanists. Helen organised the building work which provided Mill with a room he could devote to their growing collection of plants and botanical books.[81] They travelled widely in the local area and throughout Europe. In January 1862, they embarked on a six-month tour of France, Italy, Greece and Turkey. In Italy they witnessed a session of the Italian Parliament. They then travelled on to Greece, but determined not to be the typical tourists, they camped out in tents which Helen had designed herself. She had done this so that they did not have to confine themselves to the tourist trail with its inns and lodging houses. They saw no other tourists and Helen wrote to Fanny Sterling that they seemed to be the first travellers to travel in this way.[82] They were accompanied by soldiers provided by the Greek government as protection from brigands and had guides and servants who tended the mules and horses that carried their luggage and provisions. Mill wrote to colleagues back in England describing their experiences, both of the landscape and the politics of the countries they travelled in:

> We have made two expeditions of six weeks each, in which we have seen Greece more thoroughly than it has often been seen: We encamped two days at the foot of Parnassus, and two on the plateau of the mountain, climbed the mountain itself, encamped three days in the valley of the Styx, one day and two nights on Kyllene, saw nearly all Peloponnesus except the northwest corner, almost every foot of Attica and the Megarid, the north of Euboea, the coast of Phthiotis, Lamia, Thermopylæ, Œta, Phokis and Boeotia, Delphi, the magnificent coast from thence to Naupactus and the strait of Rhium, where we crossed over. I look forward to many interesting conversations with you about localities: for instance, I walked from one end to the other of Sphakteria and wondered that there should ever have been any puzzle about that matter. We both thought the beauty of Greece quite incomparable: not so the air and the sky, about which there is as much humbug current as about any purely physical subject I know. The people are very backward, and full of the faults and vices produced by long servitude, but improvement seems to be taking place, though slowly. I hardly know what is most to be desired for them at

> present. The whole people, even the civil and military officers of the government, shew an unanimity in their detestation of it which I should think has seldom existed in any country not held down by foreign forces without producing a revolution; but though all sympathized with the Nauplia insurgents, the people did not join them, but allowed them to be put down, from fear, as it is said, lest brigandage should be renewed, and the tranquillity by which they have begun to profit in their pecuniary interests, brought to an end. Most people however say that if the King does not now change his policy, there will be a revolution within a year, and nobody with whom I have conversed thinks that he will change it.[83]

After three months in Greece, they took a boat to Constantinople. From there they explored Turkey, again camping off the beaten track rather than following the itinerary of the usual European visitors.[84] On their return to Avignon, Helen wrote an article on Greek politics which Mill sent to Edwin Chadwick, the social reformer, asking him to consider it for publication in the *Penny Newsman* of which he was the editor.[85] It was published in the 22 March 1863 edition, under the title *Greece*. Helen wrote of how the dissatisfaction of the Greek people with, not their constitution but their king, had led to him being deposed five months previously. What the Greek people desired was, not revolution, but 'a freely elected assembly which would be representative of the people.' Helen judged that the choice of Prince Alfred as the new king might result in a Republic 'in all but name under a nominal monarch.' This she believed to be an advancement in democracy and much to be wished for. Greek democracy had, in the past, lacked a leader who could champion it and this was the great opportunity to improve it.

A second article written by Helen appeared in the *Penny Newsman*, 3 May 1863, entitled *The Greek Kingdom and the Ionian Islands.* Helen expressed the hope that the Greek people would have the support of Britain in resisting Turkish despotism. Britain had an important role to play in aiding a flourishing democracy following the political turmoil Greece was experiencing. Helen supported, as a means of aiding democracy and strengthening the country, the union of the Ionian Islands with Greece. This was a demand of the Greek people. The Ionian Islands had become a British protectorate at the Congress of Vienna in 1815 which had followed the defeat of Napoleon. Helen feared that British Conservatives might thwart the union of the Ionian Islands with Greece. (They would be ceded to Greece the following year, 1864, after the accession of the new Greek monarch, George). A third article penned by Helen appeared in the same paper on 24 May, *Servia and the House of Commons,* in which she criticised the British Parliament for its lack of support for the Serbian struggle for independence from Turkey.

Whilst Mill and Helen settled in the early 1860s to their lives of writing in Avignon, interspersed with travel and visits to Blackheath, Helen's brothers were both living back in Britain. There appears to have been little or no contact with Herbert who had argued so vehemently with his mother over her removal of his drunken, abusive uncle as a trustee of her own marriage settlement after the death of John Taylor. Herbert, a merchant, had married and he and his wife, Annie, and children lived in the London area. The census of 1871 records them as living in Park Side, Tyndale House, All Saints, Wandsworth, South London. They had three children Herbert, born 1854, Eleanor, born 1858 and Geoffrey, born in 1868. Little is known of his wife Annie, other than the census of 1871 records her as having been born in Devon in 1827 and that her mother, Clemence Daniel, who had been born in Canada, lived with them. [86] Baptismal records show Herbert's wife to have been christened Anna Sophie Worthington Daniel in Dawlish, Devon in 1828 and that her mother's maiden name was David. Annie and Herbert met in London. The 1851 census records her as living in Finsbury, close to Herbert's residence in neighbouring Holborn, and working as an artist/ painter. They had married in Holborn in 1853. Husband and wife would have both been 25 or 26 on their marriage. Whereas Helen would dote on Algernon's children there does not appear to have been any such closeness with her older brother's family. Herbert was permanently estranged from both Helen and Algernon and events, in later years, would strengthen the animosity between the siblings which would continue until all their deaths in the early 1900s.

Algernon and Helen, in contrast, remained close to the end of their lives. Algernon appears in censuses as 'living on independent means.' He continued to live in the house in Blackheath until his marriage. Mill had travelled back to Blackheath without Helen in 1860 and had found the house in a state of disrepair which had concerned him. Algernon, Mill wrote, was studying music. He appears to have found it hard to settle to any one thing and this worried Mill.[87] On 3 October 1860, Algernon married

Ellen Wood Gurney, aged 23. The ceremony took place at the church of St Michael of Thorn, in Norwich. Her deceased father had been the rector of All Saints in the city.[88] She was the sister of Dr Gurney, who had attended Harriet in her final days. Ellen had been born, on 16 June 1837, in Rampton, Cambridgeshire, where her father had been the vicar. The newlyweds moved to a cottage in Limpsfield on the Kent/Surrey border, just twenty-six miles from Mill's house in Blackheath and so within easy reach of Mill and Helen when they were in England. Here their first child, a daughter, Elizabeth (Nelly) was born in 1862. Also in 1862, Algernon's book *Convent Life in Italy* was published. He did not have the intellectual ability of his sister. One review of Algernon's account of staying at sixty convents criticised Algernon's writing as 'a transcript of journals never written with a view to publication' and 'generally anything but entertaining.'[89] *The Morning Herald* reviewer concluded that the book 'very rarely rises above a meagre recital of facts...He seems to want heart and fire.'[90] The following year, 1863, his son, Cyprian, was born. Hadji was a source of worry to his sister. He appears to have suffered depression and continued to be unable to settle to anything even with a growing family. In an undated letter, Helen wrote to Aunt Eliza, her father's sister, following the birth of Nelly in 1862. Helen was relieved that her brother was 'more cheerful than he used to be' but concerned that he saw no way of 'adding to his income by writing or anything else...Ellen has no expectations of increase of means from any quarter.'[91] Helen was close to her paternal aunts, Mary Travers (death unknown), Sarah Taylor (died 1868), Rebecca Taylor (died 1871) and Eliza Taylor (died 1893) who she visited whenever in England.[92] Two paternal uncles, Alfred and David had died in 1846 and 1850 and Aunt Anne in 1852. She also kept in contact with her maternal uncles and aunts, the Hardys, her mother's sister Caroline Ley (died 1864), Edward (died 1869) and Alfred (died 1870).

In the autumn of 1863, Algernon and Ellen moved to a cottage on the High Street in the Oxfordshire village of Tetsworth. Ellen died there in 1864 only eight or nine months after the birth of their third child, Mary. The closeness between brother and sister is seen in the distraught letters they exchanged as Ellen's life ebbed from her. In the early days of September 1864, Algernon wrote a number of letters to his sister as hope for his wife's life ebbed and flowed. It would appear she had an infection and was suffering chronic diarrhoea. On 9 September he wrote that Ellen seemed 'a little better' though a few days earlier it had looked as if 'she was sinking.' The doctor had been to see her sixteen times in fourteen days.[93] By 16 September all hope was lost 'the hand of death is upon her. Yesterday the sweet creature said is "Lily coming to see me?" I answered that you were in Avignon.' He told Helen that it was too late to set off for England and signed the letter 'Your broken-hearted brother.'[94] Family tragedy was never far away in Victorian England. Helen, hundreds of miles away, was distraught. She learnt of the death of her sister-in-law by letter from Ellen's sister. She found what words of comfort she could for her brother, a widower with three very young children to bring up, a 2-year-old, a 1-year-old and the young baby, Mary. She urged him to rally for their sake. 'We must live to work for others when all joy and hope is gone for ourselves. You have your children to think of and to devote yourself to.'[95] Helen loved children and would, during the following years, provide as much love and support to Algernon and his family as she could. The birth of Mary had seemed to lift Algernon, who was still prone to depression, and Helen now feared for him. In January 1864, Aunt Eliza Taylor had written to Helen of the birth of Hadji's 'little girl.' She asked her if she thought he had any means of enlarging his income to provide for his growing family. Helen believed he had not (as quoted previously) but that 'he seems more cheerful than he used to.'[96]

Helen believed that work was the only way to survive the misfortunes of life and, in 1865, her life was filled with new opportunities when Mill was elected to the British parliament as the Liberal MP for the City of Westminster. This ended Helen and Mill's relaxed life of intense writing and going for walks which she had described to Lady Amberley in the April of that year:

> Here in the perfect solitude of our little hermitage, he [*Mill*] works from morning til night with only an occasional few days botanising from time to time for health's sake.[97]

Helen loved animals and kept cats throughout her life which are referenced in letters from time to time. It was on their return to London, just before Mill's election victory on 25 July, that Kate Amberley gave them a dog which Mill called Kalos (which means beautiful or handsome in Greek).[98] During parliamentary sessions Mill now had to be in London. This gave Helen the opportunity to meet with and socialise with the growing number of women's rights campaigners in London. As the daughter of Harriet Taylor and the step-daughter of the renowned John Stuart Mill, she was welcomed into the women's rights movement with open arms. She quickly became a leading player in the campaign for women's suffrage which surrounded the lead up to the 1866 Reform Bill and the Reform Act of 1867. It also allowed her to be near Algernon and her nephew and nieces, though contact with Herbert's growing family does not appear in the correspondence. Algernon had his second book published in 1866, *Scenes in French Monasteries*.[99] Living in the shadow of his intellectual mother, step-father and sister must have been difficult for him. One critic, whilst appreciating his account was 'trustworthy' and 'impartial' found 'his remarks are too often confined to obvious and superficial characteristics...when short of facts he makes up the deficiency by reporting the general nature of his thoughts and speculation.' The 'vague conditions of his own mind' also came into question as Algernon had 'a tendency to mix up the past with the present' and 'quote poetry in the middle of his descriptions.'[100] A telling assessment in the light of Algernon's battles with mental health in the future.

Helen joined the feminists who met at Langham Place in London. The Langham Place Circle had been established by Barbara Bodichon and Bessie Rayner Parkes in 1859. The group were agitating, not only for voting rights for women, but also for women to have greater access to employment and education and better protection in law. The Kensington Society sprang from this group of middle-class feminists, many of whom shared a unitarian, dissenting family background. The society organised lectures and discussions for women on a range of educational, political and social topics, and one of the members, Alice Westlake, invited Helen to join them. Alice would later serve with Helen on the London School Board. [101] Helen's membership of the group gave Mill close contacts with suffragists whose cause he would promote in Parliament. The movers and shakers of the women's rights movement regularly came to dinner at Mill's house in Blackheath, including Millicent Fawcett, Elizabeth Garrett and Frances Power Cobbe. Cobbe recalled that it was at Blackheath that Helen gave her Mill's essay on religion to read before its publication.[102] Millicent Fawcett, who married the Liberal MP, Henry Fawcett, in 1867, retained fond memories of these evenings:

> During the months of the Parliamentary Session which we spent in London, I regarded it as a very great honour when we were invited from time to time to dine with Mr Mill and

> his stepdaughter, Miss Helen Taylor at Blackheath. These were delightful evenings, when we met Mr and Mrs Grote, Professor Cairns, Herbert Spencer and other celebrities, and heard, I suppose, some of the best talk from some of the best talkers in England. Of course, questions concerning Women's Suffrage and the general position of women not infrequently came up, and I remember a discussion between Mill and Herbert Spencer, the latter taking the 'anti' line, and basing his argumenta on the heavy handicap nature had imposed upon women.'[103]

The dinner invites allowed the women's movement to network. Elizabeth Garrett (later Elizabeth Garrett Anderson), the first woman doctor to train in Britain, first met Lady Amberley at Mill's house.[104] Helen had invited Elizabeth to dinner for this purpose as Lady Amberley wished to hear her opinions on how to achieve women's access to medical careers. Helen, who had had such limited contact with people of her own age, quickly befriended Lady Amberley. She was the former Kate Stanley whose husband was a leading Liberal supporter of women's suffrage as was Lady Amberley herself. Helen and Kate became close friends and Mill and Helen were godparents to Kate's son in 1872, the future philosopher Bertrand Russell.[105] Helen was devastated when Kate died in 1874 leaving a young family. Kate and Helen would exchange warm letters of mutual support over the next nine years and visited each other as often as circumstances would allow. It was to Kate that Helen expressed the belief which would become her mantra in her campaigning life: 'There is no other misery left in this world equal to the misery of wretched women and to fight against it is the greatest work of our generation.'[106] Slowly, in the letters between the two women, Victorian formality is dropped until, by 1870, Helen is addressing Lady Amberley as Kate. Kate and Helen discussed reform but they also discussed the Amberley children with a warmness that belies Helen's future reputation as an 'ice maiden.' Helen loved Kate's children and enjoyed their company. She wrote, on one occasion, that Kate should not fear that her children would disturb the peace and quiet when they came to visit them in Avignon, for: 'We like children and do not dislike noise. When we talk of quiet, we mean moral quiet.'[107] Helen, recalling her own upbringing, told Kate that she believed children learn best, not by formal teaching, but by sitting and listening to the grown-ups conversing and that she would have liked to have been a governess.[108]

It was for the Kensington Society that Helen wrote and delivered a discussion paper, *What are the Subjects on Which it is Desirable to lay the Greatest Stress in the Education of Women*?[109] Helen advocated for girls and boys to receive the same educational opportunities by following the same school curriculum. If women are, as society depicts them, 'ignorant, frivolous, shallow, weak, timid, partial; incapable of precision, justice, or rational argument; governable only as dogs are by the affection,'[110] Helen believed this to be as a result of their inferior education. If, however, it was true that men and women were not alike in their interests or abilities than this would manifest itself and no harm done:

> It seems to me therefore that for girls as for boys all subjects should be open; that what subjects are to be peculiarly followed up ought to depend on each individual case; and that to confine the education of women within predetermined bounds creates a class whose defects are the evident result of their teaching.[111]

This would be central to her later campaigns on the London School Board and the paper has echoes of her mother's philosophy set out in her article, *The Enfranchisement of Women*, Mill's *The Subjection of Women* and Wollstonecraft's *A Vindication of the Rights of Woman*, on the social construction of women and that their actual nature and abilities remain unknown.

Helen, during Mill's years as an MP, 1865–8, had a number of feminist articles published, In September 1866, her article *Women and Criticism* appeared in *Macmillan's Magazine*. This critiqued both the social and legal constraints imposed on women. It was published under her initials H.T.[112] The January 1867 edition of the *Westminster Review,* a paper established by utilitarian philosophers Jeremy Bentham and James Mill (John Stuart Mill's father), published Helen's article, *The Ladies' Petition*. It appeared anonymously, which was not unusual, as it was common for articles to appear in journals and newspapers without a byline. It was republished as a pamphlet, later that same year, under the title, *The Claim of Englishwomen to the Suffrage Constitutionally Considered.*[113] Although she believed that both unmarried and married women should be enfranchised using the same property qualifying criteria which were applied to men, in her publications she advocated only for single women, being careful not to go further than public opinion could accept. At the time social mores insisted that married women's interests were included in giving voting rights to their male relatives.[114] As women's suffrage would not happen without the support of the male MPs in parliament it was necessary not to move faster in suffrage demands than male legislators and society could countenance.

So Mill and his stepdaughter settled into the campaigning circles of London. As Mill entered his second year as an MP in 1866, the Liberal Reform Bill was before Parliament. This had the intent of increasing the suffrage among 'respectable' working men but opposition to it, including many Liberals, led to the resignation of the Prime Minister, Lord John Russell, the father-in-law of Lady Amberley. It would be the Conservative 1867 Reform Bill which would increase the number of voters among the working-class of urban areas, giving the vote to the male head of the household. During the debates on the doomed 1866 bill, Helen wrote to Barbara Bodichon giving her support to the idea of petitioning Parliament to include women in the Reform Bill. 'If a tolerably numerous petition can be got up, my father will gladly undertake to present it.'[115] She expected the petition to fail but it would get women's suffrage on the political agenda. The petition gathered over 14,000 signatures and Helen asked Barbara to send it direct to Mill at the Houses of Parliament.[116] When the 1866 bill was defeated and the Tories formed a government, they introduced the 2nd Reform Act of 1867. On 20 May 1867, Mill was unsuccessful in his attempt to amend the bill by having the word *man* replaced by the word *person* in the text of the bill. The word 'person' included women in its meaning and so women would have been granted the vote on the same qualifying criteria as men.[117] Mill's amendment was defeated by 196 votes to 73 and women were excluded from the 1867 Reform Act which gave the vote to one in three men who qualified under the property requirements (male heads of household and lodgers who paid £10 per year in rent).[118]

In 1867 Helen initiated the setting up of the London National Society for Women's Suffrage following the creation, the previous year, of The Manchester Suffrage Committee by Lydia Becker:

> The existence of the society is due to my daughter's initiative; its constitution was planned entirely by her, and she was the soul of the movement during its first year, though delicate health and superabundant occupation made her decline to become a member of the executive committee.[119]

It was Helen. according to Mill in his autobiography, who persuaded Florence Nightingale and Mary Carpenter to join the London National Society for Women's Suffrage by writing appeals to them that he merely signed. Helen and Mill have been blamed for ultimately causing a split in this organisation through their uncompromising and autocratic leadership. Helen has been criticised for causing arguments with her prickly personality.[120] This ignores differences in political and philosophical ideology. Liberals, including Mill, Helen and Clementia Taylor, called for the movement to campaign for both married and unmarried women to obtain the vote whilst Conservatives including Emily Davies and Frances Power Cobbe believed that current political and social opinion would only accept the vote for unmarried women. Helen, we have seen, conceded this in her writing in which she was careful to be circumspect in her demands. Helen could even rile her fellow Liberals and Lydia Becker, the leader of the Manchester Suffrage Society, broke off contact with the sister group in London due to not getting along with Helen.[121] There was great political and philosophical diversity in the women who were on the first executive of the London National Society for Women's Suffrage and clashes were inevitable. For instance, Frances Power Cobbe's Christian intuitive ethics opposed the inductive ethical stance of utilitarianism and could not accommodate Mill's core philosophy. For Cobbe morality came from God and existed independently of external materialist evidence, whereas for utilitarians morality was based on materialist empirical evidence. Mankind strove to be happy so morality was based, for utilitarians, not on an invisible God, but on whether an action would increase the amount of happiness in the world without harming others. Cobbe has been reinstated recently into the philosophical canon as an ethicist who emphasised the importance of duty as the mainstay of morality over a morality based on the pursuit of utilitarian happiness.[122] Helen and Mill's desire for a women-only committee for the group was a further cause of argument. Barbara Bodichon and others on the committee of the London National Society for Women's Suffrage were vehemently against this. Helen tried to explain the rationale behind excluding men to Barbara Bodichon: 'But to admit men into the governing body is merely to give over the whole credit into their hands, leaving women in their unusual and proper subordinate condition.'[123] Barbara disagreed and turned down this request on the grounds that a women-only committee would damage the women's suffrage campaign for the next twenty years and that Clementia Taylor was in favour of men being included and 'so are <u>all</u> the other women.'[124] In the end, it was political differences which were largely to blame for the split which left the society in the hands of Helen, Mill and Clementia Taylor.[125]

As well as suffrage, Mill and Helen were vocal in the furore surrounding the British Governor's actions in Jamaica which became the most divisive political controversy of the day. In 1865, Governor John Eyre had brutally quashed a riot in Jamaica. He was responsible for the hanging of a member of the Jamaican House of Assembly, the flogging of 600 men and women and the burning of 1,000 huts. Those who defended Eyre's actions, included the historian and philosopher Thomas Carlyle, the poet Alfred Tennyson and novelist Charles Dickens. Thomas Carlyle, formed an Eyre Defence Committee. Mill, in contrast, joined the Jamaica Committee which wanted Eyre to be charged with murder and brought to trial.[126] Other opponents of Eyre's action included the Liberal MP John Bright and the scientist Charles Darwin. Helen saw a pattern in the colonial violence. It had previously been tolerated by the English people at home when it had been employed in India:

> The Jamaican atrocities seem to me the natural consequence of those committed in India. Public opinion applauded those and so encouraged English people to fall back into the savagery and barbarism which is natural to all who don't cultivate anything better.[127]

Helen, in contrast to a great number of her contemporaries, did not subscribe to the view that the Anglo-Saxon race was superiors to all others. She commented, in the same letter, that Eyre had 'an inflated idea of his own consequence and value, and that of other white people like himself, to be maintained at all risks.' Governor Eyre was twice arrested for his actions but never tried. It was believed, by many, that Mill lost his seat in the 1868 election because of his public opposition to the actions of Eyre.[128] He had received written anonymous death threats following his high profile campaign for Eyre to be charged with murder.[129] Mill wrote in his *Autobiography* that 'there was much more at stake than only justice to negroes, the British dependencies and, eventually, perhaps, Great Britain itself, were to be under the government of law or of military licence.'[130] For both Mill and Helen their stance was a defence of democracy against the rule of tyranny.

When Mill lost his parliamentary seat, in 1868, Mill and Helen welcomed the chance to escape London and return to living in Avignon where they would be based until Mill's death in 1873. Although Helen had supported Mill putting himself forward for re-election, the freedom his defeat gave to organise their lives as they wished, came as a relief to both.[131] In Avignon, they quickly settled to working together on political and social writings. Helen was busy editing the *Posthumous Works of Thomas Buckle*, the historian, for publication. It would take her five years as Helen and Mill continued to work for women's suffrage. Arguments in the movement continued and Helen was scathing about the recently established Central Committee (for women's suffrage) as it 'consists very largely of rash people whose judgement and prudence cannot be trusted.'[132] During the last five years of Mill's life, he and Helen campaigned against the Contagious Diseases Acts. (Helen would oppose them until their repeal in 1886 and would join the newly formed Moral Reform Union, in 1881). She joined the London Committee of the Ladies Association for the Repeal of the Contagious Diseases Act when it was established in 1869 by Josephine Butler and Elizabeth Wolstenholme-Elmy. It had been Harriet Martineau, in 1863, who had first publicly raised concern over of the Acts. [133] The Contagious Diseases Acts consisted of three Acts which were passed in the House of Commons, in 1864, 1866 and 1869. In 1871 the Acts were extended to India. The government was attempting, by the Acts, to improve the health of its army by reducing the cases of syphilis and other sexually transmitted diseases suffered by soldiers. It gave authorities the power to arrest women, living near certain ports and garrisons, on the mere suspicion that they could be prostitutes. Detained women were then medically examined, against their will, for evidence of venereal disease. Infected women were then legally held in lock hospitals. Those who resisted a physical examination could be imprisoned. Men frequenting brothels suffered no such checks.

In 1870, Helen wrote an unpublished piece on the Acts in which she argued that forcing only women to undergo medical examination for venereal disease allowed men 'to lead bad lives without suffering, and this is selfish but not legitimate.[134] She believed that this resulted in 'supplying a class of women for men's wants, as public houses and public carriages are supplied, and makes it so mischievous in its influence upon the moral ideas of men and boys.'[135] It is likely that this manuscript was a speech she gave during that year, in which she also went to two protest meetings and also read the House of Commons and the House of Lords reports on the Contagious Diseases Acts.[136] Such was the extent of public disquiet over the Acts that a Royal Commission was created in 1871 to report on them. Mill gave evidence before this commission at which he voiced his opposition to the Acts on the grounds that they removed personal liberty 'from all women.' If women faced medical examination, then the men who used brothels should be subject to the same. Though even this, he made clear, would not satisfy him and the acts should be repealed.[137] For Mill and Helen the acts were an affront to women's rights. The law should deal with men and women equally. This is seen in a letter from Mill to the Secretary of the National Purity Society in 1870, in which he opposed the acts as 'utterly depraving to the mass of the population (not to speak of the gross inequality between men and women).'[138] A decade later, when she was living in London and had joined the Moral Reform Union, Helen had already acquired a detailed knowledge and understanding of the history and working of the Contagious Diseases Acts.

When not working, Mill and Helen travelled in Europe or enjoyed the terrace at Avignon. They revelled in the freedom that the loss of his parliamentary seat had given them. Helen wrote to Kate Amberley how much they were enjoying the nightingales and turtle doves singing in the garden as they sat in their 'open air sitting room.'[139] Helen was working hard on editing Buckle, and Mill was busy finishing his *The Subjection of Women* which was published in 1869. Lady Amberley and her three children visited their idyll in October of the same year. In 1870 the Franco-Prussian war made them fearful of staying in the south of France and they prolonged a stay in Blackheath to avoid the unrest. Helen confided to Kate Amberley that she feared for Mill's safety if he were at home in Avignon. Being Liberals they sided, not with France, but Germany.[140] Prussia at that time was regarded as a beacon of democracy and British Liberals cheered them on to victory against, what they saw as the despotism of the French Second Empire, headed by Napoleon III, a nephew of Napoleon Bonaparte. Charles-Louis Napoleon had been elected as the French President in 1848 but had seized power to become Emperor in 1852. It had been the French who had declared war on Prussia. The Prussian victory, following a six-month war, would unite the German states into one nation. Helen and Mill were adamant that the war was French aggression against a democratic state. The blame laid firmly at the feet of the anti-democratic actions of Emperor Napoleon. 'Prussians are fighting for their own liberty and that of Europe.'[141] Prussia, was fighting Napoleon, Helen emphasised, not the French people.

During their enforced stay in Blackheath, in 1870, Helen gave her first major speech in public at a meeting organised by the National Society for Women's Suffrage. She had spoken within the safe space of the Kensington Society but this was a large London suffrage meeting. She was incredibly nervous about the event, confiding in Kate Amberley that 'the affair of the speech is such a gigantic enterprise to me,' and that she would much rather not appear on the public stage.[142] We have a glimpse of Helen's physical appearance, aged 38, from a letter that the suffragist Catherine Winkworth wrote to her sister about the meeting:

> Miss Helen Taylor made a most remarkable speech. She is a slight young woman with long, thin, delicate features, clear dark eyes and dark hair, which she wears in long bands on her cheeks, fashionably dressed in slight mourning, speaks off the platform in a high, thin voice, very shyly with an embarrassed air, on the platform she was really eloquent.[143]

Mill had lived in Blackheath for twenty years, since the time of his marriage. It had also been Helen's and Hadji's home. In 1871, Mill and Helen, worried about its upkeep, decided to give it up and rent a smaller place in central London. Early in the spring of 1871, Helen wrote to Lady Amberley that she had found somewhere suitable; a large apartment at 10 Albert Mansions, Victoria Street.[144] It was a few minutes' walk from Victoria railway station and obviously more conveniently placed for London meetings than the Blackheath house. Mill was now 65 and in poor health. Helen worried over his loss of weight and his recurring chest problems.[145] The burden of organising the move fell to Helen. She was pragmatic, considering the new flat as 'more of a hotel than anything else.'[146] They would have three sitting rooms and two bedrooms on the top floor of a Victorian mansion, now demolished. Helen had decided to buy no 'pretty furniture' and not to spend any money making the rooms less 'prosaic' The flat was merely to be a functional place to stay when they were in London. The rooms would 'leave us free to pass most of our time in Avignon'. Herbert and Annie were living just across the river in Wandsworth, South London with their growing family. Herbert junior was 17, Eleanor 13 and Geoffrey 3.[147] Despite her love of children, the rift between Herbert's family and Helen had not healed and there is no evidence of social interaction between them. Her beloved Hadji was still living in Tetsworth. The census of 1871 records him in a property in the High Street with the three children, Nelly now aged 9, Cyprian 8 and Mary 7. He appears to have been living on his trust money from his mother's will as no occupation is given but it allowed him to employ two servants, Mary and Rosetta. The new flat in Victoria secured, Mill and Helen gave up the house in Blackheath and said goodbye to their trusted servants, who, she assured Kate Amberley, were all provided for or had found new positions.[148] They must have felt an emotional wrench as they left the last place Helen had seen her mother alive and from which Harriet had departed back in 1858, hoping to find better health in the South of France. For the next two years Helen and Mill lived mostly in Avignon, where Mill was engaged in writing, travelling to London only as campaigning work demanded, and Helen continued to edit the work of Thomas Buckle for publication.

As well as women's rights and their opposition to the Contagious Diseases Acts, Mill was involved in organisations calling for land reform, the overall of charitable endowments and the need to provide education for the children of a rapidly increasing British population in particular for the working-class. All these concerns would be ones which Helen would take up on his death as causes close to her heart. In 1868 Mill had founded the Land Tenure Reform Association which held its first public meeting in 1871. It called on the unearned profit of landlords from rents paid to them by their tenants to be taxed and for the creation of rural land cooperatives. These would facilitate greater access to the land and thereby create employment for the growing working population. At that time, few people owned the land and land reformers viewed the unearned income, by way of rent from their tenants, of a privileged minority of landowners, as utterly immoral. Land being a finite natural resource could not be left to the free market. Land reform would become one of Helen's great causes during the 1880s and during these last years with Mill she made the influential connections and gained the knowledge that would enable her to be a leading activist in the late Victorian land movement. The work Mill accomplished in these years was very much a joint venture with his step-daughter. He acknowledged this in his *Autobiography*, published after his death:

> … a great proportion of all my letters (including many which found their way into the newspapers) were not written by me but by my daughter…because I thought the letters, she wrote superior to mine, and more so in proportion to the difficulty of

> the occasion. Even those I wrote myself were generally much improved by her, as is also the case with the more recent of my prepared speeches, of which, and some of my published writings, not a few passages, and those the most successful, were hers.[149]

Helen continued to worry over her step-father's health. In 1871, in a letter to Lady Amberley, she told her that the doctor had examined Mill's chest and found no cause for concern but Helen was worried because he looked so thin 'and I don't like people getting thin without good reason for it, I am always afraid there may be some hidden reason.'[150] Perhaps she was remembering her father's death from the ravages of bowel cancer. She had written earlier that month that worrying over Mill's health was making her ill.[151] In April 1873 Mill returned in good health to Avignon from a meeting of the Land Tenure Reform Association in London. The last time his friend, Pasteur Rey, saw him was on 27 April, entering the Protestant temple in Avignon. Mill was attending the inaugural meeting of the Society for the Encouragement of Primary Education. This was a campaign for the funding of the education of Vaucluse Protestants. Vaucluse is the department of France in which Avignon is situated. Mill died ten days later on the morning of 10 May as a result of a chill he contracted following a botanical excursion.[152] Rey, on hearing of the death, went to Mill's house where he found Helen 'désolée, mais calme et ferme.'[153] Helen took Rey into Mill's bedroom to pay his respects and view the body laid out on his iron bed. She told him that Mill's last words had been 'you know that I have done my work.' Algernon, far away in Oxfordshire, England, tried to console his sister when he heard the news. He, too, had been close to Mill and was devastated. With three young children he could not up and travel to be at his sister's side. He tried to find solace in that Mill's death had been 'sudden' and expressed words of comfort for his sister in that: 'I think he met that happy death before which the Greek sage said no man could be pronounced truly happy.' He told Helen that when she could travel to England she was to come and stay with him in Tetsworth.[154] Helen was in shock. She realised the only way of coping was to immerse herself in work. She wrote to Lady Amberley:

> It was so sudden, so unforeseen, and even during the forty-eight hours I watched by his side I never lost hope up to the

> last moment… I must keep guard over his manuscripts and see they are properly published. My mind has clung to this as something certain and useful to be done and to live to do. The copying them has been and still is my occupation, and I am trying to get the printing done also while I am finishing the copying.[155]

The funeral of England's renowned philosopher and political campaigner was a very simple affair. Only Helen, his physician, Dr Gurney who travelled from Nice (the brother-in-law of Algernon), his local doctor, Dr Chauffard, Pasteur Rey and his wife formed the funeral possession from the house to the nearby cemetery of Saint-Véran for his interment beside Harriet. When they arrived at the tomb, they found that a large crowd had spontaneously formed to honour Mill as he was laid to rest with his beloved wife.[156] Helen would tend the grave devotedly for the next thirty years until she sold the house in 1905. When she left Avignon for the final time, in infirm old age, she gave the town 3000 francs to pay for the continued upkeep of the grave.[157]

Helen was prostrate with grief after her step-father's death. She had lost her mother, father and step-father and felt a great sense of loneliness. 'I do feel solitary – in heart', she confessed to Kate.[158] Like many bereaved people she could not grasp that Mill had died and she wrote to Kate Amberley that she expected him to return at any moment from a botanical expedition. She had never expected he would die during his final illness and she had always thought that she would die before him.[159] Mill's sister, Mary Colman, travelled over from England to be with her which gave Algernon some comfort, knowing she had family support.[160] He reminded his sister that her nephew and nieces were longing to see her and kept asking 'how long it will be before Auntie comes.'[161]

In July 1873, two months after the death of Mill, Helen travelled over to England to stay with Algernon. When she got to Tetsworth she collapsed. The doctor diagnosed exhaustion but she found the company of her brother and his children healing.[162] The children loved her.

Despite the long distance that was usually between them during their childhood she tried to give them the love and concern their own mother would have done but for her early death. Algernon was always mentally fragile, settling to nothing and Helen was a favourite with the children who were always, she was told in letters, 'delighted to see you.'[163] Helen sent regular presents to the family and at Christmas 1873 she sent port wine for Hadji and toys, dolls and books for the children.[164] In 1877, 12-year-old Mary thanked her aunt for the books on geography and astronomy she had sent her.[165] Kate gave her much needed emotional support in her letters. Helen visited Kate and her family during this trip to England in the summer of 1873, during which time she also stayed in the flat in Albert Mansions, Victoria. As the executor of Mill's will she had much to sort out. She was now his literary executor and none of his writings could be published without her consent. He had stipulated in his will that she had license 'to edit all or any of my literary works and to publish all or any of my manuscripts as she in her sole discretion may think fit.' It was a heavy responsibility and for the rest of her life she would guard his reputation carefully, threatening publishers with court proceedings if they republished anything without her consent. Mill had also left her as the main beneficiary of his estate. If Helen were to have predeceased him £1,000 was to have gone to each of Algernon and his three children (if they reached the age of 21) and a trust fund of £2,500 was to be set up to pay them and his sister, Mary Colman, regular dividends. The absence of Herbert or his family's inclusion in the will shows that the breach between Herbert, his siblings and his step-father was unresolvable. Mill's friends William Thornton and William Ellis were to be the executors if Helen had died. Mill's French will left the property in Avignon to Helen and also stipulated that Algernon and Helen were both to be buried with him and Harriet when their time came. This never came to pass as both are buried in England.

Helen returned home to Avignon, in the autumn of 1873, having proved the will with the London solicitor, Mr R.S. Gregson, on 5 September 1873. She busied herself, as she had told Kate Amberley she would, by editing Mill's outstanding work for publication. Helen's edited three volumes of the historian Thomas Buckle's writings had been published the previous year, in 1872, by Longman & Green, London, under the title of *Miscellaneous and Posthumous works of Henry Thomas Buckle edited with a biographical note by Helen Taylor*. Buckle, born 1821, had been influenced by the philosophy of John Stuart Mill and Augustus Comte and as a result applied the rational laws of science to historical study. He believed all civilisations, both in the past and present, had been influenced by the natural world, for example, by the climate or the food available.[166] It is easy to understand the attraction of his method to the rational mind of Helen. Anna Parnell, who we will meet later as a campaigning colleague of Helen's, avoided any mention of the names of individuals in the history she wrote of the Irish Land War 1879–82; she did not even mention, by name, her renowned brother, Charles Stewart Parnell. 'I avoided personalities as much as possible, as I consider the actions of particular individuals are unimportant in history, while the actions of groups, classes, etc of persons are more important, because the former are not met with again, and the latter are.'[167] Anna's biographer, Jane McL. Coté believed that it 'was no doubt through her friendship with Taylor that Anna first became acquainted with Buckle's theory of history, which goes far to explain her later insistence on the unimportance of individuals in history.'[168]

Editing the volumes of Buckle had taken many years and, free of this task, Helen now consoled herself with preparing Mill's *Autobiography* for publication. Mill had started his autobiography in 1853, aged 47, and had finished a draft by 1870 but had left instructions that it should be published within a year of his death. It appeared in print in November 1873. In the *Autobiography* Mill had insisted that his philosophical works were collaborative endeavours with Harriet and Helen:

> Whoever, either now or hereafter, may think of me and of the work that I have done, must never forget that it is the product not of one intellect and conscience but of three, the least considerable of whom, and above all the least original, is the one whose name is attached to it.'[169]

Helen had agonised on whether to keep this comment in on publication but did so. Both Kate[170] and the suffragist Eliza Cairnes[171] agreed with this decision though at the time, and ever since, many commentators have been divided as to the importance of Harriet's contribution to Mill's writing and her influence on the development of his political and economic philosophy.[172] It is now acknowledged, however, by many that Harriet's influence was critical to his work and that much of his output was a result of collaboration between them. Certainly, Harriet's socialism, pulled him leftwards and resulted in his support for the cooperative movement of the utopian socialists as did the 1848 French revolution.[173] Mill also insisted that he owed much to Helen's 'powers of original thought and soundness of practical judgement… Surely no one ever before was so fortunate, as, after such a loss as mine, to draw such another prize in the lottery of life.'[174] Mill had relied on Helen, as he had her mother, for organising the trivia of his life as well as for her intellectual collaboration. Harriet had often despaired at his lack of practicality – he was totally unable to do the simple things in life such as get on a train and secure a seat or understand that more coal was needed in winter than in summer to heat the house.[175] Over the next seven years Helen oversaw the publishing of his outstanding articles. The same month as his death *Dissertations and Discussions vol iv* was published followed by *The Right of Property in Land* in the July edition of the *Examiner*. His *Three Essays on Religion* appeared in print in October 1874 and as late as 1879, his final work, *Chapters on Socialism,* were published in three consecutive editions of the *Fortnightly Review*. All this Helen oversaw, editing the drafts and liaising with publishers to ensure that Mill's work appeared in print exactly as he would have wanted it. Her care over the legacy of Mill has led to some of Mill's autobiographers, including M.S. Packe depicting her, misogynistically, as a harridan:

> After Mill's death, she became the jealous guardian of all his thoughts and relics. She grew priggish and overpowering: eventually mean, suspicious truculent and sometimes half beside herself with passion. She became a great light in her various causes, women's suffrage and the London School Board. For the rest she clung on grimly at Avignon.[176]

This shows no understanding of her position after his death. Mill had given her an intellectual outlet and great emotional and mental support in all she did. She regarded it as her life's duty to strive to continue his work but this would be difficult for her as a woman in a man's world. In a society in which the public arena was a male space and women were expected to wield influence only as wives within the home she would face constant opposition. Three months after the death of Mill, Helen wrote to Kate Amberley setting out what she considered her destiny. 'I feel as though a torch has been left in my hands and I want to keep it alight until I can hand it on to someone younger than myself.'[177] What would be in Helen's favour in fighting to secure a public campaigning role would be her circumstances, namely her family background, independent wealth and being unmarried, all of which would open doors which were firmly shut in the faces of her less advantaged sisters.[178] On her death, over thirty years later, a French obituary of Helen referred to the sense of responsibility she felt as the guardian of Mill's work and reputation:

> Il semblait, selon le mot d'un de ses amis, que le manteau prophétique du grand penseur qui venait de mourir, était tombé sur ses épaules.[179] *(It would seem, according to one of her friends, that the prophetic coat of the great thinker who had just died had fallen on her shoulders)*.

Helen suffered further heartache the following year when, on 8 June 1874, her one close friend, Kate Amberley, died at only 32 years of age. Kate had caught diphtheria from her young daughter, Rachel, who also died a few days after her mother. This left Lord Stanley with two sons, Frank and 2-year-old Bertrand. Helen had been delighted to be asked to be Bertrand's godmother. Kate had hoped for a girl which she had planned to call Cordelia Helen and had asked Helen 'to be godmother… or whatever term in your and my religion would answer.' (Neither of them being adherents of the Church of England or any church themselves).[180] Alone, mostly in Avignon, far from Algernon and his family, Helen was now a middle-aged woman of 43. With Mill's work mostly published she was looking for a cause and a reason to carry on living. Kate had been Helen's closest friend and Eliza Cairnes wrote to her how she and her husband 'felt for you in your sorrow.'[181] Helen had promised to continue the work of her step-father but how was she going to achieve this?

Suffrage colleagues in London, from her days in the Kensington group, rallied round. They discussed what could be done. In October 1876, Eliza Cairnes wrote to Helen in Avignon. This letter would start Helen on the journey to a very public life over the next decade. Eliza wrote that she was happy to hear Helen had recovered from a recent illness and that;

> …it encourages me to hope that you will listen favourably to a proposal I have to make – which is that you will stand for the School Board. I saw Mrs Anderson yesterday and she was talking to me on the subject and wondering if you were properly asked you would consent to stand…Mrs Orme too is of the same opinion and is very anxious that you should become a member of the School Board. She wrote to me about it some time ago.[182]

A system of state elementary education had been created in England and Wales by the passing of Liberal MP William Forster's 1870 Education Act. The 1872 Education Scotland Act created School Boards in Scotland, and Ireland had had a system of national elementary state education administered by the Catholic, Presbyterian and Anglican churches from 1831. The 1870 Act created a dual system of state-run primary schools and voluntary aided church schools. Without this compromise the Act would not have passed. The state schools would be administered by locally elected School Boards paid for by local ratepayers. London was split into divisions for the purpose of membership. Elections would be held every three years and unmarried, rate paying women were entitled to vote under the terms of the 1869 Municipal Franchise Act. Furthermore, married or unmarried women could stand for election with no property nor residential qualifications required. In theory this opened up membership of the board to the working-class but the reality was that elections were so costly and the long hours needed to fulfil school board obligations resulted in the administration of local schools being a middle-class preserve. There was only one member of the working-class elected to the London School Board during the nine years of Helen's tenure, Benjamin Lucraft, a cabinet maker. Minority interests were protected by voters being allowed to give all their votes to one candidate rather than split them according to the number of members returned for their division.[183]

Helen was already well aware of the work of the school boards in England. Elizabeth Garrett Anderson had been elected to the inaugural London School Board in 1870, along with fellow suffragist and Kensington group member Emily Davies. Lydia Becker had also been elected to the Manchester School Board in 1870. Elizabeth Garrett Anderson had tried to persuade Mill to stand in 1870 for the London School Board and hopefully to become its chair but he had refused.[184] Mill believed that tackling the contemporary woeful standard of education for ordinary working people was the key to improving society. On it depended 'full social and political equality for women, the intellectual and moral elevation of the working-class, or fitting India for independence.'[185] Mill called for the charitable endowments left for the education of the working-class, and now in many instances misappropriated, to be returned to their original intent and he believed the better educated should be given extra votes. He wanted education to be a means to the creation of a meritocracy to which no class or sex would be excluded.[186] Mill had opposed initial aspects of the

1870 Education Act which would have allowed individual school boards to decide the tenets of the religious instruction that children in state schools would receive. The final Act did address some of Mill's educational concerns. It legislated that religious education should be non-denominational and that local rates should not be used directly to fund voluntary church schools though a compromise saw voluntary and state schools existing side by side.[187] During the first elections to the London School Board, in 1870, Mill had spoken, at an election meeting in Greenwich, in favour of the working-class receiving the same education as their social superiors. They should not be restricted to technical education for he believed that all children should leave school 'being able to understand the best books on general literature and information.'[188] He insisted that all children needed a good education, including girls, and the School Board needed both men and women members. A resolution had been passed at the Greenwich meeting in support of free, non-denominational education and the election of working-class members to the London School Board. These demands would be central to Helen's educational campaigns as a member of the London School Board.

Helen agreed to be nominated as a candidate for the South London division, Southwark, in November's elections, giving her only a month to return to England and campaign. The next decade would see her become one of the most well-known political and social campaigners in Britain. She would be to the fore in all the leading reform campaigns of the day in Great Britain and Ireland. She had written to Kate Amberley, in 1868, identifying the rights of women to be the most important political cause to work for.[189] In her work in education, political groups, land reform in Ireland and Great Britain, and for moral reform and an end to double standards in sexual conduct, she would put women and girls at the heart of her campaigning. It is to these campaigns which we now turn.

PART 2
'THE FOREMOST WOMAN OF HER TIME': A VERY PUBLIC LIFE 1879–1885

(i) Election to the London School Board

Helen arrived in London from France. She moved from the rooms in Victoria Street, which were only suitable for occasional visits to London, to nearby South Kensington. She rented a flat at 13 Harrington Road, an impressive large redbrick block of apartments which stands to this day. It was only a few minutes' walk from South Kensington train station. In 1868 the construction of the over ground Metropolitan Railway had linked South Kensington, North London and the City of London. In 1872 the Middle Circle underground service had opened which had connected South Kensington with the City of London via Westminster. This made for an easy journey from Kensington to the London School Board Offices, should she be successful in the election, which were on the Embankment of the Thames, just east of Westminster. It was an ideal location for Helen to live. Today South Kensington is one of the most expensive areas of London and renowned for its arts and culture, with the Victoria and Albert Museum (built 1852), the Natural History Museum (which would be built in 1881 shortly after Helen moved there), the Science Museum (1857) and the Royal Albert Hall (constructed between 1867–71) all situated there. It had one drawback for Helen, which it shared with anywhere in Victorian London, the air was heavily polluted with the smog from coal fired factories, trains and residential chimneys. Helen was of delicate health. She was frequently ill with chest infections and it is small wonder that she would escape thankfully from South Kensington to the purer air of Avignon as often as work and commitments would allow in the following years. A contemporary guide book to South Kensington, written in 1882, commented on the adverse effects on Londoners of the fog, smoke and damp climate. 'It is said that any Londoner may be known in any part of the world where he may die, if his lungs are examined – they being of a sooty colour.'[1]

The move to England brought her geographically close to Algernon and his family living in Thame, Oxfordshire. Thame had been connected to London, fifty miles away, by the railway since 1862.[2] In 1879, Algernon would make the short move of three miles to Haddenham, Oxfordshire, a village of thatched cottages, a thirteenth century church and a village green. Tetsworth, where his wife, Ellen, had died and was buried, was only a few miles away. In Haddenham, he bought a cottage in the area known as Townsend. His two daughters Elizabeth and Mary are recorded in the 1881 census as living there with him. Algernon had never settled to a career and all three are listed on the census as of 'independent means.' Algernon would have been still living on his share of the trust funds from his mother and father. Helen's two nieces, Nelly and Mary, were in their teens on her return to England in 1876. In 1878, Helen wished to pay for Nelly to study at the recently established Newnham College, Cambridge, as there were 'opportunities to become Head of the increasing number of girls' schools.' Algernon, however, thought this 'not desirable' as he was concerned that the academic pressure would prove too much for Nelly. Helen replied that the offer was there for his younger daughter, Mary, should she wish, at any time, to take it but her offer was never taken up.[3] Algernon's son, Cyprian, would join the British navy and serve as an Ordinary Seaman from February 1881 until 30 October 1881 on HMS *Duncow*.[4] In 1882 Cyprian would travel out to India to serve in the Royal Artillery. A letter home, written in March 1884, gave the news that he had passed an examination in native Indian dialects.[5] He would not return to England again until the late spring of 1890. In 1879, Algernon had published a third book, *Guienne. Notes of an Autumn Tour.*[6] Again reviewers of the book criticised his writing style whilst acknowledging the depth of his knowledge of the subject. Travellers would find the 'careful descriptions' in the book interesting and 'trustworthy' but it was 'not particularly attractive in style' and was 'wanting in liveliness.'[7] Algernon would always remain a source of both love and concern for Helen and the worry Mill had constantly felt for his step-son, on account of his being unsettled and drifting in life, continued to be held by Helen throughout his life. Meanwhile Herbert, the elder brother, continued to be estranged from his siblings. On her return to England in 1876 he was living only a few miles from Helen in London but she appears to have had no contact with him; the rupture after his father's death over the management of his estate, had never healed. Herbert, as we have seen, was living in Tyndale House Wandsworth south London with his wife Annie and children Herbert (17), Eleanor (13), Geoffrey (3) and his mother-in-law Clemence Daniel, aged 76. However, by 1881, Herbert had separated from his wife and was living, at the time of that year's census, in lodgings in Piccadilly.[8] Meanwhile, Annie and the children, Herbert, Eleanor and Geoffrey were living in Queens Gate, London.[9]

And so, Helen, with the support of the local Liberal party, stood as a school board candidate for the division of Southwark. Southwark returned four members to the London School Board and her fellow Liberal candidate, and supporter of non-denominational school board state education, was the Reverend John Sinclair, a congregational minister. They were up against four candidates supporting the religious schools, listed as Voluntary on the ballot paper, and one independent. The 1876 election would see thirty supporters of the London School Board policy of non-denominational elementary education elected against twenty church or independent members.[10] Helen did not expect to be victorious in the election. She wrote to fellow suffragist Alice Westlake, who would be one of the successful candidates for the Marylebone Division, that she believed she would not be elected due to her 'advocacy of gratuitous, compulsory and secular education.'[11] Even the non-denominational religious education taught in state schools was not acceptable to her. The Rev. Sinclair was fearful throughout the election that Helen's secular demands would lead to the defeat of them both. He wrote to her asking her to be more moderate in her election speeches.[12] Southwark, a very poor borough, had a large Irish immigrant church-going Roman Catholic population.[13] Helen, however, was victorious and was elected along with an, undoubtedly, very relieved Sinclair and two voluntary school supporters, Rev. Robert Maguire and Henry Heald. Helen came in as the fourth elected candidate on 6,081 votes with Maguire topping the poll with 6,568.

Coming to England and being elected to the London School Board gave Helen much needed social contact. Mill had died five years previously and Lady Amberley, four. She was now geographically close to her beloved brother Algernon. Helen was joined on the board by three other women elected in 1878, all of whom were Progressives; Florence Fenwick Miller

(Hackney), Elizabeth Surr (Finsbury) and Alice Westlake (Marylebone). The London School Board members split into two groups – Moderates and Progressives. The Moderates supported the Conservative party and church schools whereas the Progressives, made up of Liberals, Radicals and, later in the 1880s, socialists, were staunch defenders of the School Board system. Only four women in the London School Board's thirty years' existence were ever elected as moderates.[14] During the 1880s, the moderates would gain control of the board in London. Florence, Elizabeth and Helen would work closely together to promote women's rights within the board and its schools. Florence was only 22. She and Helen were close for a time, even travelling together to a suffrage event in Belfast in 1880. Helen offered to fund Florence's election expenses at the next board elections but Florence, worried that her political independence would be compromised, declined the offer. So Helen introduced Florence to the educationalist William Ellis, who had been a friend of Mill's, and he paid the election expenses instead.[15]

Florence, later, denied that the friendship was close for they were friends as 'much as that suspicious nature would allow.'[16] She was, however, a supporter of Helen's motions within the school board, particularly for better child welfare. In 1877, Florence would marry Frederick Ford, a stockbroker's clerk, and insist on keeping her maiden name. There were moves to make her stand down from the board over this but her successful defence of her right to retain her name established that a woman could keep her maiden name on marriage. Florence had passed the preliminary examination in medicine at the University of Edinburgh but had transferred to the Ladies' Medical College, London, when Edinburgh refused to start granting medical degrees to women. She only practised medicine for a short time and from then on concentrated on women's suffrage, on lecturing on the literary world, and social issues and journalism. It was as a journalist that she became best known.[17] Elizabeth and Helen would sever all contact with Florence after leaving the school board, Helen having felt she had failed to support her, when her support was needed (presumably when she was being sued for libel by Scrutton, a fellow board member, which we will come to presently), and that Florence had used the board to promote herself. Florence would write a number of text books on social economy for use in board schools, a subject which Helen vigorously opposed as being against a liberal education, for it was doctrinal. Helen voted against a London School Board motion in 1883 for its inclusion in the curriculum even though she felt it would result in 'a generation of young socialists.'[18] During the same debate Florence Fenwick Miller, in defending social economy teaching, and having a vested interest in the sale of her books to do so, had ridiculed the 'pretentions' of Henry George's political economy.[19] George, the foremost political economist of his day, and his family, as we will see later, were close friends and political colleagues of Helen's and this attack must have added coals to the fire of a growing animosity between the two women.

In contrast, Elizabeth Surr and Helen developed an enduring friendship, forged in their fight against corporal punishment in London's schools. Elizabeth, married with four children, was a writer of children's books and Helen's closest ally on the board. They were of the same generation; Elizabeth having been born in 1825. They shared a commitment to secular education and for equal opportunity for girls. With Florence and Helen, Elizabeth would expose the child abuse at St Paul's Industrial School.[20] No such lasting rapport was achieved, despite their joint women's suffrage work, between Helen and Alice Westlake who had been a member of the Langham Place Circle and had introduced Helen to the Kensington Society in the early 1860s. Alice, the daughter of Thomas Hare, was an artist and married to a barrister and prominent Liberal who would briefly serve as an MP in 1885–86. They had no children. In 1866 she had signed the petition, which Mill presented to Parliament, demanding women's suffrage and in 1876 she replaced Elizabeth Garrett Anderson as one of the members for Marylebone, achieving the highest number of votes in the election there. Alice exhibited her paintings at the Royal Academy and in Paris. She was on the central committee of the National Society for Women's Suffrage during the 1880s.[21] The National Society for Women's Suffrage was often horrified at Helen's political extremeness.[22] A loyal supporter of Liberal policies on the board, this set Alice apart from the other three Progressive women elected in 1876, who voted for motions on their merits. She did not provide support for the other women's constant attempts to challenge gendered expectations on the board and the limitations put on women members, women teachers and girl pupils. Alice would always toe the official Liberal party line on a policy including girls being subject to an increasing number of lessons in domestic subjects. When Helen, Florence and Elizabeth attempted to reduce the time devoted to the domestic curriculum (including needlework, cooking and laundry work) that only girls had to undertake, Alice suggested to women headteachers that they could reduce their heavy work load by replacing drawing and grammar classes for girls with cookery.[23]

The 1876 election over, Reverend Sinclair, despite his victory, made a complaint of election misconduct against Helen to the local Liberal Party. It would be the first of many run-ins with the official Liberal machine. Her independent stance in debates and voting would lead to her standing as an Independent Democrat in the 1879 and 1882 school board elections. Sinclair alleged that Helen had failed to acknowledge, at an election meeting, that he, too, was the official candidate of the Liberal Party.[24] He also accused her of giving money to the Southwark election committee, thus contravening Liberal rules which stipulated that Sinclair had equal status as a running partner. He made further accusations that she had issued and distributed an election handbill which expressed support for herself alone; that she had arranged an unofficial election meeting and that she had not made explicit to reporters that her opposition to religious education was not official Liberal policy but her own views.[25] She successfully defended herself at the inquiry and was found innocent of misconduct. A supporter wrote to her after the verdict, congratulating her and saying that the charges should never have been brought and that Sinclair should apologise.'[26]

At the post-election banquet held for the elected members, Helen spoke of her vision for a state education system:

> … in which neither boys nor girls shall be tied down to any conditions of religion or opinions, nay of a future destiny in life other than for which God has given them faculties…If you retard the education of girls, you will not attain liberty for the next generation for the mass of the population of the country.[27]

Her words had echoes of those of her step-father in Greenwich in 1870:

> No one was worthy to serve on the School Board who would not seek to secure attendance of every child at school, support free education and insist that the schools should not be made the means of instilling sectarian opinion.[28]

Mill, earlier in his life, had been undecided on the subject of free education and, for that reason, had not joined the National Education League in 1869 because of their advocacy of it.[29] By the end of his life, merely a few years later, he was campaigning for it. It continued to divide the Liberals with many people believing free education would erode parental responsibility.

Helen had nailed her colours to the mast at the dinner. Feminism would be her motivation.[30] Florence, Elizabeth and herself would face constant opposition in their attempts to secure equality for women board members, girl pupils and for women teachers. There would, however, be a number of men who would support them including Benjamin Lucraft and later Edward Aveling. From the outset, the three women had to challenge gendered expectations. All London School Board members were invited to the annual Lord Mayor's dinner at the Mansion House. It had, however, always been made clear to the women board members that they were not to attend. All previous women members since 1870, Jane Chessar, Alice Cowell, Emily Davies and Elizabeth Garrett, had politely declined the invitation. In 1877, Helen, Elizabeth and Florence made a stand when they accepted the invitation, and attended the dinner.[31] Alice Westlake did not attend. Alice accepted the limitations set by the male school board hierarchy on her behaviour for her loyalty was to the Liberal Party.[32] Alice, like many in the women's suffrage movement, recognised that the vote for women and improved women's rights would only be won with the consent of male politicians. The majority of British middle-class suffragists did not wish to be labelled as members of the 'shrieking sisterhood.'[33] Helen, most definitely a paid-up member of such a sisterhood, would experience rebukes by her fellow suffragists in the 1880s over much of her campaigning as they feared it would sully the reputation of their campaign for women to be granted the vote.

Florence wrote in her memoir that 'some of the gentlemen members of the Board were desirous of keeping the lady members in the inferior position proper to their sex.'[34] On four occasions she had had to insist that, being the member who had received the greatest number of votes in her division, she take the chair at local meetings when the Chairman or Vice Chairman of the Board was absent. There was 'an official ring which exercised an arbitrary authority and gave no heed to any suggestions or representations coming from outside the ring.'[35] Independently minded male members could also find themselves shunned by the ruling clique, which was comprised of, as member John Lobb described it, '…a sort of "inner circle," whose definite aim was the centralisation in themselves of all the power, patronage and expenditure of the Board; they wanted the control of everything, in addition to being the chairmen of all the committees and subcommittees.'[36] Lobb wrote a number of pamphlets in which he alleged financial extravagance and mismanagement, by this inner circle of power, of public money.

Helen, now living for most of the year in her flat in Kensington, would serve three terms as the London School Board member for Southwark, topping the poll in the next two elections as an independent candidate. This working-class area was just south of the River Thames and many of its inhabitants earned their living as boatsman or other jobs related to the river trade. These were the people whose children Helen championed on the school board. The work was arduous and involved long hours. The fortnightly school board meetings could last four hours and then there was constituency work. From now on she would only be able to escape to the tranquillity of Avignon during the summer months and the Easter and Christmas breaks. Increasingly, other political and social campaigning would compete for time with her school board work, leaving little time for leisure. Helen had a lot to learn but she had the legacy of her mother and step-father to draw on. On her election she was appointed to the recently formed Educational Endowments Committee. The misuse of charitable endowments, left by benefactors to ameliorate poverty but often now diverted from their original purpose for the benefit of the middle-classes, had been taken up by radical reformers throughout the century. Endowed schools, set up for the poor and funded by endowments, were now the preserve of the rich. The leading public-school Harrow is an example. The government had set up the Brougham Commission in 1816 which had discovered great abuses of endowment money including the funding of schools which no longer had pupils and churches without congregations. This was as a result of demographic changes, following the Industrial Revolution, which had seen populations deserting rural areas to find work in the growing cities.[37] In 1849, a Royal Commission of Inquiry had been given the remit to investigate the misapplication of endowments by charities. In 1853, the Charity Commission was established by an Act of Parliament. It was empowered to reform the parochial charities of the City of London and ensure that educational endowments in the capital were used appropriately, i.e. to fund the education of the poor. In 1873, the remit of the Endowed Schools Commission had passed to the London School Board. The school board faced a growing demand for school places as the population of London increased. If endowments were returned to their intended use, they would fund schools and teachers without further cost to the ratepayer. The Educational Endowments Committee was created by the London School Board in response to this need, to find additional funding from endowments. As a result of the Endowed Schools

Act of 1869, endowments, whose original intention was unknown or was no longer viable, could legally be used for educational purposes. Helen already had the knowledge to deal with all this. Educational endowments had been a concern of Mill's. In 1866 he had called for such a course of action:

> There are numerous charitable funds which are now, under the terms of antiquated trusts, distributed in mere doles, to persons supposed to be necessitous, but who have not always even that claim, such as it is. It would be a far more efficacious mode of alleviating the evil of indigence, to employ these funds in making war on its principal cause, the want of education.[38]

Championing the return of the endowments for the education of the working-class put her at variance with many of her fellow women suffragists who were campaigning for improved educational opportunities for middle-class girls and who saw endowments as a source of funding. Maria Grey of the National Union for the Improvement of the Education had established the Girls' Public Day School Trust in 1872 and women were admitted to degrees at the University of London in 1878. The woman's college, Newnham, at Cambridge had been established in 1871. The *Englishwoman's Review* followed these developments closely.[39] Helen, who always regretted her lack of formal schooling, had not only offered to fund her nieces' education. She had put up the money for Agnes McLaren, the daughter of the suffragist Priscilla McLaren and the Liberal MP, Duncan McLaren, to study for a medical degree in Montpellier, France.[40] During her first year as a Member of the London School Board, Helen supported a motion to apply endowment money for the establishment of board secondary schools. These schools would award places on the basis of a competitive examination. She believed such schools would enable intelligent working-class children to advance in life.

During her first term on the board, 1876–79, Helen also took up the cause of secular education which had caused so much rancour between herself and the Rev. Sinclair during the election campaign. The 1870 Education Act had made a daily bible reading in board schools compulsory but denominational religious education was not allowed. Parents were allowed to withdraw their children from the bible reading by citing the 1871 Conscience Clause. Helen was not anti-religion – we have seen how she found solace in the

Catholic mass – but she believed, as a Radical, that it had no place in education. She wrote after her 1876 election triumph:

> What I did urge strongly in speech after speech during the election contest, was that in desiring secular instruction only in state schools I was not opposed to religious teaching and least of all to religion itself. I said (what I am very strongly persuaded of) that religion should be taught by ministers of religion or by volunteer teachers, such as teachers of Sunday schools, and that the school master ought not to undertake the work of the clergyman, least of all when we have a church, the richest in the world, magnificently endowed to do its own work.[41]

Benjamin Lucraft, supported her campaign for secular education. He was a cabinet maker and trade unionist and had been a chartist. He served twenty years on the board as one of the members for Finsbury and was popular with members from all parties.[42] Helen and Lucraft, opposed the London School Board circular, issued to all schools in 1878, which stipulated that pupils should be taught 'the truths upon which their future lives depended.'[43] They feared that teachers could use this directive to indoctrinate their pupils with their own religious beliefs.[44] In 1879, Taylor unsuccessfully challenged a London School Board report, *The Religious Examination of Pupil Teachers*, which was issued to all headteachers, insisting it was a threat to the religious freedom of apprenticed teachers. Pupil teachers could find themselves coerced by their headteachers into sitting the Scripture examination to ensure that the schools did not lose government grants.

During her first term on the board Helen worked hard to create equal opportunities for girls. Girls had classes on domestic economy for between five and seven hours a week as a training for their futures as wives and mothers. Boys were given extra arithmetic lessons whilst the girls were thus engaged. In 1877, the London School Board issued a new code which increased the time allocated for girls to be instructed in domestic subjects, in particular needlework. Helen, Florence and Elizabeth opposed this move.[45] They got no support from Alice Westlake, the chair of the Domestic Subjects Committee (a gendered appointment; such matters being in the sphere of women). Alice supported the increase in domestic subjects for girls as, she believed, the working-class did not know how to cook economical, healthy meals.[46]

1879 dawned and would be an election year. Helen would face re-election in November and could count on the Liberals trying to unseat her for her constant opposition to Liberal policy on the board. She had a growing friendship with Elizabeth and relations between herself and Florence had not yet soured. She escaped to Avignon, as often as she could, where she felt close to her dead mother and step-father and she visited Algernon and his growing family, when time allowed. She always took a great interest in his motherless children, Elizabeth, Cyprian and Mary. She was as settled in her London flat as she could be, it would never be home. That was Avignon. The reporter who interviewed her for the *Pall Mall Gazette*, during her 1885 attempt to stand for parliament, described the flat as resembling a boarding house. There was little personal in her study except 'for a large basket of fresh flowers on a small side-table' and 'an illuminated address to Mr John Stuart Mill, of whom Miss Taylor was the adopted daughter, over the mantelpiece.'[47] It was functional. During this election year of 1879, Helen became involved in debates on equal pay for women teachers, against corporal punishment, and in opposing the waste of public money spent fitting out a training ship, the Shaftesbury. All this would increase the animosity of the Liberal Party towards her. The previous year the three tenacious women, Helen, Florence and Elizabeth had galvanised enough support to prevent women with children from being barred from being headteachers. This had unleashed naked sexism in the chamber. A fellow member of Florence's in Hackney, the Rev. James Picton, though a radical in politics, had declared that equal pay should not be awarded. He argued that, firstly, women teachers were not as good as male teachers and, secondly, there were more female candidates than men for teaching posts.[48]

Helen turned her attention to corporal punishment in schools during the early part of 1879. Helen had grown up in a home where domestic abuse was discussed. Her aunt had suffered it at the hands of her husband and her mother and Mill had published articles on the subject. From 1870 the London School Board had set in place strict rules on the use of corporal punishment in their schools. It could only be administered by a headteacher and its use had to be recorded in a punishment book.[49] Helen made attempts, in her first term, to have physical punishment in schools banned. Although unsuccessful, her second term would see her and Elizabeth challenging the abuse of children within the school board system to some effect.

Helen, throughout her school board tenure, attempted to hold the board accountable for its use of local tax payers' money. She challenged the expenditure of the board on the Shaftesbury training ship. Spending on the ship had been agreed back in 1877, with £15,000 being agreed for its purchase and refitting under the auspices of the Industrial Schools Committee chaired by Thomas Scrutton. It was planned to anchor the ship at the Thames estuary as an Industrial school for remand pupils. The boys would receive training for a future working on boats and ships. These remand students were not all petty thieves, some were just truanting boys picked up on the streets by school inspectors whilst their parents were out at work. The Industrial Schools Committee bought the ship for £7,000 with the remaining £8,000 being the estimate for refit and repairs. In June 1878 Scrutton asked the board to grant the project more money and an extra £7,000 pounds was awarded to the Industrial Schools Committee. The money, however, was not to be handed over until members had seen itemised accounts of the spending up to this point on the project.[50] Helen and Elizabeth had seconded the motion which retained the money and Helen claimed the debt was the responsibility of the Industrial Committee members because it had not been sanctioned by the full board.[51] When the accounts were passed to members in July 1879 the estimate for the final bill for the ship's refit was seen to have risen to £37,038. This was public money. An Enquiry Committee, of which Florence was a member, reported back to the board that even this estimate was too low and that the true cost was £40,000. The enquiry concluded that the Industrial Schools Committee had mismanaged public money. The Committee had sanctioned the buying of Chippendale chairs and oriental rugs for the captain's cabin and committee members had even taken the opportunity to buy rugs for themselves at preferential prices. An independent ship building expert had estimated that competitive tendering would have reduced expenditure on the ship by twenty five percent. The Industrial Schools Committee members had even had a free lunch, at three shillings a head, on the ship at the taxpayers' expense. Helen declared this to be 'a scandalous practice' when those same members refused to grant the poor free schooling.[52] During the furore over the spending on the ship, Scrutton had the audacity to ask for funding to employ an extra schoolmaster on the ship in view of an increase in trainee numbers.[53] Helen moved an unsuccessful amendment that the board's expenditure, on the Shaftesbury, should be paid for by a one off increase in the local rates to avoid future ratepayers paying for a training school that might no longer be in existence.[54]

(ii) Into the 1880s – A Life Leaving Little Time For Play

In November 1879, Helen was re-elected to the London School Board for Southwark as an Independent Democrat. She obtained the highest number of votes in the division, despite a vigorous Liberal campaign to unseat her. The local newspaper, *The South London Chronicle and Southwark and Lambeth Ensign*, had printed a scathing article a few weeks before the election attacking her. She had, it fumed, been elected in 1876 with the support and the funding of the Liberal party, who had campaigned for her, but she had never been loyal to the party. She had voted against Liberal school board policy and supported the opposition, the supporters of the church voluntary schools, in some divisions. The newspaper claimed she had no support in the division among the electorate and that her only support came from the local radical club which she financed. These radicals had 'a love of opposition for its own sake.' Teachers disliked her due to her opposition to corporal punishment and, it was inferred she was untruthful. She had made unsubstantiated claims of pupils being given the cane for not bringing the school fee and for truanting. Her estimates on the cost of the Shaftesbury were blatantly untrue.[55] The voters of Southwark, however, thought differently. They felt she was supporting ordinary people like themselves and she received a huge vote of confidence, gaining the highest number of votes, 5,530. Two Liberals were also successful, Alexander Hawkins and Mary Richardson along with an independent, Edward Corry. The labour activist, Francis Soutter, recounted in his memoirs the strength of support for her among the poor of Southwark and how well attended her public meetings were there. She would often pay for meals and books for poor school children herself. [56]

She was now growing in confidence. The young woman who, in 1870, had confessed to Lady Amberley that she would prefer not to appear in public to give her first speech in support of women's suffrage, would become, during the next decade, a much called on public speaker on behalf of her causes. The 1880s would see Helen at the height of her fame, or infamy according to your political bent. The words 'compromise' and 'this is as far as we can go' were not in her vocabulary for better or for worse. She increasingly had to balance campaigning interests, suffrage, education, political, land reform, Ireland and moral reform in a relentless life of campaigning for political and social change. She would travel the length and breadth of Great Britain and Ireland, during the next decade, for these causes which would climax in her attempt to become the first woman candidate in a general election to the British parliament in 1885.

She had set the tone in her first term on the London School Board and continued in the same vein, after the 1879 election, with 'her habit of calling a spade a spade utterly regardless as to whether the said spade's political bent was Tory or Liberal.'[57] She did not fear being unpopular 'for the opinion of 'society' as that term is generally understood she cared not a rap.'[58] Elizabeth Surr, would later write to the local paper in praise of Helen's campaigning on behalf of the children, saying that it was done out of a sense of morality. Elizabeth wrote admiringly that Helen 'did not work for success, she was generally found upon the losing side, fighting like a brave soldier in the cause which she conceived to be true and just.'[59] Many found Helen extremely difficult because of this black and white sense of right and wrong. It did make alliances difficult as electoral politics often calls for pragmatism and compromise. She earned the name 'the ice maiden.' amongst her detractors.[60]

The election over, Helen continued her busy life during 1880, campaigning on the school board for the return of educational endowments for the education of the poor, against corporal punishment and for free, secular education. She continued to work for gender equality in the classroom, voting against the increasing of time spent on the domestic curriculum by girls. She regarded the needlework classes, which only girls endured, as utterly pointless:

> If girls were going to do needlework, though there was far too much of it in her opinion, then it should be of help to their mothers and they should be allowed to sew items from home.[61]

She held public meetings in her division to report back to her residents and spoke at a public meeting held in support of women's suffrage, held locally in Bermondsey, along with Priscilla McLaren and Lydia Becker.[62] She also travelled to Ireland with Florence Fenwick Miller to speak at women's suffrage meetings in Belfast and Newry. [63]

(iii) A Gruelling Schedule – 1881

1880 was the last year that she would be able to give the London School Board her complete attention. From 1881 onwards she would have to divide her time between educational work, her membership of a newly formed political party, The Democratic Federation, the Land Nationalisation Society, and the Irish Land War. To Algernon's children, now teenagers, she was their beloved auntie, who they would have seen irregularly as she was so busy but it is nevertheless surprising how little they seemed to know of their aunt's fame. Towards the end of her life she was looked after by her niece Mary who expressed surprise in her diary that Auntie Helen was such a socialist.[64]

Helen continued her campaign in the School Board to abolish physical punishment. Early in 1881, herself and Elizabeth Surr made reform of the capital's industrial schools a priority and tenaciously worked throughout the year to change the system. Helen felt too many children sent to these schools as young offenders were nothing of the kind. They were ordinary children who were picked up on the streets unsupervised by truant officers whilst both parents were out at work. They should be in ordinary, not reform, schools.[65] Elizabeth visited Upton Industrial School and was horrified to find the children living without warm clothes, shoes or lit fires. Elizabeth and Helen became official visitors at St Paul's Industrial School where conditions were so bad that two desperate boys set fire to it.[66] Helen and Elizabeth both spoke in support of the boys at the subsequent trial, and Helen paid the defence solicitor's expenses. Helen described to the court what she had seen as a visitor at the school. The boys were given very little food and were subject to punishments such as having their hands and feet handcuffed and being confined in unheated rooms for long periods.[67] The court case resulted in a London School Board enquiry and the school closed after the Home Office withdrew the school's certificate. Elizabeth and Helen remained disappointed that the school manager, Thomas Scrutton, avoided prosecution through lack of evidence. Scrutton, who Helen had crossed swords with as chair of the Industrial Schools Committee over the Shaftesbury, was accused by Helen in a school board meeting of charging the board fees for boys not actually in attendance. Helen had checked the attendance registers in the Finance Department of the London School Board against the invoices of the school.[68] Scrutton, who was never prosecuted for fraud, resigned from the board in May 1882.[69] That, however was not the end of the story as Scrutton, we will see, later sued Helen for libel. Many board members, disgusted at the treatment of the boys in the school that he managed, were glad to see the back of him.[70] The Chairman of the London School Board moved that Scrutton be sent a letter regretting his resignation.

This caused William Bonnewell, a member for the City of London division, to call out the motion as hypocrisy 'when the majority of the board were glad, he had gone.'[71] The *School Board Chronicle*, however, supported Scrutton and declared him to be 'the hardest working, most zealous and most devoted of members.'[72]

1881 would see Helen move further away from the imperial feminism of the British feminist movement which prized the British Empire and imperialism.[73] They argued it was shameful that British women were treated as inferiors just like women in what they viewed as primitive native societies. The superiority of the British Anglo-Saxon people, who controlled the mighty British Empire, should prove itself by granting British women full citizen rights. When Helen began mixing in Irish nationalist circles and opposing oppressive laws passed by the Liberals to control Ireland, she drove a wedge between herself and the British suffrage movement. In February 1881, she joined the newly formed, nationalist, Irish Ladies' Land League. The Ladies' Land League would successfully continue to organise the Irish tenant farmers in their fair rent and secure tenancy campaign against the Anglo-Irish landlords after the arrest, later that year, of the leaders of the Land League, including Charles Stewart Parnell and Michael Davitt.[74]

In the late 1870s Ireland had suffered a series of bad harvests and another famine had looked likely. Michael Davitt, who, as a child, had seen his family evicted from their home in County Mayo during the Irish Famine of the late 1840s was determined the Irish would not starve again. Davitt's family had had to emigrate, like thousands of many other Irish Catholics fleeing the Great Hunger.[75] They had been evicted from their home. He grew up in Haslingden in Lancashire, England. To avoid such another disaster, Davitt had formed the Irish Land League in 1879. An active Irish nationalist, he had joined the revolutionary Irish Republican Brotherhood and had served seven years in Dartmoor Prison after having been found guilty of gun running. On his release, on license, in 1877, having read James Fintan Lalor and John Mitchel's writings on the iniquities of the landlord system in Ireland whilst in prison, he turned his attention to the plight of the Irish tenant farmer.[76]

The Anglo-Irish landlords charged their Irish tenant farmers high rents and evicted them when they could not pay. The Land League set out their three demands; fair rents, fixity of tenure and free sale and would begin a no rent campaign in October 1881 which instructed tenant farmers to withhold their rents and resist eviction. Families who took over the land of those evicted for non-payment of rents would face social exclusion. This became known as 'boycotting' after Captain Boycott whose tenants refused to harvest the grain on the estate he managed for Lord Erne. Ireland was swept with agrarian protests and unrest and it became clear, by early 1881, that the British Government was going to use the recently passed Coercion Acts to imprison, without trial, the leadership of the Land League. So that the League's campaign could continue when the men were arrested, Davitt created the Ladies' Land League. Some in the land movement opposed this, including Charles Stewart Parnell, John Dillon and Thomas Brennan. They regarded women's involvement in politics as improper. Brennan 'feared we would invite public ridicule in appearing to put women forward in places of danger.'[77] Davitt had been in the USA where he had witnessed the successful fundraising, on behalf of the Irish Land League, of the philanthropic American Ladies' Land League in New York. This had been formed by Fanny Parnell, the sister of the Irish nationalist MP and President of the Irish Land League, Charles Stewart Parnell. Davitt planned that the Irish Ladies' Land League would be similarly philanthropic. Fanny's sister, Anna, agreed to be the president of the newly formed Ladies' Land League in February 1881. An ardent feminist, she was determined it should be more than a fundraising, administrative organisation. She immediately called upon Irish women to become politically active. 'You cannot prevent the evictions but you can prevent them from becoming massacres. Form yourselves into branches of the Irish National Land League.'[78] Branches of the Ladies' organisation immediately sprang up throughout Great Britain and Helen joined the executive of the London Ladies' Land League which was formed in February 1881.[79] Just a few weeks before joining, Helen had chaired a public meeting in Bermondsey, organised by the Anti-Coercion Association, of which she was a Vice President. Two Irish Nationalist Party MPs, T.P. O'Connor and John Connor Power, addressed the meeting which was one of twenty held by the Anti Coercion League to protest at arrest without trial in Ireland.[80]

Anna Parnell travelled over to England from Dublin in March 1881 and the two women met for the first time. They warmed to each other and would keep in touch long after the Ladies' Land League was dissolved the following year. Anna came to speak at a meeting of the London Ladies' Land League branch which had been called to discuss fund raising. Here she accused the Royal Ulster Constabulary of mutilating cattle in Ireland and alleged that they had falsely accused the land leaguers of the crime.[81]

The political activism of these Irish women was an affront to the ideology of separate spheres which insisted that women's influence should be confined to the private sphere of home and family. The Bishop of Dublin, Archbishop McCabe, outraged at women being politically active, issued a pastoral letter to be read out at mass in every church in the Dublin diocese. He warned women not to join the Ladies' Land League. 'Do not tolerate in your sodalities the woman who so far disavows her birth right of modesty as to parade herself before the public gaze.'[82] The British suffrage movement was equally aghast at Helen teaming up with Anna Parnell. They feared that it would set back the suffrage movement and tarnish its respectability. They had to show men that women were worthy of the vote and the feminist movement needed to distance itself from both the immodesty of the Ladies' Land League and Irish nationalism.[83] As well as their horror at Irish women opposing the British government, they deemed it unseemly for women to be taking part in direct action. The author F.M. Holmes indeed made the link between the actions of the Ladies' Land League and the unsuitability of women being granted the suffrage in a pamphlet on the Land League:

> If the political action of the Ladies' League is to be in any sense, a sample of what we shall get when female suffrage opens the door of political warfare to ladies, may Heaven long delay the fearful period.[84]

Priscilla McClaren warned Helen at the time of this first meeting with Anna: 'I hear now and then darker surmises of how much you and some others will retard our suffrage movement by signing yourselves up with the Land League question.'[85] British Victorian feminism was fundamentally imperialist in nature with its adherents basing their claim to vote as their right as members of the superior British race, with the largest Empire on earth. Feminists, including Helen's mother Harriet, in *The Enfranchisement of Women*, used the language of racial superiority as evidence that denying women's legal and political rights was shameful. It left British women in no better a position than their colonial Indian sisters who were oppressed by their own men and the primitive society they lived in. Harriet had compared the position of unfranchised British women with the inferiority of Asian women kept hidden from society in harems.[86] Included in this sense of racial superiority was the widely held belief that the Irish were culturally and ethnically inferior. Celts were depicted, in newspapers, as uncivilised and of ape-like appearance.[87]

Support for the Irish peasant was, thus, anathema to many of Helen's fellow suffragists on both racial grounds and the fact that the Land League was an Irish nationalist, anti-British organisation. British suffragists were, in the main, unionists supporting the integrity of the United Kingdom.

Anna, her brother Charles and sister Fanny were Protestant Anglo-Irish nationalists. The leaders of the Ladies' Land League were, in contrast to the mainstream feminist movement which included such Irish women as the pro-union Isabella Tod and Anna Haslam, anti-imperial feminists.[88] The Parnells were landlords and had an estate and home at Avondale, Co Wicklow. Anna's paternal great grandfather had voted against the Act of Union in 1801 which had abolished the Dublin Parliament.[89] Her grandfather had been a supporter of catholic emancipation which had allowed Catholics to become MPs. Previously, MPs had had to swear allegiance to the queen using the Anglican oath of allegiance which they could not do as Catholics. Charles Stewart Parnell was leader of the Irish National Party MPs in the House of Commons. Anna's maternal great grandfather had fought the British in the American War of Independence. Fanny was head of the American Ladies' Land League which raised funds for the Irish Land League. Anna and her sister Fanny had both lived in New York and were well known in the anti-imperialist circles of the Irish American nationalist organisation Clan na Gael. This anti-imperialist organisation vocally opposed the British Empire and was a major fundraiser for the Irish Land League which was regarded, by Irish nationalists, as the most important vehicle for Irish independence at the time. Helen was not just joining an organisation which would improve tenant rights but one that hoped to make the first blow against the British Empire. This move, way beyond her step-father's call for improved Irish tenant rights as a means of securing the Union, thoroughly alienated many of those who had once sat organising the women's suffrage campaign with her and Mill at their home in Blackheath during the early 1860s. Many Land League supporters believed that when the landlords were driven out of Ireland so would be the British government.[90] Katherine Tynan, the poet and Ladies' Land Leaguer, later wrote that: 'The Land League, in those days, was the expression of the national spirit in Ireland,' and that people 'looked beyond the Land League to that for which Mr Parnell had taken off his hat.'[91] It was Anna who first used the term 'the famine queen' to describe Queen Victoria.[92] Anna and Helen appear to have been a meeting of minds. Both had had isolated upbringings. The Parnell's history of Irish nationalism had set them apart from their Anglo-Irish, Wicklow, Protestant, landowning neighbours and social circle. Harriet's unorthodox relationship with Mill had set Helen apart and isolated her from her peers and many in her mother's social circle during her Surrey childhood. Both Anna and Helen have, unfairly, been depicted as loners by historians but Anna's biographer referenced her friendships with Helen, Kate Malony and Jennie Wyse Power, to refute this claim.[93] Circumstances had led to their social isolation.

Both women were anti-imperialists. Taylor, herself, was a mid-century anti-imperialist, rather than an adherent to the Marxist anti-imperialism of the 1880s socialist revival. She would oppose the invasion of Egypt by Britain in 1882.[94] Her anti-imperialism was of the older radical tradition of Richard Cobden earlier in the century. Cobden had argued that taxation, rather than paying for British soldiers defending an Empire abroad, should be spent at home on measures to ameliorate the lives of the working-class.[95] Helen, in the Ladies' Land League, now began to be influenced by a more aggressive, overtly anti-British Empire anti-imperialism. She corresponded with the editor of the Irish American anti-imperialist newspaper the *Irish World*, which supported anti-colonial movements worldwide. She hoped to secure its publication and distribution in London.[96] It was reported in the press that a London publisher planned to distribute copies of this seditious paper to the trade and subscribers and this is likely what Helen was involved in.[97] Distribution of this anti-British, Irish nationalist newspaper had been proscribed, in Ireland, by the British government under Section 13 of the Prevention of Crimes Act, though it had not been felt necessary to ban it in England.[98] Helen was fully aware that she was throwing her lot in with a movement to end British rule in Ireland. The constitutional nationalist Charles Stewart Parnell, no supporter of the extremist in the movement, had made this quite clear in 1880 when speaking at a public meeting in Cork. 'If we succeed in emigrating the Irish landlords, the English government will soon have to follow them.'[99]

Helen discussed her exasperation with those Liberal suffragists, who put loyalty to the Liberal Party before the suffrage campaign, with Anna. Anna recalled this in a letter to the *Irish Times* after Helen's death in 1907:

> The late Helen Taylor told me that she had known the female suffragists, with whom she herself had ceased to have any connection, insist on giving their support to a Gladstonian MP who had voted against female franchise instead of to a conservative who had voted for it.[100]

One can imagine the two women sitting and expressing their frustrations with the contemporary women's rights movement. For two women who had often led solitary lives this rapport must have been most welcome. Anna's hatred of the landlord system went beyond the support of tenants' rights; it was a feminist crusade. She hated landlordism because many single Anglo-Irish women, herself included, lived on small, precarious annual allowances which depended on the profits of their father's or brother's estates. No profits: no allowance. She lived in near penury at various stages of her life and, on one occasion, Irish nationalists, Kate Malony, Jennie Wyse Power and John Dillon, arranged for a publisher to give Anna a supposed advance on the publication of her book of poetry. Dillon repaid the money to the publisher, when the book failed to sell, not wanting Anna to know she was in receipt of charity.[101] Anna hated the system which saw unmarried female relatives dependent on handouts from their male relatives:

> They *[i.e. the landlords' female relatives]* were, in fact, only a little less the victims of the landlords than the tenants themselves; while on the other hand they were entirely helpless, instead of being, as the tenants were, only partially helpless against the landlords. If the Irish landlords had not deserved extermination for anything else, they would have deserved it for the treatment of their own women.[102]

The anti-imperial feminism Anna promoted within the Ladies' Land League horrified the British feminists of the feminist periodical *Englishwoman's Review*, who reserved their concern for the Anglo-Irish women landlords. Women landlords, having no menfolk, were being forced into penury by their tenants withholding their rents. Anna, who called on women to oppose the bailiffs physically, became a hate figure in England, outside of the Irish immigrant circles who revered her. Her effigy was burnt by residents on a bonfire in Eltham in South London on Bonfire Night 1881.[103] The Liberal MP, Herbert Gladstone, travelled over to Ireland at his father's behest and dismissed the Ladies' Land League as 'that insane cat Anna and her silly crew.'[104] This was the company the step-daughter of John Stuart Mill was now keeping.

At the same time as she became involved with Anna Parnell's Ladies' Land League, Helen became a founder member of a new political party, the Democratic Federation. On 15 March 1881, a number of political activists, including Helen, met at the Westminster Palace Hotel in London. Their aim was to promote working-class interests and the meeting took place by '…the efforts of Mr Henry M. Hyndman, Mr Herbert Burrows, Miss Helen Taylor (step-daughter of John Stuart Mill) and some others.'[105] Hyndman had instigated this meeting, which was chaired by Joseph Cowen, the Radical MP. Hyndman's intent was to unite all the Radical Clubs of London within a single political party.[106] Hyndman was new to Radical politics having previously been a Conservative. He knew few of the people he had gathered round him but they were essential to the success of his plan for they were all leading radicals with huge influence among the working-class. The aim was to create an organised movement of English radicals against the despotic and anti-democratic Coercion Acts in Ireland.[107]

One of the organisations involved in the meeting was the recently formed Land Nationalisation Society, which Helen had co-founded along with Mr Canning Swinton, Dr Wallace and Mr T.F. Walker.[108] It was so new that it only had a provisional committee but its formation was widely noted in the press that March.[109] It was demanding an end to freehold on land and that all land should be nationalised though it advocated compensating landlords. Demand for land reform had waxed and waned for centuries going right back to the Diggers who had occupied land in Surrey in 1649 and had declared land belonged to all.[110] Mid-nineteenth century Chartists had demanded that land should be used for the housing and employment of the working-class and this would need government intervention. The Chartist Fergal O'Connor had created a ballot which had 70,000 subscribers. Those successful would receive a plot of land. Mill had believed peasant proprietorship was the answer to making more land available to the growing population.[111] He had regarded the unearned wealth gained from rent by landlords, as immoral. As regards Ireland, Mill had called for an end to landlordism and the creation of peasant proprietary i.e. farmers who owned their land. He believed that this reform was necessary to secure the continuation of the union of Great Britain and Ireland.[112] He argued that, until the passing of such land reform legislation, there should be 'fixed rents and perpetuity of interest for the tenant and the removal of competition as the determinant of rent.'[113] This pamphlet, *England and Ireland*, which Mill published in 1868, has been cited as preparing 'English liberal opinion for land reform in Ireland.'[114] It criticised excessive rents (rack renting) in England and Ireland and the profits made by landowners from rents paid by their tenants. We have seen how Mill was a central figure in the Land

Tenure Reform Association, calling for government intervention on land ownership and rents. A short-lived organisation for land reform, the Tenure Reform League emerged in 1871 created by Mill and Alfred Russel Wallace, a founder of the Land Nationalisation Society, but collapsed on Mill's death in 1873. The increasing population of industrial Britain needed more access to land for their livelihoods but it was in the hands of relatively few private landlords. Access to land became one of the leading political campaigns of the latter part of the century. The Land Nationalisation Society would become a very influential campaign group and, by 1909, 180 MPs would be signed up as vice presidents, with a further 130 as members. It would publish pamphlets to promote the cause and a monthly journal, *Land and Labour*.[115] After the First World War the land movement faded rapidly as an increasingly urban industrialised working-class transferred their allegiance from Liberal to Labour.

On 7 June 1881, the provisional committee of Hyndman's new organisation, the Democratic Federation, held its first meeting. In attendance were members of London's trade societies, radical clubs and the Land Nationalisation Society. The committee's recommendations for the manifesto of the new party, which were set before the meeting, clearly show the radical chartist heritage of the members. It would not become a Marxist socialist organisation until 1884. The committee, which included Helen, recommended the following chartist demands for adoption as party policy – manhood suffrage, triennial parliaments, equal electoral districts and the payment, from taxation, of MPs salaries and elections expenses. The Chartist Charter of 1838 had demanded the vote for all men over 21, secret ballots, no property qualifications for suffrage, payment of MPs, equal electoral district and annual parliaments. Its influence was very much in evidence at this meeting. Despite the adoption of Marxism in 1884, Hyndman found it important to record, in his memoirs, that the use of 'social democrat' for members of the newly formed Marxist Social Democratic Federation, was not influenced by the Marxist Social Democrats in Germany. It was a continuation of the term as 'used by the leading Chartist, Bronterre O'Brien, nearly fifty years ago, long before the influence of Marx or Engels.'[116] The Democratic Federation, in 1881, owed nothing to Marxism and everything to the mid-century reformers of Helen's childhood still active in the country's radical clubs. They wanted to improve democracy by increasing the number of the working-class entitled to the vote (though not all reformers supported extending the suffrage to women). Newspapers also saw the connection with the radicalism of the past. The press deemed the Democratic Federation to be 'the new radical movement.'[117]

Hyndman, was elected as chair, and distributed his pamphlet *England for All*.[118] This work was heavily indebted to Mill's *Considerations on Representative Government* in its discussion on the moral necessity of democracy which would avoid the tyranny of either the masses or the aristocratic few. The structure of the chapters of *England For All*, and its argument, follow Mill's earlier work closely.[119] Hyndman greatly admired the work of Helen's step-father. At the meeting Helen spoke for her motion that called for the party to formally support women's suffrage for she 'felt confident that there was scarcely a man present who would not as a matter of abstract right admit that women had a right to political representation (cheers).'[120] Her motion was passed despite a heated debate between supporters and opponents. Mr Matthias reminded those present that 'delegates had not been sent here to discuss women's suffrage.'[121] She was unsuccessful in a further motion she put to the meeting to include demands for a Republic to be included in the party's manifesto.[122] Newspaper reports later would call Helen a 'red republican theorist.'[123] That year, 1881, she sent 40 marks (worth £165 today) to the families of German socialists, being persecuted for their politics, through the intermediary of Eleanor Marx. Eleanor told Karl Kautsky, the Czech Marxist activist and philosopher, that Helen 'is much interested in our German movement' and asked for Helen's donation to be acknowledged in the *Social Democrat*.[124] A commitment to land nationalisation was also adopted as many of those present were O'Brienites; followers of Bronterre O'Brien who were also members of the Land Nationalisation Society. O'Brien had advocated that nationalisation of the land should be the first legislation enacted by the British Parliament after the passing of the chartist Charter into law.[125] A motion, in support of Irish Home Rule, was also passed by the meeting. Following this first meeting, Hyndman, recently converted to the Irish nationalist cause, republished his pamphlet, *England for All*, to include land nationalisation, Home Rule for Ireland, reform of the inheritance laws, nationalisation of the railways, land registration and for land sequestration for the purpose of renting it to those who needed it to work on and for housing, with landlords being compensated for the loss.[126]

Following this first meeting of the new party, the Democratic Federation sent a delegation of two members to Ireland to meet up with the Land

League and report on the progress of the Land War. Despite the demands of the London School Board, Helen travelled to Ireland that June ahead of the official delegation to meet up with the Ladies' Land League.[127] Before she left for Ireland Helen attended a meeting of the London Branch of the Ladies' Land League along with Charles Stewart Parnell at which she blamed the British Liberal government for the evictions of Irish farmers. The government had put 'the forces of the crown at the disposal of the landlords.'[128] Then she left for Ireland for which she was remembered as 'the first Englishwoman who volunteered to visit Ireland during those dark and troublesome days when the Land League agitation was at its height.'[129] The official delegation of the Democratic Federation, which included the suffragist Jessie Craigen, had been delayed from travelling owing to the sickness of a member and they did not arrive in Ireland until early July.[130] The brief of the official party was to attend a Land League meeting in Dublin and then travel throughout the country to witness the eviction of tenants for non-payment of rent.[131] Jessie Craigen wrote the report of the trip which was published later that summer. After her trip to Ireland, Helen stepped up her work on behalf of the Land League of Great Britain. Many emigrant Irish lived in Britain, forced to leave Ireland in search of work. They thanked her, at her attendance of the Southwark Branch of the Ladies' Land League, 'for her noble and constant advocacy of the cause of the Irish people.'[132] On the return of the official Democratic Federation delegation Helen attended a meeting of the North London Branch of the Ladies' Land League at which the Democratic Federation delegates described their experiences at evictions. A resolution was passed condemning the Coercion Acts. [133] Helen was now firmly an enemy of the official Liberal Party and its members on the London School Board.

On 4 August 1881, Helen chaired a public meeting at Blackfriars, London, at which the Democratic Federation delegates to Ireland reported again on their experiences there. She was juggling a heavy work schedule and was delayed due to a meeting of the London School Board.[134] Mr J. Finlay Finlayson spoke of the plight of the Irish tenant farmers who were 'housed in hovels compared with which the kraals of the Hottentots and the wigwams of the American Indians were palaces.' He described a riot at Mitchelstown and how, at a sale of land in Naas, the police had been 'present in groups of three with loaded carbines.' Finlayson put forward a resolution condemning coercion and calling for the end to the system of landlordism in Ireland. He blamed the unrest on 'excessive rents' which 'constituted the great evil under which Ireland was suffering.' Jessie Craigen, at this time a friend of Helen's though later we will see there was a falling out, called for an end to landlordism. She was scathing on the subject of Gladstone's Land Bill, which would be accepted by Charles Stewart Parnell the following year, dismissing it as 'not worth tuppence.'[135]

In September, Helen verbally attacked Gladstone at a meeting of the Democratic Federation which had been called to officially adopt its constitution. A resolution was passed condemning the attack which Gladstone and the leading Liberal MP Joseph Chamberlain had made on the Democratic Federation manifesto for the Tyrone election in Ireland. Chamberlain was an anti-home ruler and would join the Liberal Unionists in 1886 when the Liberal Party split following Gladstone's failed Home Rule Bill. The Tyrone manifesto had accused Gladstone of becoming reactionary with age and the Democratic Federation had, in protest against the Coercion Acts, put forward its own Home Rule candidate for this parliamentary by-election. The election, on 7 September 1881, of this two MP constituency, would return both the Conservative and Liberal candidates with the Home Ruler only taking 12.7 per cent of the vote but the Liberals had feared a split in the progressive vote would result in their candidate's defeat. The motion against Gladstone was defeated with only four votes in favour. Helen, however, in speaking in favour of the motion, claimed that the draconian Coercion laws, which saw hundreds of Irish imprisoned without trail during the unrest, proved that 'Mr Gladstone was equally ready to support democracy or despotism as it answered his purpose.'[136] She heaped more ire onto her head when newspapers printed that she had called Gladstone a 'dastardly recreant... who had forsaken the true policy of liberalism' for 'personal ambition and jealousy.'[137] The inaccuracy of the quote made Helen even more belligerent. She wrote an unrepentant letter to the editor of *The Echo* denying she had used that exact phrase but '...I did call him a dastard and a recreant and believe that half of England would echo those words if polled.'[138] It was further claimed in the press that she had also called Gladstone 'a hoary headed old humbug.'[139] She had increased the animosity of the Liberal Party towards her (if that were possible) and there were various attacks in the press on her. Many Liberal supporters hoped she would lose her seat at the next School Board Election to be held the following year.[140] It was likely that she was being watched by detectives from Scotland Yard at this time as it was widely believed that prominent land leaguers were being monitored by the authorities.[141]

On 23 October 1881 a demonstration against coercion was arranged by the National Land League of Great Britain to take place in Hyde Park London. Helen, who had been appointed President of the Ladies' Land League of Great Britain attended.[142] Shortly afterwards, in response to escalating agitation and unrest throughout Great Britain and Ireland in support of the Land Leaguers, the Liberal government proscribed the Land League and arrested its leaders including Charles Stewart Parnell along with many of the rank and file. Nora Lynch sent Helen a telegram from the Dublin headquarters of the Ladies' Land League informing her of Parnell's arrest.[143] Michael Davitt had had his parole licence revoked and had been in Portland prison, in Dorset, since March to serve the rest of his 1870 sentence for treason. Forster's Protection of Life and Property Act saw over a thousand men imprisoned for land league activities.[144] The Ladies' Land League now had to oversee the Land War in the absence of the men. They discovered, to their horror, that the men had only been going through the motions of a no rent campaign and that the administration of the organisation was woeful. The men had left the women no directives on how the campaign should be continued. Anna Parnell would never forgive Irish nationalist men for their lip service to what could have been, in her opinion, a defining moment in the campaign for Home Rule.[145]

Shortly after the arrests of the men, on 26 October, Helen was summoned to Ireland by Anna Parnell '…if you could come over, we should all be very glad and you would do great good.'[146] Early in November, Helen left her School Board work, in particular the campaign against child abuse at Upton House, to go over to Dublin and attend a meeting of the Ladies' Land League. It was during this trip that Helen wrote the letter from a Dublin hotel which would accuse Scrutton of the manslaughter of children at St Paul's Industrial School and land her in court the following year. It was rumoured that the British government were about to make the Ladies' Land League an illegal organisation and, during this Dublin trip, Helen and Anna formulated a plan for the work of the Ladies to continue if this should happen. Henry George, the renowned American land reformer had arrived in Ireland as special correspondent for Patrick Ford's *The Irish World*, and it was in Dublin that he met Helen for the first time. George had exchanged letters with John Stuart Mill in 1869 on Chinese immigration to California and had sent Mill a copy of the article he had published on the subject which he had based on Mill's *Political Economy*. George feared that the lower wages Chinese immigrants worked for would upset the balance of labour and capital because it would increase the latter and depress the former. He also opposed immigration from China on racial grounds for the single men who arrived did not integrate and adapt to the American way of life. Mill's letter in response was published in *The National Standard* in July 1870.[147] Mill wrote to George praising his article.[148] Mill agreed that Chinese immigration should be opposed due to the lowering of wages it would bring for the American workforce but insisted that Chinese immigrants should be granted full citizenship rights as a way of integrating them with American workers and strengthening the organised movement for improved labour conditions.[149] George and Helen shared an interest in land reform and their respect for Mill, and he and his family became lifelong friends. Helen would have read George's recently published book, *Progress and Poverty*, which advocated a single tax on land, to replace all other taxation. Unlike Helen he was not calling for nationalisation of the land but believed that the single tax would provide access to the land for the growing population because landlords would find it uneconomic to hold on to unused land. Unlike the Land Nationalisation Society, he believed that landlords should not receive compensation for the loss of their land. George's book would become the holy bible of land reformers and cheap editions would enable it to be widely read and become popular amongst the increasing number of literate working-class. George informed Patrick Ford, the editor of *The Irish World*, of the discussions between Anna and Helen. He detailed the steps they were taking to mitigate any proscribing of the Ladies' Land League which it was rumoured was the intention of the British government:

> Miss Helen Taylor came to Dublin last week to propose that she should take charge, letting Miss Parnell go to Holyhead and direct from there. Her idea was that as soon as the Government found that the Ladies' League was really doing effective work in keeping up the spirit of the people they would swoop down on the women too, and that it would hurt the Government more to arrest her (an English woman) in Ireland than it would to arrest an Irish woman, and would hurt them much more to arrest Miss Parnell in England than it would to arrest her in Ireland. Miss Taylor, who is one of the most intelligent women I ever met, if not the most intelligent, says the existence of the Gladstone Government is involved, that they will stop at nothing, rather than lose power…Miss Parnell's objection was that she could not be spared.[150]

The Dublin meeting that Helen had been invited over for saw the formation of The Political Prisoners' Aid Society which elected Helen as its president. This organisation would be responsible for fundraising to financially support the families of those land leaguers who were imprisoned under the Coercion Acts. Parnell, imprisoned in Kilmainham jail where his standing as leader of the Parliamentary Irish National Party saw him given the use of his own sitting room, had requested that such an organisation be formed.[151] Ellen McDonagh had been recently killed after having been bayonetted at an eviction by a British soldier in Belmullet, County Mayo. Helen used her acceptance of the presidency of the new organisation to make the link between the Irish Land War and the resistance of the people against government tyranny in Italy and France. Again, she attacked the Liberal government when she boldly asserted that only the government of Turkey was more anti-democratic than Gladstone's.[152]

Helen extended her stay in Ireland to travel to Belmullet as a Ladies' Land League observer at McDonagh's inquest. Anna hoped that an Englishwoman's presence at the inquest would protect those women giving evidence to the coroner from British soldiers.[153] Helen had been due to travel back to England with Anna who went without her to attend a meeting of the Liverpool branch of the Ladies' Land League on 13 November, 1881. She excused Helen's absence as a necessity, owing to Helen travelling to County Mayo because she was 'anxious to hear the truth about this terrible case.'[154] After the inquest Helen travelled on to Hacketstown in County Carlow. It was here that she helped to build the huts supplied by the Land League to shelter the evicted families of one estate. Jennie Wyse Power had been sent by the Ladies' Land League headquarters in Dublin to oversee the erection of fifty huts and to urge tenant farmers to continue to refuse to pay rent to their landlord. A policy of No Rent had been issued by the executive of the league. Jennie Wyse Powell, in whose Dublin house the Easter Rising rebels would sign the 1916 Proclamation, would later become a senator in the Irish Free State. Jennie recalled her time in Carlow with Helen in a 1909 newspaper article. She wrote that, on the evening prior to the evictions, as the two women were sitting in their lodgings planning for the next day, they were interrupted by the arrival of the police. They were obliged to give their names and addresses and the officers 'warned us against unlawful assembly.' The next morning they avoided surveillance by the police by travelling to the evictions by a circuitous route which involved climbing over ditches. The following day the police confined the women to their lodgings to stop them attending any further evictions. The reason given was that, on the previous day, guns had been stolen by land leaguers. Jennie and Helen were told that they would not be allowed to leave the house until these were recovered.[155]

On her return to England, Helen wrote to Henry George's wife, Annie, inviting the George family to stay as her guests in South Kensington when they arrived in London for George to discuss his single tax theory with members of the burgeoning British land movement.[156] Mrs George and her two daughters had just arrived in Ireland from the USA to join him. Helen was able to offer the family a sitting room and two bedrooms in her London flat.[157] The Georges arrived in London in time to celebrate Christmas and New Year. George wrote back to a friend in the USA of his pleasure at the stay:

> We are staying here with Miss Helen Taylor...There is much I would like to tell you about her. She is a noble woman giving her life to good work and she is not a Malthusian nor a materialist.[158]

Helen, regarded by some on the London School Board as the austere, difficult, tactless 'ice maiden', found the company of children much easier than adults. We have seen that she was a devoted aunt to Algernon's children and had enjoyed the visit of Kate Amberley's children to Avignon. The arrival of the George children gave her similar pleasure. Henry's daughter, Anna, remembered the joy of this Christmas in her adult life. She wrote to Helen, in 1895, fondly recalling her Christmas in London as a 4-year-old:

> One of the few recollections is of you several times at meals in a softly lighted room making me tiny spoons of tin foil and letting me put them into the sugar bowl but not into my mouth.[159]

Later, Anna remembered Helen as 'outwardly a typical English woman of the Victorian era – domestic, soft-voiced and gentle in manner, wearing – when in the house – a white lace cap on her smooth parted hair.' She had a 'love of her fellow man,' and was 'equally happy talking politics and making spoons out of tin foil for the children to dip in the sugar.'[160]

On Christmas Eve, 1881, the Ladies' Land League was declared illegal by the Liberal government and Anna wrote a letter to the press giving instructions to supporters that should she, herself, be imprisoned all correspondence relating to the Ladies' Land League should be sent to Helen in London.[161] This had obviously been agreed between herself and Helen the previous month in Dublin. The first woman to be arrested was Hannah Reynolds who was imprisoned at the end of December for inciting tenants to stay in their homes and resist eviction when the bailiffs came for non-payment of rent.[162] During the first half of 1882, regular arrests of lady land leaguers at evictions took place. Unlike the men, who were given the status of political prisoners, not common criminals, the women were denied this dignity. A statute of Edward III, dating from the fourteenth century, which allowed unaccompanied women to be imprisoned on suspicion of being prostitutes, was employed to legally validate their arrest. Anna dealt with the proscription of the Ladies' Land League by calling the British government's bluff. She arranged for every branch of the organisation in Ireland to meet at the same time, 2 pm, on one Saturday in January 1882. The meetings passed without incident. The government, not wanting a public backlash for arresting thousands of women at the same time, had backed down.[163] Anna's tactics had proved excellent and the Ladies' organisation faced no further threat from the British Government. Its destruction would be at the hands of their own Irish nationalist men, many of whom had never supported women becoming involved in the agitation.

(iv) 1882: The End of the Land War, the Scrutton Libel Case and Re-election to the London School Board

This year would see the dissolution of the Ladies' Land League, the rise of the British land reform movement, the influence of the Democratic Federation on her educational policies and Helen's re-election for a third term to the London School Board, despite the attempts of local Liberals to unseat her. In January 1882, Henry George returned to Ireland to report back to the *Irish World* on the latest developments in the Land War whilst Mrs George and the two children remained in South Kensington until the spring.[164] That month Helen travelled to Liverpool where a branch of the Democratic Federation had just been formed. Here she spoke on Ireland, believing the time was 'ripe for revolutionary changes.'[165] Her vision of

Irish independence was similar to Michael Davitt's with whom she would work closely in the Land Nationalisation Society. At the meeting, Helen declared: 'When the time came that Ireland was free, and the time she thought was not far distant (cheers) she hoped that Ireland would form part of a Britannic Federation.'[166] Davitt, later that same year, explained the difference between Home Rulers and Nationalists. Home Rulers, whilst demanding an Irish parliament in Dublin, would keep their representation in the Imperial Parliament in London. Nationalists such as Davitt, intended that that Irish would withdraw from the House of Commons after the formation of the Dublin parliament:

> I want Ireland to have a constitution similar to that in Canada – the Government to consist of a Lord Lieutenant or Governor, a Senate or Upper House and an Assembly or House of Commons…This Parliament should be elected upon the basis of Universal suffrage.[167]

Helen and Davitt saw an independent Ireland being self-governing but retaining links with Britain like Australia or Canada. Helen set out her thinking on Home Rule at a speech at Hatcham Liberal Club during the passage of the defeated 1886 Home Rule Bill which split the Liberal party. By this time, she was again moving in Liberal circles due to Gladstone's conversion to Home Rule. She dismissed the fear of many who opposed the Home Rule Bill that an autonomous parliament in Ireland might threaten Britain. She said Ireland was no closer than France and that the idea that 25 million English people should fear 5 million Irish people was ridiculous. The argument that Catholics could not govern themselves was against liberal ideas of religious freedom. She concluded by destroying the belief, held by some anti Home Rule Liberals, that the parliamentary party needed the Irish MPs' presence and support in the chamber to get their legislation through parliament in the face of Conservative opposition. It was 'ridiculous to say we needed Ireland to govern ourselves.'[168] Delaying Home Rule, which she believed to be inevitable, would result in the two countries being 'absolutely separated.'

Henry George, whilst over in Ireland, during the early months of 1882, gave Helen constant updates on the state of the country in letters to his wife who he constantly asked to inform him of Helen's opinion on these matters. The Ladies' Land League members continued to attend evictions, provide aid for prisoner's families, assemble Land League huts for the evicted tenants and administer the donations raised in the USA and Great Britain. They also secretly printed and distributed the banned Land League newspaper, *United Ireland*, which Anna Parnell later recalled as being the most rewarding and enjoyable of their duties.[169] Branches of the Ladies' Land League met regularly in Ireland and throughout Great Britain and were reported on in the Irish nationalist press, *The Nation* and *United Ireland.* Branches were named after women in the movement. There was a 'Mrs Delia Parnell Branch' in honour of Anna's mother and two were named after Helen Taylor (one in North London and one in Manchester).[170] Helen continued to travel throughout Great Britain to speak on behalf of the Land League and of her own personal experience of witnessing evictions for non-payment of rent in Ireland.[171] Annie George involved herself in Helen's public life and attended one of Helen's regular Southwark school board public meetings in March 1882. This had been organised to discuss the Industrial Schools' abuse scandal. Here, at the Drill Hall in Bermondsey, Elizabeth Surr spoke and emphasised to those present that, although she had been given much of the credit for uncovering the scandal, it was Helen who had done much of the work.[172] Annie George certainly experienced the breadth of Helen's campaigning including, in January 1882, a conference held by the Land Nationalisation Society in London at which Helen, as one of the vice presidents, spoke.[173]

Henry George returned to England, in the spring of 1882, to campaign for Land Reform. He gave his first speech in London at a public meeting organised by the Land Nationalisation Society.[174] During the early summer he and his family travelled over to Paris together, a trip which he greatly looked forward to.[175] The Georges would continue their friendship with Helen until their death. Helen was not a natural letter writer and she often apologised to friends and family, including the Georges, for not having put pen to paper.[176] Helen would write to the Georges about the goings on at the London School Board, and the animosity of the Liberal members towards her, but the letters contain little overtly personal. This is hardly surprising given Helen's social reserve. They followed each other's lives closely, however, and Helen was particularly interested in George's unsuccessful campaign to become Mayor of New York in 1886. She wrote to Mrs George then for copies of his speeches.[177] The Georges always hoped that they could persuade her to visit them in America for they felt 'much respect and admiration' and 'a warm and genuine friendship' towards her.[178] When

Henry and Annie's son, Harry, came to England, in 1893, Helen wrote to his mother of her intention to meet up with him.[179] The daughter, Anna, continued to ask her to come over to the USA after her father's death in 1895. Helen was 64 by this time and in declining health and never took the trip over the Atlantic.[180]

Back to April 1882. Charles Parnell made peace with Gladstone and accepted what became known as the Kilmainham Treaty. The 1881 Land Act created a peasant proprietary and marked the passing of the Land League into history. It also wrote off the rent arrears of 130,000 tenant farmers.[181] Parnell and all the remaining imprisoned land leaguers were released from prison. To Helen, Davitt, George, Anna Parnell, the Democratic Federation and the Land Nationalisation Society this was capitulation and a sell-out. It left landless labourers with no option but to emigrate for it did not give more access to the land for the greater number of the population. It benefited the better off tenant farmers only who already had land to work on. Parnell had never supported the foundation of the Ladies' Land League, and on his release, he cut off its funding. Parnell, ever a constitutionalist, blamed the women for the escalation in agrarian violence. He feared that the campaign was getting out of hand. Violence was not the way to win Ireland's freedom. Home Rule was to be achieved through the democratic structures of democracy not through revolutionary lawlessness. Henry George wrote to Patrick Ford that the Irish Parliamentary party were 'getting frightened at the length to which the movement was going and were disposed to unite with the Government on fixing up the Land Bill.'[182] George was back in Ireland during the end of the campaign and the demise of the Ladies' Land League. Its dissolution appeared as a notice in the 12 August edition of *The Nation*.[183] George wrote to his wife Annie, who was living again with Helen in South Kensington. 'Tell Miss Taylor that Anna Parnell is very anxious to get out and told me last night they would close as soon as possible and let the males *(missing word)* how they could get along.[184]

Anna had decided to dissolve the Ladies' Land League rather than become a secretariat for the male Land League which is what the men intended for them.[185] Anna remained bitter over the Kilmainham Treaty until the end of her life in 1911. (She drowned, aged 59, while swimming in the sea in Ilfracombe, England where she was living in lodgings under an assumed name. This was to escape the attention the Parnell name attracted after the divorce scandal her brother was named in). The Land War, she wrote in her history of it, had been a sham. The men had never been serious about carrying out an effective 'no rent' campaign, which the women had seriously tried to make a success of. The 1881 Land Act benefited the more prosperous tenants, who could afford to buy their farms, but thousands of landless labourers were forced to emigrate. In *The Tale of a Great Sham,* unpublished until the 1980s, she bitterly proclaimed: 'However, long I might live; I knew that it would never again be possible for me to believe that any body of Irishmen meant a word of anything they said.'[186]

Henry George wrote to Patrick Ford that Charles Stewart Parnell had 'thrown away the greatest opportunity any Irishman ever had. It is the birth right for the mess of potage.'[187] Davitt, too was bitter:

> …(it) was the turning point in Mr Parnell's career and he unfortunately turned in the wrong direction…He now resolved to surrender the Land League and to enter the new stage of his political fortunes as an opportunist statesman.[188]

Davitt had been elected as the MP for County Meath in 1882 but disqualified as he was in prison. He was so angry at the men's treatment of their women Land League colleagues that he refused to attend the meeting of the parliamentary party called to discuss political developments:

> But when he found at the last moment that he could not even get a resolution of thanks to the Ladies' League upon the Mansion House programme he declined to take part or have his name included in the committee.[189]

Henry George supported Davitt's actions for the parliamentary party 'never seem to have really appreciated the work the ladies were doing…there was a constant jar going on between Kilmainham and 39 Sackville Street, the men seeking to curb what they saw as the extravagance of the women.'[190] George had been at the Ladies' Land League offices in Sackville Street, Dublin, the evening of Parnell's release, where the women 'instead of rejoicing were like mourners at a wake.'[191] Helen, there is no doubt, agreed with George, Davitt and Anna who believed they had been betrayed by Parnell. George wrote to her from Dublin in October 1882:

> Anna Parnell is well but has not been to the Land League since her illness. Miss Lynch has gone to Spain. A few of the Ladies

> remain doing some work for the Mansion House Committee, but the glory has departed. The women feel really bitter towards the Parliamentary men.[192]

Anna had been very ill, grieving the unexpected death of her sister Fanny in America that August. The women had given their male colleagues 'a very frantic piece of their minds' and Virginia Lynch had threatened to throw Arthur O'Gorman out of the window. Davitt regretted ever having had 'anything to do with the Parliamentary crowd.' George tried to give Helen some hope that 'good will come out of it though and after a period of quiet a more radical and more intelligent movement will result.' Knowing that Helen would feel despondent and experience a loss of purpose at the turn of affairs, he urged her to come to America on a lecture tour. He believed, as Hyndman did, that she was wasting her 'powers.' His concern at the effect on Helen of the news from Dublin is seen in the emotional support he tried to offer her.[193] Jessie Craigen also wrote to Helen during this time following a meeting she had had with Charles Stewart Parnell, who she said, had 'sold himself to the ministry.'[194] She had previously found him encouraging of her involvement with the Ladies' Land League but this time he had been aloof and distant. 'From these circumstances I infer the truth of my information as his having turned traitor to the national cause.' Helen and Jessie had recently argued and the previous warmth between them had ended. The argument remains unknown but Jessie wished to rectify matters and resume the friendship:

> I beg you to forgive all hasty words and to read my letters. I love you more than life. I want nothing of you except that you will let me be a comfort to you as you used to tell me once that I was.

Perhaps it was Jessie becoming involved again with the British women's suffrage movement, which Helen was by now estranged from due to her political work, that had caused the argument. Priscilla McLaren wrote to Helen on 21st September 1882. The letter mentions that Helen and Jessie have argued but gives no cause. She advocates for Jessie and tells Helen that Jessie wants her to know she never intended upsetting Helen with her actions[195] The end of Jessie's and Helen's friendship has been blamed on Jessie's attack on Charles Stewart Parnell but this is certainly not the case.[196] We have seen that land nationalisers, socialists and nationalists felt like Jessie did. They had been betrayed by Parnell. In American Irish nationalist circles the Kilmainham treaty was dismissed as 'the sale of the land league.'[197] The Irish Americans of the nationalist organisation Clan na Gael were of the same opinion as was Andrew Kettle, a leading Irish nationalist. Kettle wrote in his memoirs that Anna Parnell was in sight of winning the Land War when Parnell called off the campaign:

> I found she had a better knowledge of the lights and shades of Irish peasant life, of the real economic conditions of the country, and of the social and political forces which had to be acted upon to work out the freedom of Ireland than any person, man or woman I have ever met…Anna Parnell would have worked the Land League revolution to a much better conclusion than her great brother.[198]

Ethel Leach was a close friend of Helen in the Ladies' Land League and the women's suffrage movement, and a member of the School Board in Great Yarmouth. She reveals her and Helen's state of mind in 1882 in a letter of 1890. Parnell's parliamentary career had just been ended by his having been cited in a divorce case which publicly revealed his long-term relationship with Katherine O'Shea. This had been an open secret for years but the scandal of the public outing of it finished him in politics though he strove desperately to keep control of the constitutional Irish nationalist movement until his death in 1891. Ethel wrote:

> For my part I cannot see how the matter [i.e. the divorce scandal] need affect the question of Home Rule at all, I was not working for Mr Parnell but the cause of the Irish people and if he and all his parl (sic) party disgrace themselves the need for justice to Ireland will remain…You and Miss Parnell and I would have known better than to trust him *(i.e. Gladstone)* or any of the wire pullers, he ought to have been compelled to define the principles of his bill long ago, surely he will have to do so now, and thus there may be a silver lining to this cloud.[199]

Whatever the cause of the end of Jessie and Helen's friendship there were those who could not believe that Helen was not to blame, including the suffragist, Anna Priestman:

> Helen Taylor took her up as a friend *(sic)* before anyone else in that rank of life. And Miss Craigen worshipped her and anchored her very heart upon her – soon after this Miss C came to Bristol and was received by people there as a friend and an equal.... When some of us knew what trust she put in Miss T we shivered for we knew there was grief before her – Miss Colman tried to warn her but I think this only made Miss C cling more entirely to Miss T.[200]

Helen, always a divisive figure, was believed by Anna Priestman, and no doubt many others in the women's suffrage movement, to have used Jessie for her own political ends. She accused Helen, in her letter to Priscilla McLaren, of having sent Jessie over to Ireland alone in the summer of 1881 as part of the Democratic Federation delegation, instead of travelling with her. This left Jessie in the company of men with a 'drinking habit.' Jessie paints a very different picture, in her official report on the trip. She wrote that, far from being left to fend for herself among drunken men, she was well looked after and in the company of nationalist women:

> I was during my stay the guest of the Ladies' Land League; and I have to record with pleasure and grateful remembrance the kindness I received from Mrs Lynch and her daughters, Mrs O'Reilly, Miss Hodnett and Miss Kirke, who travelled with me by turns, and from Miss Anna Parnell.[201]

She thanks Anna Parnell, in her report, for staying with her in her lodgings when she was ill despite her heavy work load which meant she should have been elsewhere. [202] The women leaders of the Ladies' Land League were from respectable middle class, mainly urban Catholic, nationalist families[203] and would not have left an English woman, who came over as their guest, to fend for herself far from home. Anna Parnell had great concern for the welfare of the young girls who staffed the Dublin headquarters of the Ladies' Land League. Katherine Tynan recalled her kindness and how she would bring sweets and cake to share between them, admire their clothes and listen to their chat.[204] It is hard to believe she would have left an English woman to fend for herself away from home and she did not.[205] There is clearly anti-Irish racism at play here. Anna Maria, later in the letter, informs Priscilla that Jessie was now unacceptable to many within the British suffrage movement because of her involvement in Irish politics and there was opposition to her re-joining the suffrage movement which she had left to work for the Irish Land League. Clearly Helen was not going to be forgiven by many British feminists for taking Jessie out of the suffrage movement to join in the anti-British Irish Land War. Jessie was an eccentric within the movement.[206] Jessie's obituary in the *Englishwoman's Review*, in 1899, refers to her lack of self-control and how she would not bow to organisational discipline:

> But that wayward soul could brook no constraint nor control; the calm dispassionate ways of the Women's Suffrage Committee were irritating to her and she swept along her way to Home Rule, to anti vaccination and other questions in which she could let her passionate emotions have full play… Her passionate craving for justice and affection blinded her to the true way of obtaining either.[207]

The winding up of the Ladies' Land League, late that summer, still left Helen's life a hectic one. She was busy all year with her School Board work and faced re-election in the November. Helen had been concerned that the establishment of School Board higher education schools would not help the working-class who could not afford the luxury of staying on at school after reaching the end of compulsory education. She wanted the board to fund higher education evening schools, which could be attended by young people after work where books and materials would be free of charge.[208] She insisted that the educational endowments should be used for this purpose. In May 1882, the Educational Endowments Committee agreed to write to the Charity Commission calling on them to employ the educational endowments in the Bethnal Green area of the city to the funding of free education for the borough's poor children.[209] Helen also tabled a motion that 'the Board petition parliament to be allowed to open all its elementary schools free.'[210] She argued that it was not cost-effective collecting and enforcing fees and that children were often sent home for the fee and so missed class. Helen claimed she knew of teachers, who were so worried about losing government grants if children were absent, who paid their pupils' fees. Helen's work on the Educational Endowments Committee increased her popularity in her Southwark school board division. When Helen spoke at a public meeting, in Bermondsey, called to oppose the closure of Bacon School, she was cheered, and 'warmly received on rising.' She called for the endowed schools, attended by the working-class, to be defended against closure for they 'had been left to them by their ancestors.'[211] She reported that the board had agreed to consider the establishment of free schools in London's poorest boroughs and that board schools would be available for Sunday schools at a low rent. She always advocated that schools should be available for community use outside of the school day and that local groups should be able to hire them for meetings.[212]

During the summer of 1882, shortly before the demise of the Ladies' Land League, Helen appeared in court on a libel charge. Back in November 1881, whilst in Ireland witnessing evictions in the company of Jennie Wise Power, Helen had written a letter accusing fellow board member, Thomas Scrutton, of manslaughter following the death of boys at St Paul's, the industrial school of which he was the manager. She claimed the boys had died of food poisoning. This letter was read out at a public meeting held on the Industrial School scandal in November 1881, in Tower Hamlets. Being away on Land League business, Helen had been unable to attend. Scrutton demanded that she withdraw her accusation that he had 'supplied some of the miserable adulterated food himself to the school and there can be little doubt in my mind that the children were kept there only to make money by their work.' Helen had repeated this claim at a school board meeting on 19 January 1882 and at a public meeting in her constituency on 7 March.[213] Helen refused Scrutton's demand that she retract and he sued her for libel. The case came to trial in June 1882 during which Helen insisted her comments were the truth and that Scrutton was a Christian hypocrite in allowing the abuse of children at the school.[214] Elizabeth Surr gave evidence which supported Helen's claims. She informed the court that she had seen, with her own eyes, a boy lying on a bed who had an uncovered abscess and that Scrutton had laughed when she had tried to discuss this with him. Elizabeth claimed that the boys were 'semi-starved' and Mrs Winch, a widow, gave evidence that her son, who was healthy when sent to the school, had died two years later of 'ophthalmia and convulsions.' Elson, a former pupil, told of a boy who, shortly before his death, had been prevented from warming his hands and feet by the fire. He gave evidence that the gruel they were given was infested with black beetles and supplemented with only 6oz of bread and milk and water per day.' Scrutton denied all these claims and gave, in his defence, the fact that the death certificates of the boys who had died at the school all gave 'natural causes' as the cause.[215] Taylor's barrister, believing the case to be unwinnable, advised that she should settle by paying Scrutton £1,000 in damages. This she did though she refused to retract her accusations and admit guilt.[216] The judge recognised that Helen had 'acted upon a sense of duty'[217] which was vindication of sorts for her and she left the court to the cheers of her supporters in the public gallery.[218] Henry George, writing a partisan report of the case in the American-Irish nationalist paper *Irish World*, blamed Helen's support for Home Rule and improved tenancies for Irish farmers for the outcome. She had no chance in a court of law, as the jury was packed with 'a number of personal and business friends of the plaintiff.' Scrutton's lawyer had drawn the attention of the jury to Helen's support of the Irish tenant farmers and her vocal opposition to British government policy in Ireland as a member of the Land League. This made the trial unfair in George's opinion. George also blamed her solicitor, an old family friend of Helen's, for presenting the defence inadequately. Evidence of mismanagement of the school was ruled out by the judge and could not, therefore, be considered by the jury. George blamed Helen's pro-Irish stance on 'the Irish question' for the lack of press support for her but he took heart that the 'common people applauded her on leaving court.' Helen left the building, George wrote, to the applause of the many working-class who had attended to support her.[219] Priscilla McLaren wrote to her after the trial:

> I was thankful to see that you had the sympathy of outsiders and that you were so warmly cheered when you left the court…I hope you will not have to pay one farthing of the £1000.[220]

In November 1882 Helen faced re-election to the School Board, again as an independent Radical Democrat supported by the Democratic Federation and Camberwell Radical Club. She recalled to Henry George, after the election, the animosity of the local Liberals to her and the campaign they waged to unseat her. They had distributed pamphlets and bills which attacked her extreme politics, thereby hoping to sway public opinion against her:

> The Liberal Association of the Borough distinctly declared that my conduct in regard to Ireland and Gladstone made it impossible for 'liberals' to allow me to be re-elected.[221]

The press had speculated that she would lose her seat as a result of the trial for libel.[222] In the run up to the election, *The School Board Chronicle* had accused Helen, Elizabeth Surr and their supporters on the London School Board who voted against the policies of the Progressive group, of being blind to 'the real enemy – the opponents of a national education system:'[223]

> Miss Helen Taylor's radicalism is of the type that does not much serve the true interests of the work, but the lady's crotchets will probably be forgiven by the constituency by reason of her democracy, her ability and her devotion to what she conceives to be the interest of the public.[224]

Undaunted Helen had held numerous election meetings in the borough and issued a letter in the local press to the electorate, clearly setting out her manifesto:

> Ladies and Gentlemen
> After Six Years' Service on the School Board, I come again to ask you to re-elect me, that I may work to secure, before all other things, the safety and kindly treatment of your children in all the Schools. And next, I want to get Free Education, in order that every child may be educated without suffering and cost to the parents when they can least afford it. And thirdly, I will work in the future as I have done in the past, against that shameful extravagance of the London School Board which raises the rates and is felt as an additional burden by every struggling ratepayer in London. And lastly, I will work to secure the Endowments for the people.
>
> Free Schools. No Cruelty.
> No Corporal Punishment. No Extravagance.
> No Payments by Commission.

Open Tender for all Contracts.
Open Advertisement for all Appointments.
Open Supervision of all Industrial Schools.
No Malversation of the Educational Endowments.
For these things I shall work if you re-elect me, and I remain,
Ladies and Gentlemen,

Yours faithfully,
HELEN TAYLOR.
Central Committee Room,
16, Southwark Street, S.E., Nov., 1882.[225]

The electorate recognised the work Helen had done, during the last six years, for the education of their children and against profligate use of public funds (as seen in the Shaftesbury debacle) and returned her at the top of the poll with 9,302 votes. Also elected was a local Church of England vicar, the Rev. Charles Lawrence (8,285 votes) and two of the previous London School Board Members being supported by the Liberal Party, Alexander Hawkins (5,932 votes) and Mary Richardson (5,904 votes). Existing member Edward Corry, standing as an economy candidate, was defeated. Helen's anger over the expenditure on the Shaftesbury training ship had not diminished by the time of the 1882 election when her outspokenness went too far. She rashly made the accusation that the supplier of seaboots for the trainees on the ship, Mr Pocock, have been awarded the contract in return for a donation to the election expenses of Mary Richardson. Helen withdrew her accusation and denied she had ever intended to imply any wrongdoing on the part of Miss Richardson but she refused to withdraw her comments that the contract had been inappropriately awarded to Pocock. It had not been open, competitive tendering. [226]

(v) 1883–1884: The Land Reform Movement Takes Off in Great Britain, the Democratic Federation Embraces Marxism and Helen Becomes the First Woman Chair of a London School Board Standing Committee

Helen was now 52 and at her peak of her political and social involvement. Living most of the year in her flat in South Kensington, school board work took up an increasing amount of time. She was successful in June 1883 in being appointed as chair of the Educational Endowments Committee, a hugely prestigious position and a first for women.[227] Despite the Liberal Party having tried to unseat her, the Liberals controlling the London School Board recognised her talent and undoubtedly sought to direct her energies into something positive which the board could benefit from. When she retired from the board in November 1885 even the ever-critical *School Board Chronicle*, which had often despaired at her extreme politics, praised her chairing of the Educational Endowments Committee which 'under her presidency has collected and presented to the Board a large amount of valuable information.'[228] The 1884 Educational Endowments Committee Report recommended that the Board should use the endowments to feed and clothe the poor.[229] It further recommended that the Charity Commission should supply the government with information on all charities feeding, clothing and providing trade apprenticeships for the poor in London. The government should then transfer these powers to the London School Board.[230] This was the work that the *School Board Chronicle* recognised as Helen's positive contribution.

Helen was appointed chair despite her earlier opposition to plans to use the endowments to benefit the middle classes. In April 1883, an endowment left by a John Carpenter came before the committee. The City of London had been using the endowment to educate four sons of Freemen of the City. The Committee judged that, as no will was to be found which could prove that this had been the intended use of the legacy, the London School Board should support the Corporation of the City of London's plan to divert the endowment to the funding of a school which would 'instruct boys in the higher branches of literature.' This was opposed by four committee members, Helen, William Roston Bourke, Charles White and George Mitchel, who added a dissenting statement to the committee's recommendation to the board:

> …that we are of the opinion it is desirable some portion of those funds be applied to the education of the poor and that we recommend requesting the Corporation of the City of London to afford us information as to the property and estates left in trust or otherwise by John Carpenter, any record as to the purposes for which the property was left, the amounts received up to the year 1834 and the value at the present time of the property known as the Carpenter's Trust.[231]

The government appointed Charity Commission was overwhelmed trying to gather information nationally on all the educational endowments. The Educational Endowments Committee was in the process of creating a register of all the charitable endowments in the capital so that it could identify the ones which could be used for education. The committee wrote to all the charities in London asking for full details of their legacies and what they were being used for. The *School Board Chronicle* supported the board's plan to use endowments to fund day time higher education schools for academically able children and ridiculed Helen's call for them to be employed to fund the education of the poor until 'they ceased to pay rates and taxes.'[232] Helen was thinking of her own constituents in her calls for more radical reform. Southwark residents were amongst the poorest in London.[233] Whole families, mother, father and children, lived in single rooms in decaying, overcrowded houses of multiple occupation.[234] The Westcott Street Board School had some of the poorest children in the capital and pupil absences were high, caused mainly by the parents being unable to pay the 'board penny' fee.[235] Many children came to school hungry. Helen saw the distress of her residents and believed free education and school meals could relieve it. Helen had joined the London Municipal Reform League at its inception, back in March 1881. This campaigned for the creation of one overriding municipal authority for London which would bring the control of public services, street paving, sanitation, water and drainage under democratic control. The present system was chaotic with the majority of these services being administrated between the Metropolitan Board of Works, twenty-three London vestries and fifteen District Boards. Although these were elected representatives, they were voted for by very few of the local population, and vestry members and District Board members elected the Metropolitan Board of Works rather than direct elections being held for them. Private companies controlled water and gas.[236] Progressives on the London School Board who were members of the London Municipal Reform League included Florence Fenwick Miller, Benjamin Lucraft and Sydney Buxton. Helen and Florence were on the General Council of the League and Buxton was its president.[237] Pressure for reform of London's chaotic system of local government would result in the creation of the London County Council as a single authority for the metropolis in 1889.[238]

Helen also continued to defend secular education throughout her final term on the board, supporting a complaint from a job applicant for a teaching post who alleged that he had been asked questions on his religious views during the job interview. Helen and her fellow socialist Edward Aveling were successful in having the claim examined by the Committee of Inquiry of the London School Board which found the interviewer not guilty of misconduct. She fulfilled a further election promise to scrutinise spending and contracts by trying to reduce costs to the tax payer. Her motion to instruct an architect to create one blueprint for all future London schools was unsuccessful, however, as members objected to all schools throughout the capital being uniform in appearance.[239] School board schools, throughout England and Wales, are instantly recognisable to this day with their large halls leading off to corridors of classrooms and their red brick and overlarge windows which give plenty of light and air, but they are not of a single, standard design. She made various unsuccessful attempts to have contracts cancelled and put out to public tender including the work to build a new school in Kilburn Lane, Chelsea[240] and the contract for coal supplies.[241] She challenged the spending on London School Board administration, insisting that 'less money ought to be spent on bricks and mortar and on patronage and more on the useful class of the Board's officers – the visitors.'[242] The visitors played an important role in supporting the poor in the education of their children. This was noted by Charles Booth in his social survey of the living conditions of Londoners, published in 1892:

> The School Board Visitors perform amongst them a house-to-house visitation; every house in every street is in their books, and details are given of every family with children of school age. They begin their scheduling two or three years before the children attain school age, and a record remains in their books of children who have left school. The occupation of the head of the family is noted down. Most of the visitors have been working in the same district for several years, and thus have an extensive knowledge of the people. It is their business to re-schedule for the Board once a year, but intermediate revisions are made in addition, and it is their duty to make themselves acquainted, so far as possible, with new-comers into their districts. They are in daily contact with the people, and have a very considerable knowledge of the parents of the school children, especially of the poorest amongst them, and of the conditions under which they live.[243]

Helen had promised to support the families of Southwark and she was doing so. She opposed the enlargement of the London School Board offices and when she was unsuccessful in this she attempted to at least get the contract for the work put out to tender.[244] She believed the half penny in the pound the building work would put on London rate payers was unjustifiable.[245] In her final months as a board member she tried, unsuccessfully, to have a motion passed which would have seen compulsory open, public tendering for all contracts entered into by the board.[246] Likewise, she tried to have all teaching posts publicly advertised to make recruitment fairer.[247]

Helen also wanted more working-class members to be elected to the board and proposed an unsuccessful motion in 1885 that the London School Board should petition parliament for legislation to be passed which would allow its elected members to receive an annual payment of up to £200. This would have made it possible for the working-class to consider standing for election and play an active role in managing the schools attended by their own children. She also attempted to have board meetings moved from 3 pm to 7 pm so that parents could attend after work, again so that the working-class would become more involved in their children's schooling.[248]

Throughout her third and final term on the board she continued to campaign for free education. She was almost successful in securing this in 1885, during her final year in office. Her motion for the abolishment of the school fee was only defeated on the casting vote of the Chairman.[249] Thomas Gautrey, who was a teacher in the capital, believed that Helen's 'impassioned speech' during the debate was a defining moment in the campaign for free state education. 'Free schools became from this time an election cry at both Board and Parliamentary Elections.'[250] The fee was finally abolished in 1891.

Helen had lost a motion in 1879 for equal pay for women teachers but, in 1883, she succeeded in getting her motion passed to have the joint assessment of married teachers' income reviewed by the board's solicitor. This was on the grounds that it possibly contravened the Married Women's Property Act of 1882. This Act legislated that married women's earnings belonged to them, not to their husbands.[251] However, only ten board members supported her motion to have the pay scales of uncertified teachers standardised so that women would be paid at the same rate as men.[252] Neither did all board women members vote for this motion for equal pay for women. Mary Richardson and Alice Westlake voted against it, showing loyalty to the Liberal whip rather than to their sex. The pay scales were finally passed in December 1883, after five years of debate. The new scales paid teachers a fixed salary which was not linked to examination results. Headteachers would, henceforth, be paid on a scale linked to the number of children enrolled at the school.[253] Equal pay for equal work for women remained elusive until towards the end of the twentieth century. Clementina Black, Secretary of the Women's Trade Union League, is remembered for achieving the adoption of a resolution for equal pay for women at the Trades Union Congress in 1888.[254] Barbara Castle finally put equal pay on the statute books of the United Kingdom in 1970, a success which built on earlier campaigns waged by now forgotten women, like Helen Taylor, who put it on the political agenda. Social progress is slow and often takes generations as it is achieved by gradually changing the attitudes of society to such a point that legislation can be passed. Even now women are taking equal pay claims to the courts.

Outside the board chamber Helen was busy, during 1883, on the executive of both the Democratic Federation and the Land Nationalisation Society. The Land Reform movement really took off in Great Britain during 1883.[255] The campaign for land nationalisation in Great Britain had gained much momentum due, in part, to the sales of Henry George's *Progress and Poverty*. The book had sold 12,000 copies by the autumn of 1882 and a second edition had been published.[256] George was not a socialist or land nationaliser, and advocated that landlords should not be compensated for the loss of land, unlike land nationalisers, but many socialists were attracted to his 'single tax' land theories. George had witnessed land speculation in California where the growth of towns had resulted in land speculation and land becoming too expensive for ordinary workers.[257] Landlords were, in his opinion, immorally profiting from rent for it which was unearned and came from the labour of those who rented the land and property that the landlords owned. He never advocated state land nationalisation but worked closely with land nationalisers as he believed that the two economic remedies, to a scarcity of land for ordinary workers to live and work on, would have the same result.[258]

Michael Davitt also turned his attention to promoting land nationalisation within the British Isles as well as in Ireland. In May 1882, on his release from prison after the Kilmainham Treaty, he and George had spoken at a land reform meeting at Manchester Town Hall and afterwards Davitt had gone to the Highlands of Scotland where the crofters were demanding fairer, more affordable rents and improved tenancies from their landlords. Davitt found himself cold shouldered by Parnell and the Irish nationalist party for his extremism in promoting land nationalisation.[259] Parnell had refused to give Davitt £500 to cover the promotion of George's land theories, as set out in *Progress and Poverty*, throughout the British Isles and Ireland.[260] It was Helen who enabled Davitt to become an influential executive member of the Land Nationalisation Society and he was still a vice president in 1900. She advocated on his behalf and overcame any reservations that the executive may have had of allowing an ex-Irish Republican Brotherhood member into their midst. During the summer of 1882 she had persuaded the Land Nationalisation Society treasurer, A.C. Swinton, to recommend Davitt to the president, Alfred Russel Wallace: Swinton wrote

> …though my public association with him [*Davitt]* would not a little startle my relations…I shall be glad to submit your proposal to him [*Wallace*] with my full sympathy and at any rate you may rely upon my doing everything I consistently can to promote Land Nationalisation under so admirable a leader as Mr Davitt.[261]

The various land reform organisations formed a coalition to work together for reform. The Land Reform Union was created in May 1883 as an alliance of Georgist single taxers, the Land Nationalisation Society and the Democratic Federation. Helen was heavily involved in this new organisation and praised both George and Davitt at the inaugural meeting.[262] The Land Reform Union immediately set about organising public meetings and Davitt and Helen travelled to Dorset together, in November, to speak at a meeting of agricultural workers in Milborne St Andrews.[263] The movement gained a further boost just before Christmas 1883 when George arrived from the USA for a lecture tour on behalf of the Land Reform Union, which Helen part funded. Helen and Davitt took the campaign for land nationalisation to Wales that year and it was noted in the press that: 'At present a lady has made the most prominent figure on the Welsh Land League platform.'[264]

However, like in all political movements, arguments between campaigners took place. The delicate balance within the coalition of land nationalisers and single taxers of the Land Reform Union was upset when the Democratic Federation became a Marxist party in 1884. The more moderate single taxers in the Land Reform Union gained control of the executive and it was relaunched as the English Land Restoration League with the Marxist socialists mainly staying in the Land Nationalisation Society.[265] However, some land reformers were in both land reform groups, believing both to be working to the same end:

> The two methods, however, are not antagonistic, but at the most alternative, as a matter of fact, many of the members of this society are members of the league also, and go in for both methods which lead to the same ends...Mr George's is the most simple method, Dr Wallace's the most direct.[266]

Helen was an executive member of both land reform groups despite believing the single tax was not a viable option:

> At the same time I wish to say that I entirely disagree in the opinion that the 'Single Tax' would restore the Land to the People in as much as, at best, it would only restore most of the revenue of the land, leaving wealthy capitalists who may choose to sacrifice large revenues (as they do at present) in order to obtain political influence which will bring them still larger sums, free as at present, to use the land as a means of compulsion or bribery. But the name 'Land Restoration' which was adopted by Mr Henry George from my suggestion, implies a wholly different theory of rights and of objects, founded on my own historical view of the subject, and I am very glad that the English and Scottish League and Union by adopting that name are carrying on the real work of educating the population to the perception of their real and historical rights which will remain intact and the need of them, I fear, as peremptory as ever after the single tax has been tried ~~and failed if it ever is tried~~. (sic).[267]

In 1883 the Democratic Federation had become the first Marxist political party in Great Britain when it published its manifesto, *Socialism Made Plain* and renamed itself the Social Democratic Federation. Helen's signature, along with the rest of the executive, appeared on the publication. It called for adult suffrage, nationalisation of the land, free compulsory education, an eight-hour day and cumulative taxes. These demands were in the radical tradition from which Helen and many of the members came. Helen, it will be remembered, had been working for free compulsory education for the last six years on the school board. The manifesto also included the Marxist demand that workers should own the means of production. The manifesto declared: 'All wealth is due to labour; therefore, to the labourers all wealth is due.' Marxism superseded the older socialist tradition of Helen's youth which Marx had derided as utopian socialism; that of the cooperative movements of Robert Owen, Charles Fourier and Henri Saint Simon. Mill had admired cooperative socialism and thought it should be tried as long as there were safeguards on individual liberty. He believed in competition and opposed the idea that the government should intervene in the market. In his *Autobiography* Mill had declared himself to be 'under the general designation of socialist.'[268] There was an exodus of radical party members, after the party's adoption of Marxism, of those who had joined the Democratic Federation to campaign against the Coercion Acts in Ireland.[269] The party's influence in radical politics had always been greater than its actual membership and Engel's estimation that, in the first ten years, membership grew to 100,000 was a gross over estimation.[270] In its first few years of existence, membership of the Democratic Federation was less than 600 and the vast majority of these lived in London. However, it influenced many people politically who came, as non-members, to its public meetings.[271] Helen, like her step-father, opposed violent revolution and class war, the rhetoric of which was becoming more apparent in the Social Democratic Federation. Like many others, she found Hyndman's dictatorial control of the party difficult. He controlled all policy and even its routine administration. Eleanor Marx foresaw the coming crisis in a letter to her sister Laura, in 1884:

> Hyndman has also succeeded in getting poor old Bax turned out of Today,[272] for Champion, who takes Bax's place, is just a tool of H's… So far he [H] has things here much his own way, but he is playing his cards very badly – irritating everyone and his little game will soon be played out.[273]

Helen and Hyndman were incompatible. Both were strong willed and sure that their way was the right way. Both were unbending, unyielding personalities. Hyndman wanted Helen to make the party her overriding concern instead of spreading herself thin on the ground with all her various political concerns. In July 1884 he wrote to her expressing exasperation that she should

> ...waste your time, energy and money on what you know, as well as I do, are mere trifling movements when the great cause of Socialism in England called for all and more than all that you could do in every way. I have heard you say that Socialism, organised international Socialism, could alone really benefit the workers.[274]

By the time of this letter Taylor was no longer on the executive of the party.[275] Her time was taken with the London School Board and the land nationalisation campaigns as she travelled to public meetings throughout Great Britain with Henry George and other leading land reformers. When she went to Staffordshire, in August 1884, to speak to striking coal miners there on behalf of the Social Democratic Federation,[276] she spoke on land nationalisation rather than focusing on the party she was there to promote. For nearly an hour she urged those present to commit to land reform, 'touching only slightly on the wages question.'[277] Hyndman was, by this time, working for a Marxist revolution and Helen, remained a mid-century old-fashioned radical whose socialism was informed by the pre Marx utopian socialism admired (with reservations concerning the protection of individual liberty) by her step-father. Mill's political and social concerns were hers and were those surrounding land, liberty, education, the strengthening of democracy by parliamentary reform, increased voting rights for the population including women, and the improvement of living conditions and opportunities for the working-class. Her Cobdenite anti-imperialism belonged to earlier in the century.[278] Hyndman had written to Helen the previous month trying to get her to focus on the party but obviously to no avail. Neither were of the character that they could compromise and find a mutual way. He demanded that she put the party first, instead of finding 'some trifling pretext or another from taking your proper share of the very heavy workload before us ...I have no hesitation in telling you that if is your duty (sic) to work with us and to help us in every way you can.'[279] Helen replied calling his letter 'hopelessly arrogant' and that there was no use at all arguing with him. She was incensed with his editorship of *Justice*, the Social Democratic Federation newspaper. She accused him of being no better than the capitalist press in his editorship for having anonymously attacked individuals in print. She pulled rank and reminded him of her history of public service and that she had 'been longer a socialist:'[280]

> If you are a socialist you have no right to say in print what you dare not put your name to…no excuse for hiding personal insult of people you don't like, under the veil of anonymous writing…With regard to 'Justice' I must say in reply to your letter that you are conducting it in a manner to make it an engine of public demoralization. It is spreading the vile morality of the capitalist press…and accustoming its leaders to the unmanly and cowardly habit of anonymous insult and irresponsible assertion.[281]

Other executive members railed, like Eleanor Marx and Helen, against Hyndman, and three months later the executive of the party split with some joining the newly formed Socialist League including Eleanor, Edward Aveling, William Morris and Ernest Belfort Bax. The Socialist League eschewed parliamentary politics, which the Social Democratic Federation hoped to influence by getting its members elected as MPs. The Socialist League believed you could not reform the existing system and only a workers' revolution would achieve socialism. Eleanor Marx wrote to her sister Laura on 31 December 1884:

> Apart from the disgraceful vilification of everyone to whom he personally objected as not being 'followers' of himself, Hyndman forced things to such a condition that it was impossible to go on working with him.[282]

Helen left the party in the autumn of 1884, but not to join the Socialist League as she abhorred violent revolution. Like many other radicals who had joined in 1881, she had found Hyndman's rhetoric of violence during meetings intolerable. She had made her rejection of violence, as a means to an end, quite clear in 1882. 'She was in favour of a republic but did not approve of anything other than peaceful means. She strongly disapproved of the use of rifles whether in the hands of monarchists or republicans.'[283] George Bernard Shaw, in a letter to Andreas Scheu, told him, 'Helen Taylor has taken herself off to run a halfpenny paper with the Georgeites.'[284, 285]

Helen would have found not only Hyndman intolerable in the Social Democratic Federation but also the lack of a commitment to women's rights which was at the heart of her concerns and touched all her campaigning. Indeed, some historians have labelled the party as misogynistic but it was rather that the woman question was never taken up as a commitment but left to individual conscience.[286] Younger feminists amongst the new Marxist socialists of the 1880s regarded Helen's mid-century feminism as bourgeois. It did not address economics and the middle-class feminists of classical feminism dared to talk on behalf of their working-class sisters with whom they believed they shared a class interest. Marxist feminists, like Eleanor Marx, believed women's emancipation was not possible without the emancipation of the whole working-class and that working-class women should campaign with working-class men in a class struggle against the bourgeoisie. They had no sisterhood with middle-class women.[287] In 1881, at its inception, the Democratic Federation had not included gender equality in its constitution. Meanwhile, in France, the French Workers' Party, Parti Ouvrier Français, had, at its first conference in 1879, added a commitment to sexual equality into its constitution.[288] Feminists in the Social Democratic Federation had to constantly negotiate their way in the party. Helen had power in the Federation as she had the wealth to fund it and strong working-class support due to her membership of the London School Board, the radical causes she espoused and the respect she had as Mill's step-daughter. She had been indispensable to Hyndman in 1881 as she brought her supporters with her into the new party and many left when she did.[289] Hyndman himself was no supporter of women's suffrage or of them working as he believed working men's wages were undercut when women joined the workforce, as they worked for less money.[290] The suffragette Sylvia Pankhurst recorded the anti-feminism which existed within the party:

> Moreover Hyndman, Belfort Bax and others of its prominent committee men, were opposed to women's enfranchisement. I remember, many years later, as a young girl, entering on Votes for Women propaganda, in London, encountering Hyndman at the house of Dora Monte Fiore. 'Women should learn to have influence as they have in France instead of trying to get votes,' Hyndman shouted at me, in a fierce tirade.[291]

Helen used her years in the party to fight the cause of women. However, she no longer supported separatism to achieve this aim and was against establishing a women's committee:

> The time is gone by for Ladies' Committees separate for public work. That is one thing at least we learn on the School Board where men and women work together on public official business and I doubt whether you will find it more easy to induce women to work on a Committee of their own.[292]

However, in 1884, she was involved in creating, with Olive Schreiner and others, a women's group in the Social Democratic Federation where women's rights could be discussed:

> Why twenty-eight years ago I was one of the eight women, with Helen Taylor in the chair, John Stuart Mill's niece [*sic*], who started in a small underground room near the Houses of Parliament, the Woman's branch of the Democratic Foundation [*sic*] – the largest socialist organization in England.[293]

Although he respected her work on the London School Board, Hyndman, as we have seen, wanted Helen to give the party her undivided attention. 'We have always regretted the amount of work given by a woman of Miss Taylor's capacity to school board work,' he wrote in *Justice*.[294] The party newspaper had, however, praised her chairing of the Educational Endowments Committee which had seen endowment funds used for food and clothing for the poor in Board Schools. *Justice* called on school boards nationwide to do the same.[295] Despite his lack of commitment to women's rights, and undoubtedly relying on her ability to fund the party and gain it popular support, he envisaged her, in 1883, playing a central role in the party. 'I should much like to talk with you seriously about the future of the Federation.'[296] He may also have feared the influence she wielded in radical circles and have been mindful of the political adage 'keep your friends close and your enemies closer.' Andreas Scheu believed that Helen was a major threat to Hyndman's leadership of the party. He knew Hyndman was aware of this and that it was clear for all to see that the two could not remain on friendly terms because of it.[297] Hyndman's jingoism, and his adherence to the widely held social 'truth' that the Irish celts were inferior to the Anglo-Saxons, would have rankled with Helen. His view was that: 'It is absurd, of course, to deny the influence of race and climate: none would contend that a Saxon and an Irishman have the same qualities.'[298]

Some executive members of the Democratic Federation were openly hostile to Helen's feminism. Ernest Belfort Bax was vehemently anti-feminist and it is no exaggeration to call him a misogynist. In his published *The Fraud of Feminism*, he used the prevalent Victorian trope of women being hysterical (emotional rather than rational). He claimed, their brains being smaller, they were less intelligent than men.[299] Bax also regarded the Criminal Law Amendment Act of 1885, which raised the age of consent for girls from 13 to 16 and provided more legal protection for women against them being trafficked for prostitution in brothels by pimps, as 'a crusade against men.'[300] He could not abide Helen and ignored her contribution to the creation of the Democratic Federation in his memoirs. He attacked her physical appearance and her air of superiority to belittle her as quoted in the introduction to this book. [301] Bax tried to end the custom of members showing her, what he deemed undeserved, respect when she entered the room. Many would rise from their seats to acknowledge her.[302] He abhorred her and her fellow feminist crusaders.

During 1884 agrarian protests in the highlands of Scotland escalated in what became known as the Crofter Wars. Highland clearances of the eighteenth century had seen the most fertile land turned over to sheep farming and many tenants were left to farm less fertile land on which they could not gain enough profit to pay the rent. Failed harvests in the 1880s had seen many evictions for non-payment of rent as in Ireland. Three reasons have been identified as the cause of the increase in agrarian unrest in Scotland; anti-landlord agitation by Scottish Liberals, the growing number of Irish emigrants in Glasgow and the widespread influence of Henry George's single tax theory.[303] George returned again to England to promote his single tax theory on behalf of the English Land Restoration League and to undertake a lecture tour. In 1884, Helen, despite her school board commitments devoted much time to speaking engagements on behalf of the Land Nationalisation Society and the English Land Restoration League. She was at the peak of her fame and attracted large audiences.[304] She used the land meetings to promote feminism, calling for women to become involved in the movement for land nationalisation:

> It was now time that the women should come to the men and say 'stand up as men, and act as men' not by fighting like brutes, but by reasoning and let them remember that what had been taken away from them by the sham pretence of the law, the reality of a just law could give back again. The audience caught up the contention of Miss Taylor that this was a women's question in so much as women had to care for the household, a sentiment that was warmly cheered.[305]

Late in 1884 George and Helen travelled to Scotland on behalf of the English Land Restoration League to promote land reform theories amongst the crofters.[306] In 1885 five Liberals lost their parliamentary seats to three independent crofters and two Highland Land League members such was the strength of the land campaign.[307] The returned Liberal government passed the 1886 Crofter Act to end the Highland land agitation. This gave tenant farmers secure tenancies and fair rents and the Crofter wars came to an end.[308] As late as December 1886, Helen was still supporting the crofters when she spoke at a meeting in Exeter Hall, London. This was attended by 500 people in protest at the imprisonment of Scottish land agitator Rev. Dr John Macpherson. The meeting passed her motion to send a memorandum to the Queen asking for his release and a collection was made for the crofters.[309] Helen, no longer a member of the London School Board after November 1885, continued her active land work into 1886 but she suffered bouts of ill health, usually bronchial, and 'the foremost women of her time'[310] had to miss the first meeting of the newly formed Welsh Land League.[311] Davitt was the architect of this organisation which was demanding the three fs secured by the Irish Land League – fair rents, fixity of tenure and free sale of the tenancy.[312] The land unrest in Wales lacked the nationalist dimension of the Irish and was more cultural and economic. The Welsh farmers were Welsh speaking and non-conformist and resented the tithes they had to pay to the Church of Wales. The Welsh farmers also did not suffer the dire poverty of their Irish counterparts. Unrest simmered until

1889 when the Liberal Land Commission agreed a reduction in rents and transferred the responsibility for tithes onto the landlords. The campaign for land reform finally died a death in the 1920s when the Anglican Church was disestablished in Wales. [313]

(vi) 1885 – The Camberwell General Election

1885 would be Helen's last year on the board. Elections were to be held in November and Helen would decide against putting herself forward for re-election. Instead she would attempt to become the first woman to stand in a parliamentary election.[314] Helen would be 54 that July and suffering increasingly bad health. Her recurring chest infections were exacerbated by the smog of London. Hyndman, back in 1883, had written to her in Avignon, where she was recuperating from severe bronchitis, urging her to 'give up some of your smaller work.'[315] The long hours on school board meant she had little opportunity to go home to the clean air of the South of France and take care of her health. On the school board she continued to work for gender equality and value for money for London's ratepayers. The domestic curriculum continued to erode equality of educational opportunity for girls in the classroom. Helen voted against a motion to make drawing an optional subject for girls on the grounds that it did not adhere to '…the principle of equal intellectual training for girls and boys . . . Let the girls have the same fair chance to have their minds and intellects educated.'[316]

Again not all women supported Helen's championing of gender equality. Rosamund Davenport Hill, who from 1882 had been chair of the Cookery and Domestic Subjects Committee, was denounced in the *Women's Penny Post* in 1888 by fellow board member, Henrietta Muller, as 'not a friend to women' for her zeal in promoting the domestic curriculum for girls.[317]

Helen's political fame peaked in 1885 when she was selected as Camberwell Radical Club's independent parliamentary candidate for the General Election that November.[318] In 1878, newspapers had reported that Helen had been chosen to fight the general election by Southwark Liberals but it did not happen. The papers, in 1878 had likened her possible candidature, as the first woman to stand for parliament, to that of Daniel O'Connell who became the first Catholic MP and David Salomons who became the first Jew allowed to take his seat. [319] Both O'Connell, in 1828, and Salomons, in 1859, found themselves debarred from parliament after being elected for refusing to swear the Church of England oath of allegiance to the queen. A successful campaign to overturn such bans had led to a change in the law. Catholics were allowed to take their seats from 1829 and Jews from 1858 on affirming allegiance to the monarch without swearing the Protestant oath.

Helen was the President of the Camberwell Radical Club on Peckham Park Road in South London, an area in which she was a respected member of the London School Board and well-known advocate for working-class interests. Radical Clubs sprang up after the increase of the electorate following the 1832 Reform Act. In the clubs, working and middle-class republican radicals discussed reform and organised public meetings for their causes. They had mobilised against the Coercion Acts in Ireland and been the first members of the Democratic Federation. The Liberal Party, which was regarded as protecting the interests of the working-class, had become more centralised as elections became more professional. The increased suffrage of 1867, which gave the vote to more working men, required canvassing and lists of followers and supporters to get out and vote at election time and there was now a slick party machine and hierarchy which side-lined their supporters in the Radical Clubs.

The radical clubs resented the 'wire pullers' of the recently formed National Liberal Federation and local Liberal Associations. The latter chose the Liberal candidates which saw radicals losing their influence over those who would represent their local communities in Parliament.[320] Hyndman, at the creation of the Democratic Federation in 1881, had seen the need for those to the left of the party elite to organise. 'The fight has begun. The liberal wire pullers, specially paid for the purpose, are at work taking the clubs from us.'[321] In the November 1885 election, the Radical Clubs of Great Britain decided to fight back against the party machine and in eighteen constituencies the clubs chose an independent radical to fight the seat against the Conservative and official Liberal candidate, much to the anger of the Liberal party. The Liberal Government had become increasingly unpopular for its invasion of Egypt in 1882, and the death of General Gordon in Khartoum who had died whilst waiting for British forces to arrive to relieve the besieged city. It was feared independent Radical candidates, who would attract the votes of the more radical Liberal voters, would split the progressive vote. This would result in a

Conservative candidate win.[322] The radical clubs were not opposing the Liberal manifesto, only the fact that they were not allowed to choose the Liberal candidate who would represent their area in the House of Commons.[323] Camberwell North was a new working-class constituency and part of Helen's school board division. Many of its inhabitants worked on the river Thames or in the tanning factories. [324] They knew and respected Helen as their School Board member. The local Liberal Association had rejected the preferred candidate of Camberwell Radical Club, William A. Coote. Coote, an evangelical Christian and working-class compositor, was Honourable Secretary of the National Vigilance Society which campaigned for the Criminal Law Amendment Act of July 1885 to be enforced. This had increased the age of sexual consent from 13 to 16.[325] Instead the Camberwell Liberal Association had chosen Richard Strong to fight the seat. Strong was a middle-class member of the Liberal establishment of the National Liberal Association. The radicals of Camberwell North found this intolerable and put up their president, Helen Taylor, as an independent candidate in protest. Similar triangular contests occurred in eighteen contests that election including Sheffield and Nottingham. However, in Camberwell North the radical club was not just challenging the Liberal establishment by putting forward their own independent candidate but also the 1832 Reform Act which had legally denied women citizenship. Women, who previously had not voted or stood for election, merely through custom, had, by this act been legally barred from doing so. There had been various challenges as to the legality of excluding women but 1885 saw the greatest challenge yet with Helen accepting the nomination. Suffragists claimed that the pronoun 'person' employed in the 1832, 1867 and 1884 Franchise Acts included women as well as men because, in other acts, it did.[326] Helen made the proviso that she would not deny a working-man the chance to represent the constituency as an independent and that she would make way if such a person came forward as a candidate. On being interviewed by the *Pall Mall Gazette*, Helen explained to the reporter that her candidature was important for the on-going campaign for the vote for women. She was 'a pioneer' and she did not believe there was any valid law which made her action illegal. The newspaper report that was written told of the strength of support for Helen amongst the Camberwell North working-class which Helen put down to the fact that working-class wives had always worked as their money was important to the survival of the family. The indications were that Helen would receive a large number of votes from the recently enfranchised working-class. Her meetings, disrupted by supporters of Richard Strong, focussed on 'shorter hours of labour, better homes, and food and clothing for children.'

Francis Soutter was her political advisor for the campaign and Ethel Leach her election agent. Helen and Ethel had much in common and grew close. A suffragist campaigner, Ethel had been a member of the Great Yarmouth School Board in Norfolk since 1881, and had been a member of the Ladies' Land League.[327] They became lasting friends, socialising and visiting each other and keeping each other up to date with letters after Helen returned to live in Avignon in the late 1880s. Ethel's emotional and physical support of Helen's 1885 election campaign would have been invaluable as Helen could not call on the support of her family. Her beloved brother, Algernon, was increasingly battling his own demons of an eating disorder which would see him in danger of his life within a few years, and her brother Herbert, although living in London was, as we have seen, permanently estranged from his sister and living the bachelor life in London whilst failing to pay maintenance to his family. Helen lacked one important aspect which would have given her the emotional support enjoyed by many other feminists of her generation. Unlike many leading feminists of her time, the Garrett sisters, the Priestman sisters, the McLarens, the Winkworths, the Ashursts, the Straceys, she had no close siblings working for the cause.[328] She had no sisters nor close relatives to share her concerns, no close cousins. (Florence Nightingale and Barbara Leigh Smith Bodichon were cousins). Neither did she have a strong romantic friendship to provide her lifetime support like Frances Power Cobbe, who lived with Mary Lloyd, nor a supportive husband as did Florence Fenwick Miller and Elizabeth Surr. Helen had no one except the friends she made to share what, at times, must have been a severe emotional strain, especially at the time of the School Board libel case or during her Camberwell election campaign. She had lost Lady Amberley, years before her public life took off, who could have provided the support she needed, Algernon required so much support from his sister because of the fragility of his mental and physical health, and could not reciprocate. He was a drain on her energy though she loved him. In any case, he took no part in her campaigning and lived, even when she was in England, outside London in the Home Counties. He seems to have inhabited a world of his own, despite having served on his local

Tetsworth and Attington School Board as Vice and later Chair for a few years from 1877.[329] He never seems to have offered Helen anything in the way of advice or support professionally and appears to have become more mentally and physically unwell as the years progressed. A constant source of anxiety for his sister.

Helen and her election team issued a manifesto:

> To the Electors of North Camberwell
>
> A fair day's wages for a fair day's work
> 6 hour working day which will give work to men where now there is none
> Local government cooperation and workshops under elected managers
> Restoration of the land
> Direct taxation and graduated income tax none under 300 and rising by degrees to 19 shillings in the pound
> No wars that are not voted for by the people,
> Free justice
> Restoration of the endowments for free clothing, food and education
> Free education
> Home Rule and legislative independence for Ireland
> Universal suffrage, annual parliaments and payment of members[330]

Much of this manifesto was that of the Social Democratic Federation, which many radical club members and Helen had parted company with. Some were old chartist demands and some echoed the manifesto of Helen's Liberal opponent, Richard Strong, who supported Joseph Chamberlain's *Unauthorised Manifesto* which demanded free education, land reform, disestablishment of the Church of England, a graduated system of income tax, death duties, universal male suffrage and elected County Councils. Strong was a supporter of Home Rule as was the Conservative candidate Wilfrid Blunt. Blunt had supported the Irish Land War and would be imprisoned in 1888 for his chairing of an anti-eviction meeting in Galway.[331] Blunt, like Helen, was an anti-imperialist and had supported Egyptian nationalism. He was a Tory Democrat, committed to progressive social policies to alleviate poverty whilst supporting the monarchy, the Church of England as the established national church and the heredity House of Lords.[332] Helen differed from Catholic, Wilfrid Blunt and Richard Strong in her commitment to secular, non-denominational state schooling.[333]

And so, Helen, with nine years' experience on the London School Board as a member for Southwark, well-known in the area for her socialist politics and president of the local radical club, was styled the working-class choice for parliament by her election team:

> The People's Candidate
> Vote for
> Miss Taylor
> The Tried Friend
> Of
> The People
> And
> Their Children[334]

Both national and local Liberals were incensed at the affront of the Camberwell Radical Club putting up a candidate against them and a woman to boot. She was attacked for both splitting the anti-conservative vote and for being a woman who dared to enter politics. The local paper printed a letter, from 'a Liberal elector, Peckham' which attacked the club as 'a mischief-brewing clique.'[335] Acceptance of women as members of School Boards was more widespread for surely, as wives and mothers, they were most suited to attending to the welfare of children but this was a woman who dared enter the public sphere of national government. The House of Commons only allowed women to view the proceedings of parliament from the Ladies' Gallery which screened them, by means of a metal grill, from the sight of all. Anna Parnell had called this 'the Ladies' Cage.'[336] Helen was called a 'wilful woman'[337] and 'an unsexed female agitator.'[338] She was also attacked for her extreme politics for she was 'a pushing and active agitator and she likes to keep her name before the public.'[339] So dangerous was her socialist, land nationalising feminism that it was feared that local Liberal voters would desert the party at the ballot box, 'for the stoutest Liberal would probably prefer to see Mr Blunt rather than Miss Taylor in the House of Commons.'[340] Such was the fear of this that she could not be ignored as the Liberals, who had tried to defeat her twice in the School Board Elections, were well aware of the support of working-class voters for her:

> That the great majority of the Radical working men will support her need hardly be doubted. On the other hand, there is a section of Liberal less advanced, and perhaps more fastidious, who may decline to sanction so startling an innovation, to say nothing of their dread of a politician of the most extreme type…The world outside the United Kingdom sets us down as a people of eccentricities, and surely there will be abundant scope for wit at our expense as soon as we shall have a Legislature of mixed sexes…The House of Commons is not a place for the softer sex.[341]

Helen's campaign team, headed by Francis Soutter, set up a number of public meetings to promote their candidate.[342] As local Liberals tried to disrupt them, Soutter had to organise security to protect Helen and the speakers on stage. On one occasion he protected the stage with a barrier of forty volunteer stewards and placed another forty in the hall to keep order. Despite this security presence, protestors tried to drown out the speakers and the women had to leave the stage when chairs began to be thrown at them.[343]

The mainstream British suffrage movement again despaired at Helen, fearing she was bringing the campaign into disrepute. Helen's school board colleague, Alice Westlake, begged Helen not to stand at this election and delay until after the second reading of a suffrage bill for 'we feel anxious about any step that will endanger it.'[344] Suffragists were hoping that the Reform Bill of 1886 would include votes for women. The *Englishwoman's Review* refused to acknowledge that Helen's candidature was a step towards the suffrage, sneering that it only proved that '*men* shall be allowed to appoint what candidate they choose whoever that candidate might be.'[345] The Liberal MP, Richard Pankhurst, did share a platform with her, much to the horror of his wife, the suffragist, Emmeline, when she saw that Helen was wearing trousers.[346] It is likely what Emmeline took for trousers was the divided skirt promoted by the Rational Dress Society.

However, Helen's former political colleagues in the Social Democratic Federation, members of the land movement and some leading Irish nationalists rallied to support her. All those outside the accepted political establishment who wanted to give Gladstone's government a kicking.

Jessie Craigen, though no longer a close friend, formed the 'Miss Taylor Election Independent Aid Committee.' She distributed handbills, which while making it clear that this was not official election campaign material, informed voters of the legality of Helen's candidature as no statute had been passed which explicitly excluded women from Parliament. The legality of Helen's claim, Craigen insisted, rested on the established fact that Henry III and Edward III had sent the order for abbesses to attend Parliament.[347] Women had, therefore, already sat in parliament. Craigen, in referencing Helen's work against the Contagious Diseases Acts, insisted that the national legislative needed womanly attributes.[348]

> In that House womanhood has been outraged by laws which, with cold brutality, made the daughters of the poor mere animal instruments to gratify the lusts of men. That degrading insult to us is still on the statute book. Send up a woman from North Camberwell to give utterance in the senate, for all womanhood in the land, to the hot shame and anger which every woman feels at it. Give womanhood a voice in the House of Commons to demand the repeal of the Contagious Diseases Act.[349]

Henry George, back home in New York, wrote congratulating her on her candidature.[350] Her former Social Democratic Federation colleague, William Parker, the Social Democratic Federation candidate in Central Hackney in another three-way contest, joined her at one of her election hustings. Helen travelled to support John Burns, the Social Democratic candidate in the triangular contest in Nottingham West, at one of his election meetings which he believed would 'strengthen materially my candidature for the West Division.'[351] Helen promoted herself as a socialist, and referenced Mill's *Chapters on Socialism*, which, she declared, set out 'those principles of socialism which she hoped the people of England would soon be prepared to carry out.'[352] As the local candidate, she advocated strongly for 'a federated government for London with a general council to control such matters as the police, gas, water, electricity, steam tramways and railways.'[353]

Anna Parnell came over to England to support her and Michael Davitt wrote hoping to come if his work allowed. Helen's campaign team turned Davitt's letter, offering to chair a meeting in her support, into a handbill. Davitt was a hero amongst the immigrant Irish working-class of Camberwell for his campaign against the landlords and the time he had spent in prison for the Irish cause. He wrote emphasising Helen's credentials for he was 'satisfied that Ireland would not have a truer friend or a more staunch supporter in Westminster.' He also believed the candidature to be a step towards women's suffrage for he was a feminist himself. There was a sizeable Irish vote to win over and all three candidates were vying for it. The conservative, Wilfrid Blunt, was the preferred candidate of Charles Stewart Parnell. Parnell, despairing of Gladstone's delay of putting a Home Rule Bill before Parliament, had issued a manifesto to the Irish in Britain to give their vote to Conservative candidates except in a handful of exceptional circumstances where the Liberal had proved himself a supporter of the Irish cause.[354] Anna Parnell and Michael Davitt, both frozen out of the organised Irish nationalist movement by Parnell for their extremism, were openly able to voice their dissent by supporting Helen.

A letter from Anna Parnell to Helen was published in the press. It reminded the Camberwell North electorate of the hard work, the 'distressing drudgery,' Helen had undertaken during the Land War as a member of the Ladies' Land League. Helen was a great friend of Ireland for 'the most enthusiastic and self-sacrificing patriot could have done no more for Ireland than you did.'[355] Helen called for Home Rule and likened the plight of contemporary women with that of English Catholics of fifty years ago before Catholic emancipation. Thus making the link between herself, aiming to become the first woman MP, and Daniel O'Connell who was elected as a Catholic MP before a law was passed enabling him to take his seat. Anna, addressing the Irish in the crowd, at a meeting she attended with Helen, emphasised the contribution Helen had made to the Ladies' Land League and how she had undergone physical labour in building Land League huts to house those families evicted for non-payment of rent.[356]

Anna's life subsequent to the Land War is a sad indictment of the plight of many intelligent women of her generation who, denied full citizenship, had no outlet for their talents. A leading historian of her more famous brother believed her to be 'one of the most likeable, and possibly the most admirable, of the Parnells.'[357] Anna took no further part in Irish politics after the Land War as that avenue was cut off for women for a generation. She would lead a nomadic life in various lodgings throughout England and Ireland, typical of many impoverished Anglo-Irish ladies. Helen sent Anna a typewriter which delighted the recipient.[358] A letter written on it in 1887 shows Anna practising her typing and her wry sense of humour. Having heard of a ferry sinking in the English Channel, Anna typed: 'Were you on board the Dieppe boat that was wrecked? If so were you drowned?' She goes on to ask Helen her opinion of potash water and lime juice as a drink.[359] Anna has used the typewriter so much she has had to buy a new ribbon for it. She goes on to thank Helen for the copy of *The Standard* and the speech from Lord Randolph Churchill, she had sent to her. At Christmas 1889 Anna sent a card with a picture of a cat on it and asked after Helen's dog and talked about her own cat. A friendly exchange between good friends showing a more human relaxed side of two women who have, at times, been portrayed as members of the 'shrieking sisterhood.'

To return to 1885. The voting period for the general election ran from 24 November until 18 December.[360] Helen arrived to present her nomination papers to the presiding officer on the opening day who promptly declared them invalid under Section 4 of the Franchise Act which explicitly used the male pronouns, 'his' and 'him.' Helen argued with him but he was having none of it.[361] The case was clear cut she was a woman and thus ineligible. However, this ruling was not universally accepted as correct. The *Englishwoman's Review* believed that Helen's candidature was possibly legal for in other Acts of Parliament 'his' and 'him' included women. John Chapman of the National Liberal Club also asserted that Helen's papers should have been accepted.[362] The *Law Journal* believed that there was a case to be made that the presiding officer would have been legally obliged to accept her nomination papers had they been presented by a third party 'but she preferred boldly to avow her sex.'[363] Richard Strong, the Liberal, won the election as the vote was not split. He would only serve until 1886 when the Liberal government fell after the defeat of the 1886 Home Rule Bill which split the party. The seat would then be taken by John Richards Kelly, the Conservative candidate.

PART 3
THE TWILIGHT YEARS, 1886–1907

These years saw a gradual decline in Helen's physical involvement in campaigning as she spent increasing amounts of time in Avignon. At first, she kept involved through letters but these declined as she entered her 60s and began to suffer increased ill health. In 1888 all her campaigning was halted when Algernon became very ill. Algernon's mental instability had resulted in him starving himself through following too restricted a vegetarian diet. He had become obsessive with what he was eating.[1] Helen went to his cottage in Haddenham to nurse him back to health. She then returned to Avignon to recover. In March 1889 he wrote to her there on his intent to leave Haddenham and move to Devon to 'one of the numerous vegetarian lodging or boarding houses which now receive lodgers or boarders which the secretary of the vegetarian society might be able to recommend. I care about vegetarianism more than any other subject or cause.'[2] The cottage and garden in Haddenham had fallen into disrepair during his illness and was 'a very wilderness of desolation.' In July 1889, Helen travelled back to England to check on the house which Algernon had refused to sell by public auction on his move to lodgings at the Vicarage in Chudleigh, Devon. He is marked in the 1891 census as living on his own means as a boarder of the vicar of Chudleigh, his wife, children and other boarders. Algernon wrote to his sister that he was enjoying his new life in Devon but constantly worried about the sale of the Haddenham house; its state of repair and the unpicked fruit in the orchard. [3] He asked Helen to write to his daughter Nelly, who was presumably living close by the old house, and ask her to keep an eye on the tomb of his beloved wife in nearby

John Stuart Mill and Helen Taylor.

Harriet Taylor Mill.

Anna Parnell c.1878.

Maison de Stuart Mill.

Helen Taylor and three others.

Helen Taylor standing for parliamentary election in 1885.

Above: Mill and Helen's home in Avignon,1858-1873. Helen's home until 1905. Damaged by fire in 1956 and demolished in the early 1960s.

Right: Irish Land League Poster for the No Rent campaign, c.1880s.

London School Board Offices, demolished 1929. (Public Domain)

Camberwell Comber Grove School, built 1877. (Nigel Cox Camberwell-Comber Grove School, SE5 CC BY-SA 2.0)

Helen’s Grave Obelisk in Torquay Cemetery.

Helen's Grave Inscription.

Tetsworth, which he feared was overgrown.[4] Helen was constantly spending mental energy on advising Hadji about the house and presumably suggested letting it as he wrote that he was against the idea. He reasoned that because it was such a small cottage 'it is not likely to attract a very substantial class of tenant.'[5] Helen travelled again from Avignon, in October 1889, to visit her brother in Devon. He made his will appointing Helen as the executor. Helen continued to spend her declining physical energy on travelling to England to sort out Algernon's affairs. She travelled again to Haddenham in May 1890 and was asked by her brother to tidy his wife's grave in Tetsworth.[6] Nothing is expressed about his health at this time but he seems to have needed constant support which Helen, always of delicate health herself, must have found mentally and physically exhausting. She had written to a friend about how she had had to flee, totally exhausted, to the peace and quiet of Avignon after supporting Hadji through his 1888 bout of self-starvation.[7]

Meanwhile, the estrangement of Herbert with his brother and sister continued. In a letter, with no year, but sometime in the early to mid-eighties, Algernon had written to his sister asking if she had seen news of Herbert's bankruptcy in the newspapers and that 'his wife was the principal creditor.'[8] His bankruptcy appeared in the lists of provincial papers as well as the London Press. He was listed as a London merchant, living in Piccadilly, and trading as David Taylor and Sons. He had liabilities of £125,530.[9] Following bankruptcy Herbert had set up in business again and Algernon informed his sister that he had heard rumours that Annie was bringing a law suit against her estranged husband for non-payment of the £1,500 a year he had agreed to pay her. In a letter, marked not sent, written in 1888, Helen vented years of frustration, no doubt remembering his slighting of his mother on her marriage to Mill. She railed against her eldest brother; 'a man who makes such an agreement, leaving his children to his wife and himself leads a bachelor life in Piccadilly while bankrupt does not inspire me with confidence.' He had got their aunt, Eliza, to draw up a new will leaving everything, but a few legacies, to himself

> …instead of to her nephews and nieces as she had previously arranged…He had guided her hand to sign it. …a man whose very name brings to my memory with an undying pang all that he inflicted on my beloved mother and the shadow that his heartlessness cast upon my youth…Bad son, bad brother and now it would seem bad husband and bad father.[10]

Helen was concerned he would not pay out the legacies on Eliza's death. Indeed, she later had to instruct a solicitor to act to recover a legacy left by Eliza to a servant which Herbert was refusing to pay and she instructed the lawyer to use her own legacy to pay for its recovery.[11] The rift between Herbert and Helen was to be permanent. The 1891 census shows Herbert living as a lodger and working as an American merchant in central London. The same census shows his wife as living nearby in Chelsea, London with two of their children Geoffrey, aged 23 and listed as an actor, and Eleanor, aged 33, a writer and translator. Annie Taylor was 'living on her own means.' In 1894 Herbert wrote to his brother, Algernon, about his financial plight. Aunt Eliza had lent him 'more money' which he could not repay and he was concerned that his finances would soon appear in the 'Gazette.' Failing to repay his aunt would leave her in financial difficulties. Herbert suggested that if Algernon and Helen would agree to send a hundred pounds a year to their aunt this 'would put it all right, and as she is ninety-three this month, it could not, in all probability, continue very long. Will you write to Helen about this? It is no use my writing.' We can guess what Helen thought about Herbert's coldness in passing the solution to his own financial problems to them with the comforting proviso that their aunt would not live too long to be a financial burden to his siblings.[12]

In 1897, Herbert wrote to Mary Stuart, a relative, that he had had no contact with his sister for seven years.[13] Herbert's oldest son, Herbert junior, emigrated to America. He wrote to Helen from 294 Fifth Avenue, New York, in 1893. He sent the letter to the London School Board to be forwarded on, obviously not knowing her current address. He addressed her as 'My Dear Aunt Helen,' sending her a portrait of his daughter Ethel who was 18 and regretting the circumstances which had led to the family estrangement. He was planning a visit to Europe, in December, as Ethel was to enrol at a finishing school in Paris. He judged family arguments 'of your generation' to have been 'fatal to the fortunes of our family.' His own finances, he assured her, were good as a result of his marriage. He hoped Helen would agree to meet Ethel when she was in Europe and write to her. It was many years since they had been in contact but Helen had met Ethel once at Aunt Eliza's house:

> I am writing this feeling our family has been much estranged through causes now so distant as to render further allusion to them unnecessary.[14]

There is nothing in the archives to show that this softened Helen's attitude to the family feud whatsoever. In 1900 Ethel wrote to Helen from New York informing her of the death of her father, Herbert, Helen's nephew. She too recalled the meeting at Aunt Eliza's house in Stoke Newington which she dated as 'about eleven years ago.' Herbert and his wife and daughter had lived in New York for a decade and her stepmother and herself were in business 'and anticipate staying here several years more.'[15]

The friendship between Helen and Elizabeth Surr endured though distance would separate them. Elizabeth Surr left the London School Board in 1882 and emigrated to California with her husband and daughter Minnie. Helen used her friendship with Henry George, to secure lecturing engagements there for Elizabeth before the Surr family emigrated.[16] The two women continued to exchange affectionate letters up to 1898. Helen sent updates and gossip on old London School Board colleagues and they reminisced fondly over the old days. Helen wrote believing that the support of fellow London School Board member, Henrietta Muller, when Helen was successfully put forward for the chair of the Educational Endowments Committee, was self-motivated. Henrietta wanted to be chair of a special committee drawn up to report on the adoption of Swedish Exercise in London's schools. No woman had ever chaired any committee. If Helen were to be appointed chair of a permanent committee, Helen claimed, in the letter, this would ease Miss Muller's way to obtaining the chair she so desired. Helen would have set a precedent which Henrietta Muller would be able to follow. Helen was successful in being elected as chair but Henrietta failed to follow in her footsteps much to Helen's and Elizabeth's delight when reminiscing in their letters. Helen enjoyed the irony of this failure when she wrote to Elizabeth that:

> Miss M succeeded in helping to put me <u>for her own sake</u> (sic) into a place of dignity I did not seek or want and failed for herself who did. Yet I do not think she will learn the lesson, to cast aside personal objects, any more than did Mrs M [*Florence Fenwick Miller*] who <u>ratted</u> (sic) from me when she thought I was down.[17]

This 'ratting' is likely a reference to the time that Mr Scrutton took Helen to court for libel after she accused him of the manslaughter of pupils at the Industrial School he managed.

Elizabeth, also, had not forgiven Florence Fenwick Miller for some slight to her friend and ceased corresponding with her, despite Florence sending letters and pamphlets out to California, 'for I always had a feeling that she did not behave well to you.'[18] We saw how at one time, Florence and Helen had been close and had travelled to a suffrage meeting in Belfast together in 1880. Helen had given Florence a pair of diamond earrings and invitations to dinners during the early years of their acquaintance after being elected to the London School Board in 1878.[19] Florence, herself, in her unpublished memoirs indicates that the friendship was not deep and that Helen's nature hindered real intimacy '[20] Helen was, however, more scathing in her assessment of Florence in her letters to Elizabeth Surr and claimed that the younger woman's 'object in life was money' and that she was on the School Board 'selling herself to the government now she has by opposition become worth buying.'[21] Helen had not forgiven Florence for a lack of support at a time of crisis.

Helen and Elizabeth Surr were not alone in their dislike of Florence. Elizabeth Wolstenholme Elmy and Florence had an initial period of friendship, in the same way as had Helen and Florence, but it floundered in the same way when Elizabeth became convinced that Florence was making the Women's Franchise League 'a stalking horse of personal ambition.'[22] Elizabeth shared Helen's view of Florence:

> Mrs Miller had far too early in life, as a nice girl of 18 or 19, personal successes which turned her head, and that for the rest she lives on and by rich people, mixes with them whilst poor and is corrupted thereby. She longs to be rich.[23]

Ursula Bright, the suffragist, also found Florence unpleasant[24] so it may be, in this case that Helen had some grounds for her dislike of Florence rather than the 'acid tongue' attributed to her. Florence asked Helen's niece, Mary, for her letters to be returned to her after Helen's death so the surviving correspondence between the two women in the Mill Taylor archive is sparse. It is restricted to Florence's gratitude and excitement when Helen invited her to join her and travel to Ireland in 1880 to speak at a number of women suffrage events.

By 1888 Elizabeth Surr was addressing Helen as 'my very dear friend.'[25] By 1892 this has become 'my dear old friend.'[26] In 1898 Helen sent financial aid to the Surrs when they suffered financial problems during the Californian recession.[27] She also provided support when Elizabeth's grown-up daughter, Minnie, who had emigrated with her husband and parents, suffered terminal cancer. Sometimes the chat was more lighthearted. Elizabeth would ask after Helen's cats wondering if they were the same ones she had known or their offspring.[28] Elizabeth, a great lover of cats, had written a children's book about them.[29] Neither distance nor time broke the friendship forged in the battle against child cruelty in the committee room of the London School Board and the correspondence petered out as Helen became too mentally frail to put pen to paper. Elizabeth died in 1901 in Coronado City, San Diego, California. The census of 1900 had showed her living there with her husband, Joseph, two sons, a daughter in law and her grandchildren.[30]

Ethel Leach and Helen also kept in touch after the 1885 election. Helen spent Christmas 1886 with the Leach family which Ethel remembered fondly the following April: 'It needs but your presence to make our party comfortable as it was at Xmas.'[31] Ethel clearly missed her friend. In 1888, on passing Helen's former flat in South Kensington she remembered the happy times they had spent there together.[32] That same year she wrote to Helen regarding the visit of the Irish nationalist MP, John O'Connor, to her home in Great Yarmouth where they discussed the votes for women campaign. 'I have been trying to convert him to women's suffrage.'[33] Ethel was a fluent letter writer, much more so than Helen. She provided much support in her letters and they discussed both politics and Ethel's family life. When the local government county councils were established in 1888, Ethel wrote wishing that Helen would have agreed to be a candidate. Frequently the correspondence was gossip between two close women friends as when Ethel passed on to Helen the news that Anna Parnell's dog had developed anxiety and started to bite people.[34] At other times they returned to more serious discussion of politics, the School Board and the land campaigns.[35] They also discussed the divisions in the suffrage movement and their disillusionment with political life.[36] Often these letters, written to Helen in Avignon, must have been a source of encouragement and support as she became increasingly infirm and isolated. Letters became less formal over the years and Ethel was delighted when Helen began using her Christian name in addressing her:

> I had rather be loved by you than by any dozen other people and the very greatest misery that could befall me would be to lose your respect and affection.[37]

Ethel, a secular freethinker, would appear in court in 1904 for opposing the 1902 Education Act which granted tax payer's money to elementary schools for religious instruction. In 1920 she became Great Yarmouth's first female Justice of the Peace and the town's first female mayor. She died in 1936.[38]

Anna Parnell and Helen, as we have seen, also kept in touch though by the 1890s the correspondence had dried up. For a time Anna lived in an artist colony in Cornwall for she had trained at the Royal Academy as an artist. She wrote occasional letters to newspapers and in 1900 sent money to the daughters of Erin who were organising a patriotic children's tea party in protest at the visit of Queen Victoria to Ireland. Her final appearance in public was in support of the Sinn Fein candidate in Leitrim during the parliamentary election of 1907. She wrote her bitter critique of the Land League in 1907, *The Tale of a Great Sham*, and tried unsuccessfully to find a publisher.[39] The manuscript was then lost until 1959 when it was discovered in the belongings of a Sarah Fraser. It was in a parcel addressed to the Irish nationalist, Helena Molony which had been handed over to her. Molony tried, unsuccessfully, to have it published as did the Irish Republican, Maire Comerford, who worked on editing the manuscript. Comerford handed it to the historian, T.W. Moody who deposited it in the National Library of Ireland. It was finally edited by Dana Hearne and published in 1986.[40]

(i) Land Reform Work

Helen continued her involvement with the Land Nationalisation Society although, as the 1890s progressed, this was mainly by way of letters. In 1888, the society published Helen's pamphlet *Nationalisation of the Land*.[41] This was sold to supporters at the huge land meetings. Helen opened with a reference to her step-father who had argued that as land was a limited resource its use needed government intervention to ensure that the population had access to it and that it was not in the hands of a few landowners. Mill had been a supporter of peasant proprietorship, but Helen believed that nothing less than nationalisation of the land would solve land scarcity for common use. Many would be unable to afford to buy their farms. The present system of tenants paying rent gave the tenant no incentive to improve the condition of the land as this would lead to his rent being increased. She stressed the urban dimension of the land problem, referencing the appalling living conditions of the urban working-class who were living in dilapidated overcrowded properties. The only solution was government intervention in the form of land nationalisation. Maintaining the status quo, in the hope that good Christian landowners would see the moral right of fair, affordable tenancies, was never going to work. Neither would private ownership of land by individual farmers because this would still leave the poor, without the means to buy, excluded from land use. Neither would the single tax advocated by George and his supporters work because the increased tax would fall as a burden on the tenants as the landlords would increase the rent to offset the increased taxation demanded of them. The only solution to the scarcity of land for society to satisfy the demand for housing and work was, she claimed, nationalisation.

> It follows that the land should be the common property of the nation as a whole… No individual should be able to lay down the conditions under which another may dwell or labour on the land of their common birth.[42]

Helen continued to use her land campaigning to promote her feminism. Speaking at the Annual General Meeting of the English Land Restoration League in 1885 'she claimed for the people the restoration of all the value they had by their labour put in the land, and reminded the meeting that no small part of that labour was due directly or indirectly to women.'[43] She blamed the loss of the land, through Enclosure Acts, on the exclusion of women from national government. It was men who had put the land into the hands of the few: '... she sometimes thought that it would not have been stolen from them if the men had not in the first instance denied equal rights to women.'[44]

Helen continued to work with the single taxers and in 1890 the English Land Restoration League published her pamphlet, *The Restoration of their Homes to the People, An Appeal to Women*. She argued in this work that it was a natural part of women's domestic duties to have a say in the laws regarding land and housing. It was part of their care of their families to be involved. [45] Land Boards, were being advocated by land reformers to control land and Helen demanded, as a moral duty, for women to be included as members of these:

> In the days when the foundations of our national liberties were laid, men and women met together at the annual assemblies

> which were afterwards consolidated into the House of Commons. Probably had women never been deprived of or neglected to claim their ancient right to sit in the original Parliament of the country, the nation would not so easily have been deprived, either by open violence or insidious fraud, of their right to the land of their fathers. For it seems in human nature that the women should take the deepest interest in the home and be its most watchful guardians. It is time that the women of England should open their eyes to this matter; the poor that they themselves, their neighbours, and their children, may have safe, pleasant, and healthy homes to live in; the rich that they may do their duty to their poorer fellow-creatures in securing for them that haven of a peaceful home which is one of the first blessings of a civilised life.[46]

Helen's support for land nationalisation incensed some of those in the women's suffrage movement. Millicent Fawcett spoke on the evils of land nationalisation in two lectures on behalf of the university extension movement, calling it 'folly or robbery.' The Land Nationalisation Society paper, *Land and Labour*, reported on these and judged that it was 'difficult to imagine the possibility of exhibiting greater ignorance on the subject than was manifest in these discourses.' Fawcett had erroneously thought that only agricultural land was to be nationalised.

In 1889, Helen travelled from Avignon to lecture for the Land Nationalisation Society and the English Land Restoration League (and to sort out her brother's domestic arrangements following his move to Devon). She was hopeful that land nationalisation would be achieved and she undertook a further tour in 1890 which were reported on in *Land and Labour*. From then on, she spent more and more time in Avignon and her involvement in the land movement was mainly in the administration of it by letter. She financially bailed out the movement on a number of occasions. In 1883 she paid the salary of Mr Knight who was employed on a year's contract by the Land Nationalisation Society. She insisted that, as a paid employee, he should resign from the governing executive so that there should be no conflict of interest.[47] When Knight did not take up the offer she refused to fund a Mr Aldridge instead as she feared he was putting the security of his family at risk by accepting a temporary appointment.[48] The Land Nationalisation Society apologised to her, in

1894, for suggesting that she agree to pay any future deficit that *Land and Labour* might incur. She was not prepared to cover unknown future expenses.[49] In 1897 she helped to fund the £1,000 a year van fund which was in deficit, owing the secretary of the Land Nationalisation Society, Mr Vereinder, £150.[50] In 1893 she also loaned £20 to the sister of Joseph Hyder, Secretary of the Land Nationalisation Society, to be repaid at the rate of £1 per month.[51] Five years later, however, she refused to loan his sister money a second time, advising Mr Hyder to stop taking on his sister's financial problems. She did not want to receive begging letters from her.[52] She did send her £52 but made it quite clear that this was the last time she would help her out.[53] In 1897 she funded the vans of the English Land Restoration League so that they could continue touring Great Britain promoting land reform. [54]

(ii) The Liberal Women's Association

Helen, so long at loggerheads with the Liberal party for the causes she espoused, became reconciled with the party after 1885. This would have been very much influenced by Gladstone's conversion to supporting Home Rule. Gladstone introduced his Home Rule Bill to Parliament in 1886 but it was defeated. This led to a split in the party into the Liberals and the Liberal Unionists. In 1887, Helen, who had been so vocal in her disgust at Gladstone's Coercion Acts, felt able to speak at a meeting celebrating his birthday in Eastbourne, where she praised his Irish policy.[55] She remained a radical within Liberalism. She was elected as a Vice President of Portsmouth Radical Club in 1886 as well as being the President of Camberwell Radical Club.[56] However, some Liberals would not forgive her opposition to official liberalism even when she returned to the fold. For example, whilst she declined the offer of Hatcham Liberal Club to be one of their candidates for the Greenwich Division for the London School Board elections of 1888,[57] the Vice President of the Liberal Association of Great Yarmouth had refused to invite her as a speaker in 1887. He deemed her unacceptable on '…the grounds that she had treated T. Scrutton so badly.' Ethel Leach, writing to inform Helen of this assured her that 'some of the other members thought it was the other way round.'[58]

Helen joined the Liberal League. (This was not the Liberal League, established in 1902 by Liberal Imperialists opposed to the policies of

Campbell Bannerman). The earlier Liberal League was formed in 1886 as an organisation in which men and women worked together to campaign for the Liberal Party. It was created to deal with the threat of the Primrose League in which men and women Conservatives worked to increase the influence of the Conservative Party.[59] Helen, as usual, was able to give financial aid to this new organisation. In 1890 Mr Talbot, the Honourable Secretary, asked her advice as the League owed £350. Committee members had promised to donate to clear the debt but now the Liberal MP, Arnold Morley, had come forward with the money.[60] Helen wrote a stiff reply, horrified that the League were even considering having anything to do with the Liberal establishment who must surely believe they had something to gain by clearing the League's debts:

> I was much surprised to hear from you that you have been in communication with Mr Arnold Morley respecting the affairs of the Liberal League, as I understood from yourself and others that it was owing to the hostile and disingenuous action of the Liberal whips and party wire pullers that the difficulties of the Liberal League had chiefly arisen.[61]

She advised the Liberal League executive not to worry and if she, herself, were to receive a summons for the debt she would;

> … make it an opportunity of saying my say both about Liberal whips in general and Mr Arnold Morley in particular in their dealings with the Radicals. And also, about tradesmen 'running' political associations.[62]

It was the League's commitment to women's rights which would have enabled Helen to join this Liberal organisation. The local Liberal clubs had, from the early 1880s, admitted women as equal members.[63] At the inaugural dinner of the Tolstoy Lodge of the Liberal League in, 1887, Helen emphasised the fact that men and women were working together:

> The Liberal League is an organisation consisting now of eighty-five associations of men and women (or women only) with upwards of four thousand members, all bonded together for the two-fold purpose of liberal organisation and education.[64]

She regarded women as an important moral force for good in politics, a core belief of mid-century classic bourgeois feminism which we have met before:

> It was the first anniversary of the Liberal League which was the first political association in any country which had given absolute and complete equality to men and women…It had put into its programme that it would put principle before party, and it demanded morality on the part of public men and she hailed in that fact the first fruits of women's work in politics… Justice, honesty, morality: these were the things which women had to urge on men.[65]

During the late 1880s, Helen accepted many speaking engagements to the Women's Liberal Association. The suffragist Anna Maria Priestman had set up the first Women's Liberal Association in Bristol back in 1881.[66] It had immediately refused to campaign for Liberal men who were opposed to women's suffrage.[67] It called for men and women to be treated equally in divorce law and the repeal of laws which prohibited women from working in certain jobs and professions. By 1886 there were fifteen Women's Liberal Associations and six thousand members. (This would increase, by 1892, to 307 branches and 51,000 members).[68] On 27 May 1886, at a London conference, these associations were brought under the umbrella of the newly created Women's Liberal Federation.[69] The Federation was formed as a campaign group:

1. To promote the adoption of liberal principles by the Government.
2. Just legislation for women and protection of the interests of children.
3. The advancement of political education by literature and meetings.
4. The promotion of a Women's Liberal Association in every constituency and the admittance of women to membership of any Liberal Association.[70]

Clearly the Women's Liberal Federation aims were to both support the party's Liberal MPs and to promote feminism within the party. Its feminism has been described as a 'Trojan Horse' as it entered the Liberal party under the guise of working for the elected male MPs.[71] In 1892 the Federation officially added the demand for women's suffrage to its constitution. Following this move the Women's Liberal Federation started to campaign for the Liberal Party to officially support votes for women.

Helen's topics for her speaking engagements with the Women's Liberal Association included Home Rule for Ireland and land reform. Eva McLaren invited Helen to address the recently formed Women's Liberal Association in Crewe. Eva wrote to ask whether her preference was for an all-woman or mixed sex meeting and informed her that the 1,100 members were 'sound on all the questions which you feel so strongly.'[72] Ethel Leach formed the Women's Liberal Association in Great Yarmouth. She wrote to Helen that, although it was more a philanthropic rather than political group, 'I suppose such an organisation might do good work in helping women to form sound opinions on questions affecting the wellbeing of the Community.'[73] Ethel expressed regret that Helen had declined to stand as a candidate for the newly formed County Council elections. She criticised the women's suffrage movement which had 'shown such apathy in the matter.' They had failed to 'press the claims of women voting and holding seats when the bill was going through.'[74] The County Councils had been created by the Local Government Act of 1888 and the first elections were held in January 1889. As in other local elections, women ratepayers were qualified to vote.[75] These would have been unmarried or widowed women in charge of a household. Helen would have seen the justification of much of her 1880s campaigning in the causes of the Women's Liberal Federation. In 1891 it passed a resolution in favour of national free education and self-government for Ireland.[76] Support for Home Rule led to a split in the Women's Liberal Association, as it had the Liberal Party in 1886. Resolutions were passed both for and against Home Rule throughout the branches. For example, Chesterfield Women's Liberal Association passed a resolution in support. [77] In the north of Ireland, a schism occurred as the Ulster Women's Liberal Unionist Association was formed to oppose it, led by Miss Tod.[78]

(iii) The Moral Reform Union

The Moral Reform Union had been formed, in 1881, by Dr Elizabeth Blackwell and Mrs S.W. Browne to promote 'pure family life' and 'the spread of pure literature bearing on social and political morality.'[79] Helen was one of sixty-eight members who had joined in the first year.[80] Like many who joined the Democratic Federation that same year Helen, we have seen, was a mid-century radical and moralist. She was a generation away from the younger women who joined Hyndman during the early 1880s like Eleanor Marx and Olive Schreiner. Eleanor was in a free union with Edward Aveling who had worked alongside Helen on the London School Board. Olive was a friend of the socialist homosexual Edward Carpenter[81] and a member of Karl Pearson's Men and Women's Club which debated the relations between the sexes. Traditional marriage and sexual mores were being challenged. Meanwhile Helen, in the Moral Reform Union, would uphold the institution of marriage and oppose easier divorce. The Moral Reform Union called on men to show the same restraint in sexual relations as women were expected to, not for women to embrace the same current sexual standards as the opposite sex. Helen did not approve of fellow suffragist Elizabeth Wolstenholme-Elmy living, unmarried, in a free union with Ben Elmy. Mrs Browne, then Honourable Secretary of the Moral Reform Union, wrote to Helen that Mrs Elmy did 'not base her morality on the same source as ourselves.'[82] Free love was immoral for it did not give women any security. It allowed a man to up and go, leaving his family destitute. It was not equality. The Moral Reform Union published a paper by Miss Chapman: 'Why we should Oppose Divorce.'[83] In its 4th Annual Report the organisation set out to 'wage an unremitting war' on free love, which was mere lust.[84] It publicly opposed Sir Charles Dilke's return to public life. He had been involved in a notorious divorce and the Moral Reform Union disapproved when the Women's Liberal Association in the Forest of Dean became involved in organising Dilke's local meetings. The Union insisted that Dilke should keep to his promise that he would not return to public life until it was proved that he had not had an extra-marital affair with his sister-in-law's married sister.[85] Dilke, who had once been thought of as a possible future Prime Minister, had been the Liberal MP for Chelsea from 1868 to 1886 when he was rejected by his constituency because of the scandal. The Liberals in the Forest of Dean approached him to be their candidate in 1889, an offer he accepted in 1892 when he was returned to parliament. He held the seat until his death in 1911.[86]

The work of the Moral Reform Union against the Contagious Diseases Acts, in England and the Empire, provided Helen with a link with the past and the campaigning world of Mill. We have seen Mill's opposition to these Acts in the 1860s. Campaigning had continued against them during the subsequent decades and they were finally repealed, in Britain, in 1886. The campaign continued after this to have the Acts repealed in India. In 1888, Walter McLaren MP, the son of Helen's friend and women's suffrage colleague, Priscilla, successfully tabled a parliamentary motion to repeal the acts in India.

Despite this, the 1889 Containment Act India saw the sub-continent continue to be subject to the Contagious Diseases Acts. The Moral Reform Union had sent repeal literature to India and Ceylon, in 1888, and a petition for repeal to the House of Commons.[87] The Union believed that women's suffrage would improve the morality of lawmaking in Parliament. 'This battle, which was, year by year, so bravely fought for sixteen years in Parliament, would have been won much sooner had women possessed the vote.'[88]

In 1890, Mrs Woolcott Browne retired as Honourable Secretary of the Moral Reform Union and Helen agreed to take on the role. The Moral Reform Union was, however, already in decline as an effective campaigning organisation. The repeal of the Contagious Diseases Acts in Britain and Ireland had largely removed its raison d'être and it was starved of funds. Helen was the major donor. The Treasurer, E.L. Miers, wrote to Helen that, without her financial support, the organisation could not continue to exist.[89] Indeed this blow fell, in 1895, when Helen resigned from both her position as Honourable Secretary and membership of the Union. By 1895, Helen was 64, living in Avignon, and spending very little time in England. She dealt with matters concerning the Moral Reform Union by way of letters between herself and the secretary, Miss Albert, in London. The relationship between the two women was not good and Helen was frequently incensed with Miss Albert's refusal to follow instructions. Miss Albert had issued circulars and letters without getting the approval of the Executive Committee or Helen, the president.[90] Helen resigned making it quite clear that the actions of Miss Albert were responsible for her decision. Miss Albert was impossible to work with.[91] This is rather rich coming from Helen who had driven colleagues in various organisations to despair at her inability to see another's point of view. Other executive members though agreed with Helen and also resigned although the Moral Reform Union ineffectively soldiered on for a number of years. The newspaper, jointly published by the Moral Reform Union and the Social Purity Alliance, *The Pioneer*, folded in 1898.[92] The world of her mother and step-father was long gone and the next generation of feminists, with freer attitudes to sexuality, had replaced them. By the 1890s, the 'new woman' feminist, mainly middle or upper-class, was challenging the sexual limits to her independence.[93] She was demanding an autonomous life and equality in sexual relations, marriage, education and professional opportunity with men. Helen's ending of her involvement in the dying organisation of the Moral Reform Union was the end of her active involvement in politics.

(iv) Retirement from the Public Stage

We have seen how, by the 1890s, Helen was conducting business for the Moral Reform Union and the land reform organisations by letter from Avignon. In 1890, a newspaper commentated on her disappearance from public life. 'Miss Helen Taylor who up to a year or two ago was one of the foremost political women in London ...but who now seldom appears on a public platform.'[94] During the 1890s she lived in the house she had shared with John Stuart Mill, looked after by loyal servants.[95] She no longer lectured and travelled to England only rarely, and then to see her brother Algernon rather than renew her campaigning. Letters went unanswered as infirmity increased. Despite this, she continued to fund land reform until at least the turn of the century. Hyder, the secretary of the Land Nationalisation Society, wrote to her, in 1900, acknowledging her 'extremely liberal subscription last June.' [96] In 1900 Christina Bremner, who had known Helen when she was a member of the London School Board, wrote to her, '...you seem to have retired so completely from all connection with public life.'[97] Mary, her niece, noted the rapid decline in her aunt's health during this decade after her trusted maid got married and moved away. In January 1898, Helen wrote to her fellow moral reformer Alfred Dyer:

> Weak health prevents me from doing sustained work. I have neither illness nor suffering and I am happier than I have ever been in my life before and in my little cottage with beautiful views and the mountains and a garden and terrace-roof. [98]

In the same letter she displays a shocking level of antisemitism. She talks derogatorily of Gladstone 'incited by his task masters the Jews...with all its faults England is the nation that now leads the world in morals and religion. There are twenty honest men and women for one in every country. They ought not to let the Jews drag them down to the level of the others.'[99] Jews were regarded as conspiratorial people, taking over the world through capitalism for world domination. The Eastern Question of 1875 had increased anti-Jewish feeling as world powers sought to avoid instability in the Balkans and increased immigration of Jews to Britain was regarded by many as an alien invasion. Liberalism had at its heart tolerance of the beliefs of others and freedom of religious expression but it was not immune to antisemitism. In Bethnal Green in 1901 the Liberal and Radical Club would pass a resolution barring Jews from applying to be election candidates and the left too were antisemitic. Beatrice Potter's report on poverty in East London displayed racist stereotypes of Jewish immigrants.[100] In her comments on Jewish influence in the government Helen was tapping into the widespread racism and trope, still current today, that the Jews were conspiring to take over the world.

Her contact with former friends and colleagues outside of official business became infrequent. Helen and, the previously mentioned, B.M. Dallimore (we do not learn of her Christian name) had formed a friendship during the London School Board years. Dallimore had been the headmistress of a London school. Letters, between them in the late 1880s, reveal that Helen had helped Dallimore financially and had also supported her sister by having her to stay when she needed a rest.[101] Dallimore's letters are written in a gushing romantic tone, a common convention at the time. Helen had been ill in Avignon and Dallimore wrote to her wishing she could go and see her immediately. 'I seemed to realise all at once, the probability of losing you and the mere thought was agony.'[102] She goes on to beg Helen to send a portrait of herself,

> …and some <u>little thing</u> you have been accustomed to use, as a 'memento' not in the sense of a reminder but I feel I need not explain myself – you will understand and I believe appreciate my motive.

Clearly the two women were emotionally supporting each other. Dallimore wrote to Helen on the stress of being a head teacher in a London school.[103] The letters express ties of love and friendship but there is one striking superficiality in the correspondence of Dallimore and Helen which points to a lack of real closeness between the two women. During the time when Dallimore is writing of her love and anguish at Helen's illness she tellingly writes, in response to Helen's account of coming to England to nurse her brother Algernon, in 1888, that, 'I did not know you had any such near relations to cause you anxiety.'[104] This casts doubt on how deep the friendship was exactly and evidences that professions of devotion and love could often be conventional expressions of regard and friendship rather than any evidence of emotional closeness. As Philippa Levine has illustrated, in her work on Victorian romantic friendships, the social barriers set up between men and women made friendships between women extremely important to their emotional wellbeing.[105] It gave Victorian women rights' campaigners, for instance, a sense of community and allowed them to form feminist networks.[106]

By the early 1900s Helen appears only to have kept up a regular correspondence with Algernon's daughter, Mary, who did not realise the true extent of her aunt's failing health until Helen travelled to England to visit her ailing brother. Mary lived with her father in the lodgings in Devon. Algernon, after almost starving himself to death in 1888, had continued in poor health. He had suffered, for over a decade, with his eating disorder and had become obsessive again over his strict vegetarian diet. Mary had written to her aunt in 1890 and 1897 detailing her father's ill health. Both times the doctor had diagnosed 'starvation.'[107] He had sold the house in Haddenham by auction in 1894. The *Bucks Herald* carried the announcement of the sale of the 'brick built' cottage with 'parlour, sitting room, front and back kitchen, cellar, four bedrooms, garden, barn and orchard'. The furniture, fixtures and fittings were also in the auction. Algernon had never settled to a job but he had obviously lived very comfortably on his trust fund.[108] In 1895, he had published a book of memories of his life, *Memories of a Student*, which contained interesting details of his life when young living with his stepfather and mother in Blackheath. He was also a member of the local Anti-Vivisection Society at this time.[109] Mary returned to Avignon with Helen in 1900 after the latter had visited her brother in early March. Algernon had greatly looked forward to his sister's visit.[110] Mary was no stranger to Avignon. It is not known how often she visited her aunt, or if Algernon visited in later years, but Mary had enjoyed a trip to see Helen in 1890 accompanied by an M. Wigmore. Miss Wigmore was the governess of the family where Mary and her father lodged at the Vicarage, Chudleigh. [111] Helen's niece, Nelly, it would appear, seemed to plough her own furrow in life. There is almost nothing in the archive to enlighten us on the years of her maturity. In 1897 Mary wrote from Devon to Helen in Avignon hoping that Nelly had written to her aunt. Mary had sent her sister the message Helen had included for Nelly in her last letter to Devon. Mary informed her aunt that her sister was still living at Dows House, Boscombe, Bournemouth and that she sent her love to her.[112] In 1899 Nelly joined Mary and her father in Ilfracombe for three weeks where they had gone for Algernon's health, and they then all returned to Torquay together. [113]

The 1901 census shows Algernon living, as a boarder, at Warmhill Farm in the village of Hennock, near Newton Abbot in Devon. Sometime during the early 1900s his elder daughter, Nelly, came to live with him, presumably to look after him. His will of November 1903 places her at the same address he moved to before his death, Moorlands, Bovey Tracy. His son Cyprian had been committed as insane to an asylum in Exminster, Devon. Algernon had written to Helen, in May 1900, detailing Cyprian's deteriorating mental health. He had developed religious mania and obsessively tore up books.[114] He had been committed after interrupting an Anglican church service and shouting his disapproval. A Member of Parliament in the congregation who had witnessed the incident, had signed the committal papers.[115] Algernon's health was failing and Helen managed the journey back to Devon in 1902 to visit him. By this time she had completely disappeared from public view. A columnist in the *Labour Leader*, writing in praise of Mill as 'a rare soul' of the type unfortunately no longer present in politics, mused that he had recently heard that Helen was still alive. 'She seems a link with the extreme past. She must be very old.'[116] On her return to Avignon, she took her niece Mary and her friend, Molly, with her. Molly was Mary Ann Trimble. Mary had first mentioned her friend in a letter to Helen written on 18 February 1900. She told her aunt that her friend, Miss Trimble, was staying with them in Devon for two weeks. Molly had recently returned from New Zealand, where she had relatives. In the same letter she tells Helen that Nelly had been 'lodging with three lady friends at Crowborough, Sussex' but was now in Tunbridge Wells to be near them as they had moved. She assured her aunt that Nelly was 'wonderfully improved, so much more sympathetic, in fact very sisterly. Friendship has done a great deal for us both.'[117] Both sisters and Cyprian, it would appear, had suffered from the death of their mother and the social isolation of having a father who had his own mental health problems all his life and who settled to nothing. In July 1900, Mary was able to update Helen that living with friends in Tunbridge Wells had proved greatly beneficial for Nelly who had been very self-contained all her life. Mary felt, she wrote, that their father had discouraged them from expressing themselves when young. They had learnt to be circumspect in expressing their emotions and to check the correctness of their thoughts and expressions. They had been taught to only say to each other what it was seemly for others to hear. It had obviously had an effect on all the children's mental development and emotional health. In the same letter Mary is referring to Miss Trimble as 'her other half.'[118] Nelly's mood improved so much that in September of that year she visited her sister and father, staying in Mary's room whilst Mary stayed with Miss Trimble in Torquay.[119] Molly Trimble also had a sister living in neighbouring Newton Abbot.[120]

Nothing is known of the first year of Mary and Molly's stay in Avignon but between 1904–1906 Mary would keep a diary which gives us a window into their lives. In June 1903, Mary received a telegram from her father back in England that he was about to have an operation. In October Mary and Molly returned to England to nurse her dying father taking the French house maid, Catherine, with them. Helen had been reluctant to let Catherine go as she had never been further than Carpentras in her life. Helen herself was getting more frequently confused, often misplacing items including money which Mary would have to find. When Mary arrived in Bovey Tracey, she did not yet know what was wrong with her father and had to ask her sister Nelly to tell her. Algernon died, aged 73, on the 14 November 1903 and probate was granted to his daughters Nelly and Mary and their cousin, the Reverend W.F.C. Gurney, chaplain to the British consulate in Marseille (and presumably the son of the doctor who had attended Harriet Taylor in her last illness in Avignon and also Mill's funeral). Algernon left an estate worth £7,807 net. Algernon was buried with his wife, Ellen, in Tetsworth on 18 November 1903 as would have been his wishes.[121] His obituary in the local Devon newspaper, noted him as 'an earnest vegetarian, an opposer of vivisection and an accredited authority on church architecture.'[122] Mary and Molly stayed on in Devon. After various legacies to relatives and 100 pounds to Rev. Gurney the estate was divided into three equal parts between his three children. Cyprian's bequest was held in trust for him as he was mentally incapable. Algernon left his brother Herbert, £100.[123] Herbert would survive him for less than two years. He died on 24 August 1905 at 17 Upper Cheyne Walk, London, unreconciled with his sister. He left an estate of £58,617.00 to his son Geoffrey Taylor and a friend Harry Garraway in equal shares. To his granddaughter Ethel May Taylor, he gave £100. There is no mention of his daughter Eleanor and his other son, Herbert, had died in America in 1900. His former wife, Annie, had died in 1901 in Chelsea where she had been living with her son Geoffrey. Geoffrey's occupation is given in the census of that year as 'newspaper editor.' Although the family had been estranged from his father's siblings since before his birth, Geoffrey took great pride in his grandmother, Harriet Taylor, and aunt's campaigning and writing. Replying to an obituary in the *Morning Post* of his uncle Algernon, in 1903, he reminded the editor that

Mill's work, *On Liberty*, was a 'joint work' with Harriet and drew attention to his aunt's campaigning work.[124]

Mary and Molly stayed on in Devon to help sort out Algernon's affairs whilst Catherine returned home to Avignon. There was a legal dispute with the will which kept them in England longer than expected. However, in February 1904, with the dispute settled, they could start to plan their journey back to Avignon. Mary drew up her will and arranged for Cyprian, still in the asylum, to be looked after. On the 4th of March she sent a cheque for £2 to Dr Daris to be spent by the clerk of the asylum on her brother's behalf and on 5 March they set off for Dover for the return trip. Before sailing, they saw Mary's aunt, her mother's sister, the former Annie Fowler Cecil Gurney to whom Algernon had left fifty pounds. She was now Mrs Annie Harris and living in Bedford Cottage, Barton Road, Dover with her son George Britain (aged 25, a musical composer).[125] Widowed twice, she had married a George Britain, the father of her children, in 1873 in Marylebone He had died in 1880. Annie and George came to see Mary and Molly at their hotel. Aunt Annie and George waved them off on the boat on 7 March 1904 for the long journey back to Avignon. The train trip from Paris to Avignon took twelve hours and they arrived unexpected as Helen had thought they were coming the following week. They had been gone for five months. Mary found worrying developments in their absence. It would seem, at least from Mary's one-sided diary account which is all we have to go on, that Helen had feared that her two English companions were not returning and she had written an unsigned will leaving all her money and property to the servants, Marguerite and Catherine. Mary suspected that the servants had hidden a signed copy which they would produce on the death of her aunt. Unmarried women at the time faced financial hardship and we must not judge Mary by modern standards in her desire to secure her place in Helen's will. Even with the money left to her by her father, she lived precariously and did not have enough for an independent life. The will in favour of the servants, who she feared had taken advantage of her absence, upset her greatly and she wrote in her diary a passionate, 'Oh for a peaceful settled home with my Molly free of various cares.' Helen, always a prickly person, was getting increasingly difficult to deal with in her mental decline. Today, she would be recognised as having a form of dementia. She was refusing to hand over the trust money she owed to Algernon's executors and had administered, during his lifetime, on his behalf. The life Mary had returned to in Avignon was unremittingly depressing. Mary wondered how she would be able to endure it for the years and years stretching ahead of her. They rarely had visitors, except for the occasional local resident asking Helen for money for various causes. The house was dirty and dilapidated and many of the rooms were now unused and kept under lock and key. The garden, in which Helen and Mill had delighted, was now overgrown and Helen spent her days shuffling around in it collecting leaves to burn on the fire at night. Molly and Mary shared a bedroom and a bed in which they spent hours talking about the situation and trying to get the courage to tell Helen that they could no longer endure this life and wanted to leave. In April, Mary decided to stay and look after her aunt because 'of what my aunt has done for me lately and I mean to be happy.' The solitude was broken, that month, by a visit from her cousin, Willie Gurney, the co-executor of her father's will. Willie a clergyman, had come to Avignon to conduct the funeral service of an English man who had died in the same hotel as Harriet had all those years ago, Hôtel d'Europe.

The visit provided relief from the daily stress of coping with Helen whose behaviour was often unbearable as that intelligent mind crumbled. One night, while playing cards, Helen lost her temper when Mary won and accused her niece of cheating. She screamed at her she should leave her house. Another time, when Mary took Helen to visit old friends of both her and Mill, Pasteur Rey and his wife, Helen refused to enter the house when she got there. She only calmed down when she reached home and saw 'our trees;' the avenue of trees which lined the drive. That night Mary let her aunt win at cards to keep the atmosphere congenial. With modern eyes and a knowledge of how dementia robs the person of their self, it is easy to understand the daunting role Mary and Molly had taken on in caring for Helen. They were in a foreign country with no support network and limited knowledge of the language. Mary was increasingly at her wits' end with 'the monotony of the days that succeed each other.' She also had her brother, Cyprian, to worry about in the asylum in England. Cyprian was asking her for money. Mary had received a cheque with the balance owing to her and Cyprian from her father's estate, but Cyprian's doctor had advised her not to send any to her brother. Molly and Mary bought bicycles to give themselves some freedom and began to enjoy rides round the neighbourhood. Helen did not usually come out into the garden from her bedroom until lunchtime when she would demand great attention and devotion. She lived in the past when she had been a public figure and expected her niece and Molly to listen to her tales. They tired of having to feign interest in the repeated stories of thirty years ago 'dreaming about which forms her chief pleasure.' Helen frequently lost her temper. She accused her companions of not leaving enough meat for the servants at meal times even though there was precious little on their own plates. Helen allowed the servants to take liberties and the house became increasingly filthy. Yet, in the moments when her mind cleared, Helen could be her old generous self, once giving Mary a cheque for £5 to send to Aunt Annie in Dover.

However, during the summer of 1904, Helen's rages, caused by her mental condition, became more frequent and she constantly picked quarrels. Mary got Helen a dog, thinking it would make her aunt happy, but this was a disaster. Helen became jealous when the dog preferred the company of Mary and Molly and it had to be sent back when it became obvious how much it missed its previous owner. By July 1904 Helen was eating little and fainted with hunger one day. Mary wrote, in her diary, of the unappetising food served by the servants and they began to invite their aunt up to their bedroom last thing at night to give her a 'nourishing drink' of milk chocolate. They got Helen another dog but again it pined so much for its previous owner they had to return it. It is clear to see Mary and Molly were trying so hard to do what was best for Helen but everything they did failed to improve matters, for, indeed, there was no improvement to be had in this cruel illness. The summer dragged on and on and was the hottest since 1823 in the South of France.

Towards the end of July they found a third dog, Papillon. Helen had always loved animals so Mary and Molly persevered in their quest to bring some means of happiness to her. Many, many years ago now, she and Mill had adored Kalos, the dog given to them by Lady Amberley, and Helen had always kept cats. Mary was desperately trying to make the old lady happy. Mary used her diary to let off steam and the entries can appear harsh but the strain they were living under, as carers, was intolerable. Mary felt her sole existence consisted of 'keeping a bad-tempered, selfish, conceited old woman in as mild a frame as possible.' By August Mary was gravely worried about her aunt's diet and the fact that she was refusing to have her room cleaned. She had to be cajoled into changing her clothes. Helen accused the two women of refusing to give her food and was jealous that the new dog preferred the company of Mary and Molly who it slept with. Helen constantly picked arguments with the women and told them to leave. Sometimes she would summon them to her room and then forget why she had called them. Yet, at other times, she would be pleasant and talk about writing a new will and leaving her money to Mary rather than the servants. Mary grasped at this fleeting lucidity to try and get her aunt to write this new will. She pleaded the case of her Uncle Herbert who Helen had not spoken to for nearly 20 years, following his divorce, bankruptcy and his behaviour regarding Aunt Eliza when he had abused his trusteeship of her money.

Mary had suggested that Helen leave her uncle 500 pounds, using her father's example of his leaving his brother 100 pounds as a softener. Helen refused, as she did Mary's request that her sister Nelly be left some money.[126] Mary also tried to get Helen to leave some money for the concierge, the caretaker of the house in Avignon. Mary had learnt that it had been a Miss Fisher, who had stayed in the house when Mary and Molly were away in Devon, who had persuaded Helen to change her will. Miss Fisher had suggested that, after the death of her father, Mary had no need of any further inheritance. She also discovered that the servants, Marguerite and Catherine were trying to persuade Helen to buy a piece of land from Catherine's nephew at what Mary estimated three or four times its value. They asked for 18,000 francs well knowing that Helen had 19,000 in her bank passbook. Mary was horrified. It was clear to her that the servants were hoping to benefit as the land would form part of the will in their favour. Cyprian continued to be a source of very great concern. In September he wrote asking for the consent of the executors of his father's will for his being received into the Catholic church. Mary was concerned that his priest-confidant was preying on her mentally ill brother in order to get him to go into a monastery. This would enable the church to have control of the money left to him by his father rather than the trustees of the will. Cyprian was too vulnerable to make this decision, in Mary's opinion, and her sister Nelly agreed. His sisters thought he was safer in the County Asylum than in an enclosed monastery at the mercy of the religious order. Cyprian's request was declined for his own well-being on the grounds that he was not mentally competent. Mary lamented that she had no profession which would have enabled her to live independently and not depend on inheriting from her aunt. 'My own income derived from my dear father's estate, is comfortably sufficient for one, but what comfort is there in a lonely life when one has tasted a double one.'

Helen would often argue with Molly and once asked her to leave after an argument. Mary felt aggrieved that her aunt had never even asked her dear friend, and presumably lover's, surname. Helen's rages subsided as quickly as they came. That same evening, after earlier telling Molly she would have to go from the house, all was pleasant again as Helen listened to Molly's tales of life in New Zealand with great interest. Little is gleaned from Mary's diary of Molly's past life, only small snippets such as these appear in the diary. Molly Trimble had lived in New Zealand but had an aunt in Ireland so it would be presumed she was the daughter of Irish emigrants. Her baptismal name was Mary Ann and she had two sisters Fanny and Kate back in New Zealand who she tried desperately to get to come and visit them but they never came. Where Mary and Molly/Marion/Mary Ann met is unknown. Her full identity is only gleaned from the will of Helen Taylor who left a legacy to her. 'I give to Mary Ann Trimble at present residing with me an annuity of eighty pounds for her life.' This was at the time Helen, Mary and Mary Ann were all living together in Devon shortly before Helen's death. In the census records of 1901, a Mary Ann Trimble, aged 40, was living in Lyme Regis Dorset and working as a governess. She was registered as having been born in County Tyrone (though we know that if this is indeed the same Mary Ann she had lived and had family in New Zealand). A Mary Ann Trimble is recorded, in birth records, as being born in Armagh, Co Tyrone in 1867 which would match the year of birth of the governess in the Devon 1901 census but Trimble is a fairly common name in the north of Ireland. In the same census of 1901, Mary is registered in nearby Totnes, Devon, as a visitor in the household of James Milton, a congregational minister, and living on her own means.

It was the unpredictability which greatly frayed Mary and Molly's nerves. Mary knew that Helen never really wanted the two women to leave her. The younger women sought solace in learning French at the 'college des jeunes filles' and not returning home until 4 pm each afternoon. They enjoyed the lessons and Mary revelled in being a school girl at the age of 40 as she had never gone to school. Algernon, it will be recalled, had declined Helen's attempts to fund both nieces' education.

Matters came to a head in December 1904. Helen was having night terrors and was afraid of sleeping alone. The house, her beloved home and refuge from political life in England since her mother had died over half a century ago, seemed to now frighten her. Mary saw the opportunity of getting Helen away and suggested going to spend the night in the Hotel d'Europe. Once there Helen, refusing to take off her hat and coat, began to dwell fondly on England. Mary and Molly made a quick decision that this was the moment to rescue both Helen and themselves from this intolerable life. Leaving everything they possessed in Avignon, they took the train to Lyon. From there they travelled on to Paris. As soon as they got to Paris Helen's mood lightened, though she developed diarrhoea, which delayed them in the French capital for six long days. From the safe distance of northern France, they wrote dismissing the servants and travelled back home to Devon. They found lodgings and Helen began to mentally improve. She started to get up early and do some needlework, making 'petticoats for the wives and children of the unemployed at Westham' in London. She regained enough clarity of mind to make her will and appoint Mary her power of attorney giving her responsibility for her financial and legal affairs. She even thanked Mary and Molly for getting her back to England. They visited friends in Torquay and Helen was convivial. She went to church. By the beginning of February 1905, the three women were living in lodgings in Torquay. They rented rooms in a house called Peploe, in Higher Terrace, an imposing Victorian building above the harbour. During this year, 1905, Herbert died aged 78 in Chelsea.

Molly returned to France with their friend Mrs Joll to settle their affairs there. Helen and Mary took omnibus excursions around the area. On one such trip they visited Trinity Church. Sometimes Helen would get confused when she was out and begin to worry that Mary was taking her back to France. This would make her cry. She would always be relieved to arrive home. They went to public lectures but Helen's increasing deafness was a problem. Mary recorded them as going to the Morning Service at Trinity church. Holy Trinity was an Anglican church. So even late on in her life, there is no evidence that she converted to Catholicism as Florence Fenwick Miller and Ernest Belfort Bax claimed she had before her death.[127] In early March, Mary Ann returned to Torquay. She and Mrs Joll had cleared the house in Avignon of unwanted possessions. They had packed eighteen boxes for delivery to England and sold some of the books. Helen gave the women's college, Somerville in Oxford, 1500 books from Mill's library.[128] Mary and Molly found the landlady at Peploe rude as when the door broke, she blamed her tenants. So they moved to a house on Babbacombe Downs at two and a half guineas a week including linen. There they had a dining room, drawing room and bathroom as well as the bedrooms. Despite an improvement in her mental health, Helen's physical health continued to worsen and the doctor diagnosed a weak heart and prescribed drives instead of walks. He also syringed Helen's ears of wax which left her hearing the best it had been for sixteen years, in Mary's estimation. Sometimes the three women took the motor omnibus instead of the pony carriage. Helen took great enjoyment from these trips out and her mental state improved enough for her to agree to change her clothes. On 14 April 1905, a relieved Mary commented in her diary:

> We have no difficulty in getting her to change her under linen and she is quite pleased to wear the nice things I get her. She is wearing a lovely braided coat lined with squirrel fur and when we want her to have a new bonnet, she just comes with us into a shop to choose one.

Helen's mind, the night terrors gone, cleared enough to decide to sell the French house with the help of Mary as power of attorney. On 5 May the local Devon paper, *The Western Daily Press*, reported that Mill's house in Avignon was to be sold by auction.

With life settling into a pleasant pattern, after the stress of recent years, Molly took a short holiday in Ireland that late spring, visiting her aunt in Belfast. Mary, who had used the diary to vent her frustrations, wrote fewer entries. She did record, on 26 July 1905, that all the French property had now been sold and most of the money for the sale had been received. Helen and Mill's staunch friend in Avignon, Pasteur Rey, had been most helpful. He had been given power of attorney by Mary to sign for the sale of the Avignon property and had been most assiduous in protecting Helen's interests. Helen had loved her home in Avignon which she had first entered as a young woman in her early thirties, forty-five years ago. He knew how much it had meant to both her and Mill. 3,000 francs were donated by Helen to the town for the perpetual upkeep of her mother and stepfather's graves in Avignon.

On Molly's return from Ireland, they were visited by Molly's Irish nieces. In late July, the days of long ago were brought to mind for Helen when an admirer of John Stuart Mill came to the house. He refused to come in, not wanting to intrude, but left a 'magnificent bouquet of roses.' By October, Mary's diary shows all the women to be really enjoying their new life in Torquay. Torquay, on the English Riveria, has a mild climate and was a fashionable resort. Mary, using her power of attorney, bought a house for £1,050, called Santry on the cliffs overlooking the town. Chelston Road was a street of Victorian villas which still retains its charm. The name of the house is no more, but may be one of the care homes on the street which many of the large villas, high above the town, have been turned into.

The last entry in Mary's diary is on 23 December 1905 after the move to Santry. She describes Helen's joy in the house and how she loved to sit and eat on the balcony. She had always been a lover of the natural world even before her days of botanising with Mill. Perhaps she recalled the sounds and sights of her childhood garden in Walton which she had described in her adolescent diary. As she had in Walton, she sat happily in the garden of the house in Torquay, gazing at the flowers and the views beyond. She rarely argued now with her companions and Mary and Molly had time to devote to their own interests. They became socialists, corresponding with Alfred R. Wallace, Helen's old friend and colleague in the Land Nationalisation Society. Mary began to appreciate her aunt's past, who she discovered, 'had long been deeply tinctured with socialist sentient though I had not quite understood her hints in that direction.' Mary would only have been in her late teens in the early 1880s when Helen was at the peak of her political involvement. Mary and Molly read the *Clarion*, *Labour Leader* and Henry George's *Social Problems*. Mary recorded that Alfred Wallace's book *Bad Times* helped them to understand socialism. After reading this they sent a subscription to the Labour Party, which had been formed in 1900. Mary had an article 'Does England Deserve to be Prosperous?' published in the *Literary Guide and Nationalist Review*. This was against the British trade in opium. It was as if Helen had passed her the baton of campaigning handed to herself by Mill.

And there we leave Helen as there are no further entries in her niece's diary to record the last thirteen months of her life. The rest is silence. The next time we learn anything of her is through the obituaries and letters written after her death, but we can leave her in her garden, high above the cliffs of this most pleasant Devon town, enjoying the sights and sounds of an English garden, with occasional trips by motorbus around Torquay.

(v) In Memorandum

Helen died on 29 January 1907 at her home in Torquay at the age of 75 with Mary by her side. Her death certificate recorded the cause as senile decay and syncope. The latter was most likely losing consciousness due to heart failure. Her death was mercifully quick. Her niece, Nelly, wrote to Mary expressing shock at the sudden passing. 'I am so sorry for you. It must have been a great shock to you – aunt's sudden and quite unexpected death.'[129]

Helen was buried three days later, on 1 February, in the cemetery on the hill overlooking Torquay.[130]

With the speed that Nelly had written to Mary, the day following her aunt's death, she was still living in England. Sometime between her aunt's death and 1918, Nelly Taylor emigrated to Canada. She was living there at the time Mary made her will in 1918. Her address is given 1256 Walnut Street, Victoria, British Columbia. No mention is made of Nelly in her sister's diary recording Helen's life in Torquay before her death. In July 1916, Lydia S. Whitfield had written to Mary from 1268 Walnut Street, assuring her that 'we are all going on nicely. Lydia regretted that Mary had no religious faith and did not 'have the joy of knowing Jesus.' Lydia's religious fervour takes up most of the letter and she has enclosed religious pamphlets for Mary. Mary had visited them both in Canada previously and Nelly had proved difficult:

> 'I am sorry you had such a long and expensive journey for so little compensation….it showed your kind love and affection to your dear sister although perhaps she did not seem to appreciate your kindness, yet I think she was very pleased about it…We were all very pleased to meet you and shall always remember your visit to Victoria.'[131]

The 1921 Canadian census records an English woman, Mary Elizabeth Taylor, living in the city, who had entered Canada in 1911. She was recorded living alone as head of household. (A Lydia Whitfield, Presbyterian, who had entered the same year as Elizabeth, 1911, is recorded as a servant in Nanaimo, British Columbia, sixty-nine miles away). Nelly's sister, Mary, was the sole beneficiary of Helen's will. She had also appointed her as her literary executor and also Mill's. Mary took this seriously and arranged for a volume of Mill's letters to be published for which she wrote the forward. This was edited by Hugh S.R. Eliot and published in 1910 as *The Letters of John Stuart Mill.*

After Helen's death Mary became involved in the growing campaign for women's suffrage. She joined the Women's Social and Political Union which was a militant woman-only suffrage group headed by Emmeline Pankhurst and her daughters Christabel and Sylvia. Unlike the more moderate, National Union of Women's Suffrage headed by Millicent Fawcett, the suffragettes of the Women's Social and Political Union committed acts of violence against both property and opponents of women's suffrage and many endured hunger strike in prison. In November 1910, Mary Taylor was arrested along with other suffragettes of the WSPU after a march on the House of Commons. This had taken place after a suffragette meeting in Caxton Hall. On reaching the British parliament they tried to force their way into the building. The *Birmingham Mail*, 19 November 1910, under the heading 'Suffragette Riot,' recorded the arrest of suffragettes including a 'Mrs (sic) Mary Taylor, granddaughter of Mrs John Stuart Mill.' Charges were later withdrawn as Winston Churchill, the Liberal Home Secretary, did to want to make martyrs of the women and, thereby, give them more publicity.[132]

Mary died on 6 November 1918 in an asylum, Northumberland House, in Finsbury Park London. Northumberland House had been opened in 1829 as a lunatic asylum for upper- and middle-class ladies and gentlemen. In 1916 the weekly charges started at 3 guineas.[133] Mental health had troubled her father, brother, and possibly her sister and, in the end, Mary herself. Probate gives her last address, before the asylum, as Kings Heath, Birmingham. Her net estate after taxes was £10,788. She left most of her personal possessions to her sister Nelly in Canada. She bequeathed to her bank all documents, photographs, manuscripts, correspondence and the copyright relating to works by John Stuart Mill, Harriet Taylor and Helen. The bank had permission to grant access, at their discretion, to any writers who wished to consult them. No mention of Mary Ann Trimble is made in the will. Mary left Emmeline Pankhurst £100 'to be applied at her discretion for the cause of women's suffrage and its extension.' To 'my friend' Elsie Howey of Malvern, near Birmingham, 'in respect of all she has endured and accomplished in the fight for women's suffrage,' she left £50. Elsie was a militant suffragette who was arrested many times for acts of violence and who endured hunger strike for the cause during imprisonment. Mary's estate came mainly from that of John Stuart Mill through her Aunt Helen. Fifty years after Mill's death he was still financially supporting women's rights although he would not have supported the violence of the suffragettes and neither would have Helen. A further legacy of £100 'for the cause of antivivisection' is a reminder of her father's support for this cause. A long list of cousins also benefited from small legacies in the will and she left an annuity of £50 to her brother, Cyprian and £200 to Nelly. The residue of the estate was in trust for the needs of her brother. Mary Ann Trimble for some reason, emigration, death or estrangement was no longer in Mary's life. The last record of her is on a passenger list of those leaving the United Kingdom in 1908, the year following Helen's death. An M. Trimble, spinster, travelled out on the 21 October from Liverpool on the Suevic. The ship was bound for Sydney, Australia. Also, on the passenger list was a Miss M. Taylor and a Mr W.H. Trimble. Most likely Mary Ann was en route to her relatives in New Zealand. A letter that she wrote to the *Labour Leader* in September mentions this forthcoming trip. The editor referred to her letter as 'from one of our shareholders' and it is almost certainly from Helen's niece. An impoverished old man had been imprisoned for stealing fruit and she wrote of her intention to set up a bank order to pay him five shillings a week on his release from prison.[134] In 1906, Helen and Mary had contributed ten shillings each to the Independent Labour Party's Huddersfield Election Fund which the paper had acknowledged.[135] Mary returned to the United Kingdom but there is no record of Mary Ann after this. Elizabeth Mary (Nelly) Taylor died, aged 62, in Victoria, British Columbia on 26 April, 1924. Cyprian, however, lived until early 1939. He died, aged 76, in Bridport, Dorset.

With Helen's death the last link with the world of non-conformist, mid nineteenth century reformers were broken. The Secretary of the Land Nationalisation Society, her old friend Joseph Hyder, acknowledged this in a condolence letter to Mary: 'Her death snaps another link with the past.'[136] The *Labour Leader*, the newspaper of the Independent Labour Party, which had affiliated to the newly formed Labour party in 1906, reported her death. It mourned the passing of 'one of the pioneer spirits of the present-day Socialist movement. She was one of the original members of the Democratic Federation.' The paper went on to remind readers of her work for the Land League and land nationalisation, her interest in the Independent Labour Party and her financial contribution to the Special Effort Fund. [137] Socialist campaigning for political and social reform was now led by the Labour party and its affiliates, replacing the generation of nineteenth century campaigners who had successfully improved opportunities in education and work for middle-class women. In the world of the New Woman, Mill's influence on feminism was being lost to memory and his political star had faded. Helen's mind-set was that of a bygone age. Helen never supported violence and would not have approved of the militant suffragettes nor the armed Easter Rising of 1916 in Ireland, though the two causes were close to her heart.

The decline in the importance of Mill's feminism from the 1880s onwards was lamented by the feminist writer Olive Schreiner. Olive, from South Africa, had the greatest respect for Mill and was shocked at the decline in his reputation among younger feminists during the 1880s. In 1892 she wrote:

> I am conscious of owing a profound and unending debt to John Stuart Mill; when I got home to Europe and found men and women whose views coincided with indifference to his works or ridiculing them as old fashioned, it was keenly painful to me.[138]

Helen's causes, such as land reform and moral reform, died with her, as did the political ideology of her generation.[139] The campaign for land nationalisation more or less disappeared after the First World War as a result of urbanisation. The industrial working-class began to vote Labour not Liberal, believing the former was looking after their class interests. The latter's political fortunes declined rapidly after 1918. The County Councils took over the remit of schooling and the school boards were dissolved. The London School Board disappeared in 1903 and the London County Council became responsible for state schooling in the capital. Helen's world had disappeared even before her death.

After her death, Helen, so famous during the 1880s, faded from public memory. She left little for prosperity, save the few pamphlets and writings discussed in this book. Neither was she in the tradition of a great Victorian letter writer. Her letters are functional, to the point, and she often apologised for the lack of them. She mixed with the movers and shakers of the day but left little on them that could appear in their biographies. Her strength was the power of her spoken word at public meetings and in the school board chamber but these too are now lost as they were before the advent of film and tape. Yet her campaigning was an important step in the road to sexual equality. On the London School Board, she had campaigned for equal pay and conditions for women teachers, for equal access to the curriculum for girls, free education, an end to corporal punishment and for school crèches to be set up as girls were missing school due to caring for their younger brothers and sisters at home. In her work in the Social Democratic Party she had worked for a fairer society by means of democratic socialism. She had opposed British imperialism and the belief in the racial superiority of the Anglo-Saxons by supporting the Irish Celts in their struggle for land reform and an Irish parliament in Dublin. She worked for a redistribution of land through land nationalisation which would have created a more equal society. Above all she worked for sexual equality and for women to be allowed to become full citizens by voting for Britain's legislators and being able to stand for office.

When she did appear in the histories of the time it was often as a dislikeable, pretentious, over privileged woman. This we have seen in the comments about her being 'priggish' by her step-father's biographer, M.S. Packe, who sneered at her 'causes.' These 'causes' were actually the radical causes of the time, not the individual peccadillos of a socially privileged lady. Yes, she did sometimes have the 'genius for turning friends into foes.'[140] Her early life, living mostly in seclusion with her mother in Walton, had made it difficult for her to open up to people. She told Emily Hill, as noted earlier, that it took a decade before you could count on someone as a friend.[141] She was ill at ease in society and knew it. She had opened up to Kate, Lady Amberley, and admitted that she was much more at ease with children than adults who she did not know well.[142]

She was stubborn. She refused to withdraw libellous comments against Scrutton and had paid an out-of-court settlement of £1,000 rather than retract her allegation of manslaughter. Her principled stance on the London School Board made her truly independent. F.W. Soutter, summed up her political and social involvement in that it '…was marked by earnest attention to the exacting duties of the office, an exceeding plainness of speech and a resolute obliteration of the ordinary party-politics.'[143] She had stubbornly presented her general election nomination papers herself, which the Law Society blamed as the cause of their refusal. Her intractability would try the patience of a saint. Her friend in the Moral Reform Union, Emily Hill, wrote her obituary in the *Englishwoman's Review*. It summed Helen up rather well:

> A rare and striking personality. Mentally and morally she was on grand lines…Her love of truth and justice and hatred of oppression amounted to a passion. Compromise she could neither tolerate nor understand. She used to say of herself that she had no tact. What she seemed to fail to recognise was that life could not be lived on principles of pure logic. Everything Miss Taylor, did, said or wrote had an air of distinction and individuality. She was a formidable antagonist.[144]

The Social Democratic Federation, mourning her passing in the party newspaper, *Justice*, remembered her as 'one of the most earnest devoted, disinterested and gifted champions of the working-class which the country has ever had.'[145] Her political advisor during the failed 1885 election campaign, Soutter, lamented, in 1923, that the contemporary women's rights campaigners made no mention of Helen. He believed that the success of the 'votes for women campaign' and the extension of the suffrage to women over 30 in 1918 owed much to the generation that had gone before and should have been acknowledged. Modern feminists, he wrote, 'often reap where others had sown.' Such was the importance he gave to Helen that he devoted a chapter of his memoirs to her 1885 campaign.[146] Helen, who had fought so hard for ordinary working people to access education and to live lives free from poverty, had been quickly forgotten. She had fulfilled her destiny as the daughter of Harriet Taylor and the step-daughter of John Stuart Mill and had used her birthright to work tirelessly for improved democracy and social and political rights for both the working man and the whole of her sex. The epitaph inscribed on her tomb in the cemetery, high above the town of Torquay, reads simply: 'She fought for the people.'

ENDNOTES

Introduction

1. This work is indebted to previous published and unpublished work by the author. The following sources are acknowledged as having been used throughout. Full details in bibliography:

   Smith, Janet, 2020, *Crossing the Border of Citizenship: Helen Taylor, the Independent Radical Democrat Candidate for Camberwell North, 1885.*

   Smith, Janet, (forthcoming) '§25: Feminism and the Rights of Women UK,' in Jensen, Kipton & Keefe, Jenny (eds.), *Grundriss der Geschichte der Philosophie: Nineteenth Century British and American Philosophy* (Schwabe Verlag)

   Smith, Janet, 2023, *Feminism and Women's Rights in Great Britain and Ireland: Tracking Developments and Debates through the Case of Helen Taylor*

   Smith, Janet, 2019, *First Woman Parliamentary Candidate, Helen Taylor 1885.*

   Smith, Janet, 2016, *Helen Taylor's Anti-Imperialist Feminism: Ireland and the Land League Question.*

   Smith, Janet, & Morris Stern, Claire, 2017, *Helen Taylor becomes Miss Trevor, actress.*

   Smith, Janet, 2017, *Helen Taylor's Work for Land Nationalisation in Great Britain and Ireland, 1879-1907.*

Smith, Janet, 2018, *'She fought for the people,' Helen Taylor's Work for the Advancement of Socialism and Feminism on the London School Board, 1876-8.*

Smith, Janet, unpublished PhD, 2014, *The Feminism and Political Radicalism of Helen Taylor in Victorian Britain and Ireland*, London Metropolitan University.

2. *Lloyds Weekly Newspaper*, 1 November 1885.
3. *The Hull Packet and East Riding Times*, 30 October 1885.
4. Letter dated 15 January 1877, Mill Taylor Collection (hereafter M.T.C.), L.S.E, file 15, no.100.
5. E. Belfort Bax, 1918, *Reminiscences and Reflections of a Mid and Late Victorian*: 110.
6. Henry George (jnr), 1904, *The Life of Henry George*: 361.
7. *The Lancashire Evening Post*, 19 October 1886.

Part 1: An Apprenticeship for a Campaigning Life.

1. For detailed studies on the development of Victorian British feminism see Barbara Caine, 1996, *Victorian Feminists*, Kathryn Gleadle, 1995, *The Early Feminists: Radical Unitarians and the Emergence of the Women's Rights Movement*.
2. Charles Booth, 1892, *Life and Labour of the People of London, Vol 1: Streets and Population Classified.*
3. Hansard, 27 July 1831.
4. F.A. Hayek, 1951, *John Stuart Mill and Harriet Taylor: their friendship and subsequent marriage*: 51.
5. For the evidence on the possibility of Harriet having syphilis and details on the marital separation see Jo Ellen Jacobs, 2002, *The Voice of Harriet Taylor Mill*: 11 & 143. See also Josephine Kamm, 1977, *John Stuart Mill in Love*, for the early relationship of Harriet and Mill.
6. Mary Taylor's introduction to Hugh Elliot, (ed.), 1910, The *Letters of John Stuart Mill, vol.1*: xi.
7. Ibid: xiii.
8. Helen Taylor to Lady Amberley, 11 September 1869, in Bertrand Russell & Patricia Russell, (eds), *The Amberley Papers,* vol. 2: 312.
9. Diary of Helen Taylor, 1842-46, M.T.C., file 24.

10. Jacobs: 2002: 86.
11. Josephine Kamm, 1977, *John Stuart Mill in Love*: 12.
12. Draft letter from Helen Taylor to Algernon Taylor, marked '1888 not sent,' M.T.C, file 24, no. 756. She is probably alluding here to his opposition to his mother removing her brother-in-law from the trusteeship of her own will which will be mentioned later after the death of his father.
13. Carol Dyhouse, 1981, *Girls growing up in late Victorian and Edwardian England*: 3.
14. Mary Taylor's introduction in Hugh Eliot, *The Letters of John Stuart* Mill: xiii.
15. Jacobs, 2002, refutes the charge that Harriet was 'a bad mother' made by Mazlich (1975), Kamm (1977) and Packe (1954).
16. Letter Helen Taylor to Kate Amberley, 24 October 1864, Bertrand Russell Archive, Ontario, Canada.
17. J.S. Mill, 1859, *On Liberty*.
18. J.S. Mill, 1873, *Autobiography*: 129.
19. Identified in F.A. Hayek, 1951, *John Stuart Mill and Harriet Taylor: their friendship and subsequent marriage*.
20. Helen Taylor to Algernon Taylor, 25 July 1844, M.T.C. file 24, no. 696.
21. Louis, Rey, 1937, *Le Souvenir de John Stuart Mill en Avignon*, conference paper given in 1921. Pasteur Rey was a personal friend of Mill and Helen in Avignon and pastor of the Protestant church in the town.
22. June Purvis, 1991, *A History of Women's Education in England*: 64.
23. Helen Taylor to Lady Amberley, 20 February 1865, in Bertrand Russell & Patricia Russell (eds), *The Amberley Papers,* vol. 1: 372.
24. See Helen McCabe, 2023, *Harriet Taylor Mill*.
25. John Stuart Mill, 1873, *Autobiography*: 223.
26. Helen Taylor Diary, M.T.C., file 24, 22 January 1845.
27. The nature of nineteenth century feminism throughout this book is indebted to Janet Smith, 2023, 'Feminism and Women's Rights UK' in Moland, Lydia & Stone, Alison Laura (eds), *The Oxford Handbook of American and British Women Philosophers in the Nineteenth Century,* and Smith, Janet, (forthcoming) '§25: Feminism and the Rights of Women UK,' in Jensen, Kipton & Keefe, Jenny (eds.), *Grundriss der Geschichte der Philosophie: Nineteenth Century British and American Philosophy* (Schwabe Verlag)
28. William George Ward | Victorian Era, Anglican Church, Theology | Britannica

29. Helen Taylor to Lady Amberley, 11 September 1869, in Russell & Russell (eds.), *The Amberley Papers,* vol. 2: 312.
30. See Florence Fenwick Miller, *An Uncommon Girlhood,* unpublished memoir, and Bax, 1918.
31. Diary of Mary Taylor, M.T.C., file 58.
32. Algernon Taylor, 1895, *Memories of a Student*: 23.
33. Information on Helen's actress aspirations and her time as an apprentice actress, later in this chapter, is indebted to Janet Smith & Claire Morris Stern, 2017, *Helen Taylor becomes Miss Trevor, actress.*
34. See Tracy C, Davis, 1991, *Actresses as Working Women: Their social identity in Victorian culture* and Christopher Kent, 1977, 'Image and Reality: The Actress in Society,' in Vicinus, Martha (ed.), *A Widening Sphere*: Chapter 5.
35. Kathy Chamberlain, 2017, *Jane Welsh Carlyle and Her Victorian World*: 288.
36. Jacobs, 2002: 117.
37. Algernon Taylor, 1895.
38. The information on middle class attitudes to reading is from Kate Flint, 'The Victorian Novel and its Readers' in David, Deidre, (ed.), 2001, *The Cambridge Companion to the Victorian Novel*: Chapter 1: 18.
39. Purvis, 1991: 66.
40. Kate Flint, 1993, *The Woman Reader 1837-1914*: 57.
41. Helen Taylor diary, May 26,1846.
42. Harriet appears on the London Library Subscriber list of 1846 in *Laws and Regulations of the London Library ... with list of subscribers*, 1846.
43. Jennifer Simpson's introduction to M. Wilson, 1987, *A European Journal*: 8.
44. Ibid.
45. Pasteur Louis Rey, 1913, *Le Roman de John Stuart Mill.*
46. Mill Taylor Collection, London School of Economics.
47. Helen Taylor to Lady Amberley, 13 June 1871, Amberley Letters, Bertrand Russell Archive.
48. Jacobs, 2002: 165.
49. Jacobs 2002: 148.
50. Jacobs, 2002: 117.
51. Blackheath Village | Case Studies | Ideal Homes (ideal-homes.org.uk).
52. Greenwich Industrial History: Blackheath Station 150 years.
53. Taylor, 1895: 144.

54. M.S. Packe, 1954, The *Life of John Stuart Mill:* 360.
55. J. S. Mill, *Collected Works, vol XIV*: 114, fn. 1, The Collected Works of John Stuart Mill, Volume XIV - The Later Letters 1849-1873 Part I | Online Library of Liberty (libertyfund.org).
56. These articles are reprinted in A.P. Robson & J.P. Robson (eds), 1994, *Sexual Equality*: 53-100.
57. Robson & Robson, 1994: 178. The article is reprinted in full: 179-203.
58. For a detailed study of Helen's battle to become an actress and her experiences in the theatre see J. Smith & C. Morris Stern, 2017. 21-43. Quotes from correspondence of this time are taken from the article.
59. Algernon Taylor, 1895: 5.
60. Helen Taylor to Algernon Taylor, M.T.C., file 18, no. 24.
61. Letter quoted in Smith & Stern: 29.
62. For attitudes to Harriet Taylor Mill in academic publications see Jo Ellen Jacobs, 1994, '"The Lot of Gifted Ladies is Hard:" A Study of Harriet Taylor Mill Criticism' in *Hypatia*, Summer 1994, Vol 9, No 3: 132-162.
63. J.S. Mill to Dr Cecil Gurney, *John Stuart Mill, Volume XV - The Later Letters of John Stuart Mill 1849-1873 Part II,* 28/02/2020. http J.S. Mill to Helen Taylor, 21 October, *John Stuart Mill, Volume XV - The Later Letters of John Stuart Mill* ps://oll.libertyfund.org/titles/252#Mill.
64. Helen Taylor to Algernon Taylor, undated, M.T.C., file 24, 702.
65. Ibid.
66. N. Capaldi, 2004, *John Stuart Mill, A Biography*.
67. Pasteur Louis Rey 'Le Roman de John Stuart Mill : 522.
68. Ibid.
69. Ibid: 525.
70. See the entry in the *Stanford Encyclopaedia of Philosophy* on Harriet Taylor for a summary of attitudes to Harriet Taylor. https://plato.stanford.edu/entries/harriet-mill/, as well as Jacobs cited earlier.
71. Quoted in Emily Hill to Helen Taylor, 5 November 1895, M.T.C, file 10, no. 43.
72. Florence Fenwick Miller, *An Uncommon Girlhood*: 453.
73. Press cutting, MTC, Box 7. The poem is by the American poet, William Maxwell, (1784-1857). Helen kept two copies of these lines only, not the complete poem. The poem, however, entitled *To a Fair Lady* starts: 'Fairest mourn not for thy charms, circled by no lover's arms, while inferior belles you see, pick up husbands merrily.'

74. J.S. Mill, Additional Letters, Collected Work, vol xxxii. https://oll.libertyfund.org/title/mill-the-collected-works-of-john-stuart-mill-volume-xxxii-additional-letters?ht.
75. For an account of this episode see Kamm: 134.
76. J.S. Mill to Helen Taylor, 14 February 1860, *Complete Works of J.S.M.,* vol XV The Collected Works of John Stuart Mill, Volume XV - The Later Letters 1849-1873 Part II | Online Library of Liberty (libertyfund.org).
77. H. Eliot (ed), 1910, *Letters of J.S. Mill, vol 1*: 262.
78. Ibid.
79. Helen Taylor to Lady Amberley, 11 September 1869, *Amberley Papers vol* 2: 111.
80. John Stuart Mill to Duncan McLaren MP, 3 January1869, Eliot, *vol 1*: 173.
81. John Stuart Mill to W. R. Thornton (though the letter has been identified as having been written by Helen), 16 January 1869; Eliot, *vol 1*: 54.
82. Ann Robson, 1994, 'Helen Taylor and John Stuart Mill: Travels with a Donkey,': 336.
83. J.S. Mill to G. Grote, 11 June, 1862, Collected Works of John Stuart Mill, vol 15, https://oll.libertyfund.org/titles/252#Mill_0223-15_845.
84. Robson, 1994: 341.
85. J.S. Mill to Edwin Chadwick, 24 April 1863, *Collected Works of John Stuart Mill, vol 15*, https://oll.libertyfund.org/titles/252#Mill.
86. The census gives her place of birth as Canada. Although transcribed on the census as Clemence, Annie's baptism certificate records her mother's Christian names as being Clementine Elizabeth. The 1851 census transcribes this as Clemena and that she was living as a housekeeper at the College of Surgeons in Finsbury, London with her daughter. It states her birthplace as the Gulf of St Lawrence, Canada in 1795.
87. Mill wrote four letters to Helen during his absence in 1860. *Collected Works of J. S. Mill, vol XV*: 659- 660.
88. *Norfolk News*, 13 October 1860.
89. *Press (London)*, 21 June 1862.
90. *Morning Herald,* 15 August 1862.
91. Helen Taylor to Eliza Taylor, undated, written from Avignon, M.T.C., file 24 no. 719.
92. Helen Taylor to Algernon Taylor, 18 November, 1868, M.T.C., file 24, no. 723.

93. Algernon Taylor to Helen Taylor, 9 September, 1864, M.T.C., file 24, no.720.
94. Algernon Taylor to Helen Taylor, 16 September 1864, M.T.C., file 24, no. 721
95. Helen Taylor to Algernon Taylor, 25 September, 1864, M.T.C., file 24, no. 722.
96. Eliza Taylor to Helen Taylor, 22 January 1864 and Helen's draft of a reply, M.T.C., file 24, no. 240.
97. Helen Taylor to Kate Amberley, 22 April, 1865, Amberley Papers. In the same letter Helen comments that Mill had refused to canvas in Kensington.
98. Helen Taylor to Kate Amberley, 25 July 1865, Amberley Papers. The letter is written from Blackheath.
99. *Bookseller*, 31 October 1866.
100. *Lincolnshire Chronicle*, 15 December 1866.
101. Diane Worzala, 1974, *The Langham Place Circle*: 283-4.
102. Frances Power Cobbe, 1904, *Frances Power Cobbe: As told by herself*: 411.
103. Millicent Fawcett, *What I Remember*: 60.
104. Helen Taylor to Elizabeth Garrett, 9 June 1866, Autograph Letters, Women's Library, L.S.E.
105. Helen Taylor to Lady Amberley, 1 July 1872, in Russell & Russell, (eds.) *The Amberley Papers* vol. 2: 495.
106. Helen Taylor to Lady Amberley, 13 February 1868, in Russell & Russell, (eds.) *The Amberley Papers* vol. 2: 102.
107. Helen Taylor to Lady Amberley, 24 October 1869, *Amberley Papers*, Bertrand Russell Archive.
108. Helen Taylor to Lady Amberley, 24 July 1871 and 25 July 1873, *Amberley Papers*, Bertrand Russell Archive.
109. Reprinted in Robson and Robson, 1994: 112-16. Helen's published work on feminism is discussed in more depth in Janet Smith, 2023, *Feminism and Women's Rights (UK*).
110. Robson and Robson, 1994: 115.
111. Ibid: 116.
112. Ibid. *The Ladies' Petition:* 216-33 and *Women and* Criticism: 103-111.
113. Helen Taylor, 1866, The Claim of Englishwomen to the Suffrage Constitutionally Considered. (indiana.edu).

114. See discussion on Helen's literary output in Andrea L. Bloomfield, 1997, 'Walking a Narrow Line. Helen Taylor's Literary Contribution to the British Women's Rights Movement.'
115. Helen Taylor to Barbara Bodichon, 9 May 1866, *Autograph letters,* 7.bmc/3/8fl646, Women's Library L.S.E.
116. Helen Taylor to Barbara Bodichon, 6 June 1866, *Autograph letters,* 7.bmc/b2, Women's Library.
117. 'The Admission of Women to the Electoral Suffrage' reprinted in Robson and Robson (eds.): 234-246.
118. Martin Pugh, 2009, 'The Liberal Party and Women's Suffrage 1866-1918.'
119. J.S, Mill, 1873, *Autobiography*: 170.
120. D. Worzala, 1974: 293.
121. Sandra Stanley Holton, 'Women and the Vote' in June Purvis (ed.), 1995, *Women's History: Britain 1850-1944*, chapter 11: 281.
122. Alison Stone, 2022, *Frances Power Cobbe.*
123. Helen Taylor to Barbara Bodichon, 10 June 1866, *Autograph Letters,* 7/bmc/bc, Women's Library.
124. Undated letter, Barbara Bodichon to Helen Taylor, M.T.C., file 12, no. 54.
125. Sandra Stanley Holton, 1995, *Women and the Vote.*
126. Catherine Hall, 1992, *White, Male and Middle Class*: 265.
127. Helen Taylor to Mrs Grote, 20 December 1865, in Russell & Russell (eds.), *The Amberley Papers vol. 1.*
128. As late as 5 May 1905 *The Western Daily Press*, reporting that Mill's house in Avignon was to be sold by auction, blamed his 1868 defeat on his stance on Governor Eyre.
129. Helen Taylor to Kate Amberley, 29 May 1870, *Amberley Papers vol* 2: 345.
130. J.S. Mill, 1873, *Autobiography*: 166.
131. Helen Taylor to George Grote, 25 September 1868, in Eliot, *The Letters of John Stuart Mill*: 254.
132. Helen Taylor to Lady Amberley, 21 March 1872, M.T.C., file 19, no. 54.
133. For the campaign against the Contagious Diseases Acts see Lisa Sapiro Sanders, 2015, 'Equal Laws based upon an Equal Standard: The Garrett Sisters, the Contagious Diseases Acts, and the Sexual Politics of Victorian and Edwardian Feminism Revisited.'
134. Reprinted in Robson and Robson: 127-129.

135. Ibid: 129.
136. Helen Taylor to Lady Amberley, 12 April 1870, Amberley Letters, Bertrand Russell Archives, Canada.
137. J.S. Mill, 'The Contagious Diseases Act 1871,' in *The Collected Works of John Stuart Mill*, vol. xxi, online at oll/libertyfund.org/ :4.
138. J.S. Mill to W. Malleson, 18 January 1870, cited in H.S.R. Elliot (ed.), *Letters of John Stuart Mill*: 238. William Malleson was the Hon. Sec. of the Social Purity Alliance during Helen's time in the M.R.U. (see *The Pioneer*, the newspaper of the S.P.U.).
139. Helen Taylor to Lady Amberley, June 1869, Amberley Letters, Bertrand Russell Archive.
140. Helen Taylor to Lady Amberley, 17 August 1870, Amberley Letters, Bertrand Russell Archive.
141. John Stuart Mill to Henry Fawcett in Eliot, vol 2: 166–67. It was written from the safety of Blackheath. Helen wrote this letter which Mill copied out before sending.
142. Helen Taylor to Lady Amberley, 5 March 1870 and 21 March 1870, Amberley Letters, Bertrand Russell Archive.
143. Catherine Winkworth to Emily Winkworth, 31 March 1870, in Margaret J. Shaen (ed.), Susanna and Catherine Winkworth, 1908, *Memorials of Two Sisters*: 275.
144. Helen Taylor to Lady Amberley, 28 March 1871, Amberley Letters, Bertrand Russell Archive.
145. Helen Taylor to Lady Amberley, 21 June 1871, Amberley Letters, Bertrand Russell Archive.
146. Helen Taylor to Lady Amberley, 13 June 1871, Amberley Letters, Bertrand Russell Archive.
147. UK Census 1871.
148. Helen Taylor to Kate Amberley, 13 June 1871, Amberley Letters, Bertrand Russell Archive.
149. John Stuart Mill, 1873, *Autobiography*: 171-2.
150. Helen Taylor to Lady Amberley, 21 June 1871, Amberley Letters, Bertrand Russell Archive.
151. Helen Taylor to Lady Amberley, 13 June 1871, Amberley Letters, Bertrand Russell Archive.
152. Pasteur Louis Rey, 1913, *le Roman de John Stuart Mill* : 26 & 27.
153. Pasteur Louis Rey, 1937, *le Souvenir de John Stuart Mill en Avignon* : 13. In English, 'desolate, but calm and steadfast.'

154. Algernon Taylor to Helen Taylor, 11 May 1873, M.T.C., file 24, no. 730.
155. Helen Taylor to Lady Amberley, Amberley Letters, Bertrand Russell Archive.
156. Pasteur Louis Rey, 1921, *John Stuart Mill en Avignon :* 13.
157. Ibid: 15
158. Helen Taylor to Kate Amberley, 11 May 1873, Bertrand Russell Archive.
159. Helen Taylor to Kate Amberley, May 1873, Russell & Russell (eds), Amberley Papers vol 2: 549.
160. Algernon Taylor to Helen Taylor, 20 May 1873, M.T.C., vol. 24 no. 35.
161. Algernon Taylor to Helen Taylor, 18 June 1874, M.T.C., file 24, no. 734.
162. Helen Taylor to Kate Amberley, 25 July 1873, Amberley Letters, Bertrand Russell Archive.
163. Algernon Taylor to Helen Taylor, 29 June 1872, M.T.C, file 24, no 758.
164. Algernon Taylor to Helen Taylor, 4 December 1873, M.T.C., file 24, no. 758.
165. Mary Taylor to Helen Taylor, 2 October, 1877, M.T.C., file 25, no. 725.
166. Henry Thomas Buckle | Encyclopedia.com.
167. Anna Parnell, 1986, *The Tale of a Great Sham*: 17.
168. Jane McL Coté, 1991, *Fanny and Anna Parnell: Ireland's Patriot Sisters*: 186
169. J.S. Mill, *Autobiography*: 148.
170. Kate Amberley to Helen Taylor, 20 October 1873, M.T.C., file 19, no. 162.
171. Eliza Cairnes to Helen Taylor, 7 July 1874, M.T.C., vol 19, no. 331.
172. For an excellent summary of historical attitudes to Harriet Taylor see Jo Ellen Jacobs, 1994, '"The Lot of Gifted Ladies is Hard,": A Study of Harriet Taylor Mill Criticism,' in *Hypatia, Summer 1994, Vol 9, no.3*: 132-162.
173. Helen McCabe, 2020, 'John Stuart Mill: market socialist,' in *Review of Social Economy,* published online 25 June 2020, doi.org/10.1080/00346764.2020.1781923.
174. J.S. Mill, *Autobiography*: 148.
175. Jacobs, 2002: 100-1.
176. M.S. Packe, 1954, *The Life of John Stuart* Mill: 413.
177. Helen Taylor to Lady Amberley, 1 August 1873, Amberley Letters, Bertrand Russell Collection.
178. Jane Martin used Stacey and Price's sociological model to assess the women members of the London School Board's successful involvement

in politics. This revealed that they mostly shared similar privileged backgrounds, i.e. they were from politically active middle- or upper-class families, were financially independent, or were supported by their families, and had few family commitments. See Jane Martin, 1999, *Women and the Politics of Schooling in Victorian and Edwardian England*: 53.

179. *Le Mistral,* 6 February 1907, M.T.C., box 7. *Le Mistral* was the local paper for Avignon and the Provence region.
180. Quoted in Ann Robson, 'Bertrand Russell and his godless Parents,' *Russell: The Journal of Bertrand Russell Studies, vol. 7, 1972: 3-9*: 5. Project MUSE, https://doi.org/10.1353/rss.1972.0012.
181. Eliza Cairnes to Helen Taylor, 7 July 1874, M.T.C., file 19, no. 298.
182. Eliza Cairnes to Helen Taylor, October 1876, M.T.C., file 19, no. 301.
183. Information on Helen's School Board years is taken throughout from Janet Smith, 2018, "She fought for the people:' Helen Taylor's work for the advancement of socialism and feminism on the London School Board, 1876-1885.' For detailed discussion on the women members of the London School Board to which I am indebted see Patricia Hollis, 1989, *Ladies Elect: Women in English Local Government*; Jane Martin, 2005, To Blaise a Trail for Women to Follow Along, Sex, gender and politics of education on the London School Board (1870-1904). For an overarching view of the gendering of the school board system and education in Victorian Britain see Felicity Hunt, (ed.), 1987, *Lessons for Life, The Schooling of Girls and Women 1850- 1950*; Jane Martin, 1995, 'Fighting down the idea that the only place for women was home,' Jane Martin, 1999, *Women and the Politics of Schooling in Victorian and Edwardian England;* A. M. Turnbull, 1987, 'Learning her womanly work. The Elementary School Curriculum 1870 –1914.'
184. Elizabeth Garrett Anderson to Helen Taylor, 9 December 1870, M.T.C., file 15, no. 54.
185. A. Ryan, 2011, 'J.S. Mill on Education': 654.
186. Ibid: 654-663.
187. Bruce L. Kinzer, 1997, 'The 1870 Education Bill and the Method of J. S. Mill's Later Politics:' 232 & 244.
188. *The Times*, 9 November 1870.
189. Helen Taylor to Lady Amberley, 13 February 1868, in B. Russell & P. Russell, (eds.) *The Amberley Papers vol. 2*: 102.

Part 2: 'The Foremost Woman of her Time:' A Very Public Life.

1. Moncure D. Conway, 1882, *Travels in South Kensington*: 15.
2. Risborough~Oxford Railway – Aston Rowant & Chilterns Spring Line Villages (wordpress.com).
3. Algernon Taylor to Helen Taylor, 20 September 1878, M.T.C., file 24, no. 796 and Helen Taylor (draft) 22 September 1878, M.T.C., file 24, no. 797.
4. *England and Wales Merchant Navy Crew Lists 1861-1913*, The National Archives.
5. Algernon Taylor to Helen Taylor, March 1884, M.T.C., file 24, no. 4.
6. *The Scotsman*, 9 October 1879.
7. *Pall Mall Gazette,* 16 October 1879.
8. Algernon Taylor to Helen Taylor, 26 August 1888, file 24, no. 118.
9. U.K. Census 1881.
10. *Huddersfield Chronicle,* 4 December, 1876.
11. Draft letter, Helen Taylor to Alice Westlake, 26 September 1876, M.T.C., file 16, no. 181.
12. John Sinclair to Helen Taylor 17 October 1876, M.T.C., file 16, no. 147.
13. Charles Booth's 1886 survey of London identified poverty in Southwark as at 67 per cent of the population. Charles Booth, 1892, *Life and Labour of the People of London, vol. II, Streets and Population Classified.*
14. Martin, 2000, To 'Blaise Trail for Women to Follow Along:' 169.
15. See Florence Fenwick Miller, *An Uncommon Girlhood*, unpublished memoir, Welcome Institute.
16. Florence Fenwick Miller: 453.
17. Rosemary T. Van Arsdel, 2004, 'Miller, Florence Fenwick,' in *Oxford Dictionary of National Biography*, https://doi.org/10.1093/ref:odnb/37764.
18. *School Board Chronicle*, 21 July 1883.
19. Ibid.
20. J. Martin, 2004, 'Surr (nee Grabham) Elizabeth' in *Oxford Dictionary of National Biography*, https://doi.org/10.1093/ref:odnb/48591.
21. Mitchell, Rosemary, 'Alice Westlake' in 'Andrews, Marian (nee Hare; pseud. Christopher Hare, 1839-1929,' *Oxford Dictionary of National Biography*, doi-https://doi.org/10.1093/odnb/9780198614128.013.59077.

22. Helen, as we will see, had a fraught relationship with this organisation due to her support for the Irish Land League, her socialist politics, campaigning for better tenant rights for farmers and opposing the Liberal government's Irish policies, in particular, the Coercion Acts.
23. Martin, 2000: 175.
24. *Bermondsey and Rotherhithe Advertiser,* 30 December 1876.
25. Ibid, 23 December 1876.
26. A. Moss to Helen Taylor, undated 1876, M.T.C., file 16, no. 113.
27. Helen Taylor's speech at her post-election banquet, as reported in the *Bermondsey and Rotherhithe Advertiser*, 27 January 1877.
28. Mill's speech to ratepayers in Greenwich and Deptford before the first London School Board Elections, *The Times,* 9 November 1870.
29. J.S. Mill to Henry Fawcett, 24 October 1869, M.T.C., file 1, no. 159.
30. Although the term 'feminist' did not come into use until the 1890s and Helen would have talked of 'women's rights' not feminism, it has become an acceptable term to use in the historical study of the earlier nineteenth century.
31. Fenwick Miller, *An Uncommon Girlhood*: 950.
32. Martin, 2000: 172.
33. This phase for strident women's rights campaigners was coined by the anti-feminist author and journalist Eliza Lynn Linton in her article 'The Shrieking Sisterhood,' *The Saturday Review*, 12 March 1870.
34. Fenwick Miller: 949.
35. Ibid: 632.
36. John Lobb, 1889, *Extravagance and Mismanagement of the London School Board*: 4 & 9.
37. J.J. Fishman, 2005, *Charitable Accountability and Reform in Nineteenth Century England. The Case of the Charity Commission.*
38. Written in 1866. J. S. Mill, 'Report of Commissioners on Education in Schools in England 1867-8,' in Robson (ed.), *The Collected Works of John Stuart Mill, vol. xxi.*
39. *Englishwoman's Review,* August 1878.
40. See correspondence between Helen and Agnes, M.T.C., file 14, nos. 17-42.
41. Draft letter, Helen Taylor to Miss Hart, 1876, M.T.C., file 15, no. 82.
42. Thomas Gautrey, 1936, *Lux Mihi Laus. School Board Memories*: 59. As well as supporting campaigns for secular education, Lucraft supported the women's campaign against corporal punishment and organised a deputation of working-men to the LSB to protest against the proposed

legislation which would allow assistant teachers to inflict corporal punishment

43. *School Board Chronicle*, 8 June 1878.
44. Ibid, 8 June 1878.
45. Ibid, 28 March 1877.
46. *School Board Chronicle*, 1 June 1878.
47. *Pall Mall Gazette*, 21 November, 1885.
48. *School Board Chronicle*, 3 May 1879.
49. *The Bury and Norwich Post,* 27 June 1871.
50. Information on the growing scandal in 1878 is taken from Florence Fenwick Miller, *An Uncommon Girlhood*: 929-30.
51. *School Board Chronicle*, 1 February 1879.
52. Ibid, 29 March 1879 and 5 April 1879.
53. Ibid, 5 July 1879.
54. Ibid, 14 May 1881. She lost by 20 votes to 8.
55. *South London Chronicle and Southwark and Lambeth Ensign*, 8 November 1879.
56. F. W. Soutter, 1923, *Recollections of a Labour Pioneer:* 84.
57. F.W. Soutter, 1925, *Fights For Freedom*: 147.
58. F. W. Soutter, 1923: 84.
59. *Bermondsey and Rotherhithe Advertiser*, 11 March 1882.
60. Martin, 2000: 170.
61. *School Board Chronicle*, 17 July 1880.
62. *Sheffield Daily Telegraph,* 2 December 1880.
63. *Northern Whig*, 20 September 1880.
64. Diary of Mary Taylor, M.T.C., file 58, no. 4.
65. *School Board Chronicle,* 26 February 1881.
66. *The School Master*, 1 July 1882.
67. *School Board Chronicle*, 5 November 1881.
68. Helen Taylor to Elizabeth Surr, 24 October 1881, M.T.C., file 23, no. 681.
69. *School Board Chronicle*, 6 May 1882.
70. Ibid, 6 May 1882.
71. Ibid, 13 May 1882.
72. Ibid, 6 May 1882.
73. For a discussion on this and all aspects of Helen's feminism see Janet Smith, 2023, Feminism and Women's Rights. This section is also indebted to Janet Smith, 2025, 'Feminism and the Rights of Women (UK).

74. Information on Helen's involvement in the Land War and background to the personalities involved is taken from J. Smith, 2016, *Helen Taylor's Anti-Imperialist Feminism: Ireland and the Land League Question.*
75. Known in Irish as An Gorta Mor (the Great Hunger), many argued, then and since, that there was no famine in Ireland. The potato crop, the staple diet of the Irish peasant failed, whilst corn and cattle continued to be exported to England. Aid was diverted by Charles Trevelyan, Assistant Secretary to the British Treasury, to Scotland. See John Mitchel, 1882, *The Last Conquest of Ireland (perhaps).* Mitchel, declared, 'The Almighty, indeed, sent the potato blight, but the English created the famine:' 219.
76. See Philip Bull, 1996, *Land, Politics and Nationalism: A Study of the Irish Land Question,* Michael Davitt, 1904, *The Fall of Feudalism in Ireland,* Roy Douglas, 1976, *Land, People and Politics: A History of the Land Question in the United Kingdom 1875 – 1952* and Barbara Solow, 1971, *The Land Question and the Irish Economy 1870-1903.*
77. Michael Davitt, 1904: 299.
78. *Freeman's Journal*, 5 February 1881.
79. *The Nation,* 26 February 1881.
80. *The Times*, 2 February 1881 & 5 February 1881.
81. *The Nation,* 19 March 1881.
82. Jane Coté, 1991: 169.
83. *The Nation*, 18 June 1881.
84. F.M. Holmes, 1881, *History of the Irish Land League, Impartially Reviewed*: 122.
85. Priscilla McLaren to Helen Taylor, 15 March 1881, M.T.C., file 13, no. 234.
86. Antoinette Burton, 1994, *Burdens of History.*
87. See Liz Curtis, 1996, *Nothing But the Same Old Story: Roots of Anti-Irish Racism.*
88. Margaret Ward, 2001, 'Gendering the Union: Imperial Feminism and the Ladies' Land League,' *Women's History Review*, 10:1.
89. Dana Hearne, 1986, editor's notes in Anna Parnell *The Tale of a Great Sham*: 28.
90. Ibid: 29.
91. Katherine Tynan, 1913, *Twenty-Five Year Reminiscences*: 72.
92. Beverly Schneller, (ed.), 2005, *Anna Parnell's Political Journalism: Contents and Texts*: 244. Schneller writes that Anna wrote objecting

to the visit of Queen Victoria to Ireland, in 1900, using the term and that Irish nationalist Maud Gonne copied Anna's phrase 'the Famine Queen' to headline her editorial on the visit in the *United Irishman* on 7 April 1900.

93. Coté: 230.
94. *Freeman's Journal,* 3 November 1881.
95. The nature of anti-imperialism in the C19 is discussed in J. Smith, 2020.
96. Henry George to Patrick Ford, 23 September, 1882. Henry George General Correspondence 1852–1897, *(*HGGC). Helen sent her regards to the Fords who had received letters from her.
97. *Globe*, 18 February, 1882.
98. *York Herald*, 14 March 1882; *Waterford Standard*, 20 December 1882.
99. *Cork Examiner*, 28 March 1880.
100. *Irish Times,* 7 December 1907.
101. Coté: 240.
102. Anna Parnell: 86.
103. Katherine O'Shea, 1914, *Charles Stewart Parnell: His Love Story and Political Life:* 56.
104. Herbert Gladstone, 1970/71 'Diary,' in *Irish Historical Studies,* vol 17: 521 – 548: 533
105. S. Webb, 'Socialism in England,*'* in *American Economic Association, vol. 4, no. 2, April 1889*: 7-73: 10.
106. For the history of Radical Clubs see J. Davis, 1989, 'Radical Clubs and London Politics 1870–1900,' Feldman, D. and Stedman Jones, G. (eds.), *Metropolis: Histories and Representations of London Since 1800*: chapter 5.
107. H. Lee's introduction to the 1912 edition to Henry Hyndman and William Morris, 1884, *A Summary of the Principles of Socialism.*
108. John Edwards (ed.), 1909, *The Land Reformer's Handbook*: 86.
109. *Western Morning News,* 21 March 1881 for example.
110. Alan Howkins, 'From Diggers to Dongas, the Land in English Radicalism,' *History Workshop Journal, vol 54, 2002:* 1-23.
111. See Roy Douglas, 1976, *Land, People and Politics: A History of the Land Question in the United Kingdom 1875 – 1952.*
112. Philip Bull, 1996, *Land, Politics and Nationalism: A Study of the Irish Land Question*: 30.
113. Ibid.
114. Ibid: 32.

115. Ibid: 46.
116. Henry M. Hyndman, 1911, *Record of An Adventurous Life*: 225.
117. *Huddersfield Daily Chronicle*, 21 March 1881.
118. M.S. Wilkins, 1959, 'The non-Socialist Origins of England's First Important Socialist Organisation,' *International Review of Social History*, vol. 4 (1959): 205.
119. Seamus Flaherty. 2019, 'H M Hyndman and the Intellectual Origins of the Remaking of Socialism in Britain, 1878-1881,' in *English Historical Review, vol 34 no 569*: 855-880: 860. Flaherty identifies Willard Wolfe, 1975, in his *From Radicalism to Socialism, men and ideas in the formation of Fabian Socialist doctrines, 1881 – 1889* as the only historian who has acknowledged the influence of Mill's book on Hyndman's later work.
120. *Freeman's Journal*, 9 June 1881 & *Pall Mall Gazette,* 9 June 1881.
121. *Manchester Times,* 11 June 1881.
122. *Freeman's Journal,* 2 June 1882.
123. *Ipswich Chronicle,* 29 November 1884.
124. Eleanor Marx to Karl Kautsky, 7 October 1881, *Eleanor Marx Papers*. Thanks to Eva Rosenhaft for the information that 40 marks was worth £2 in 1881.
125. Information on the O'Brienite influence within the Democratic Federation is taken from M. Bevir, 'The British Social Democratic Federation 1880–85; from O'Brienism to Marxism,' in *International Review of Social History, XXXV, 11, (92)*: 207- 229.
126. M.S. Wilkins, 1959: 205.
127. *The Nation*, 18 June 1881.
128. *Freeman's Journal,* 23 June 1881.
129. F.W. Soutter, 1924: 40.
130. *Irish Times*, 29 June 1881.
131. *Irish Times,* 24 June 1881.
132. *The Nation,* 7 July 1881.
133. *Freeman's Journal,* 24 July 1881.
134. *Daily News,* 5 August 1881.
135. Ibid.
136. *Pall Mall Gazette,* 19 September 1881.
137. *Birmingham Daily Post*, 17 October 1881.
138. Draft Letter, no date, M.T.C., file 18, no. 17.
139. *The Echo*, 17 October, 1881.

140. *Birmingham Daily Post*, 17 October 1881.
141. Ibid.
142. The *Morning Post*, 24 October 1881.
143. Nora Lynch to Helen Taylor, 15 October 1881, M.T.C., file 18, no. 72.
144. Jenny Wyse Power, 1909, 'My Recollections of Anna Parnell,' in *Sinn Fein Weekly*, 19 October, 1909.
145. See Anna Parnell: 89-90.
146. Anna Parnell to Helen Taylor, 26 October 1881, M.T.C., file 18, no. 75.
147. Henry George to John Stuart Mill, 22 August 1869, M.T.C., file 1, no. 138. See also Henry George jnr., 1904, *The Life of Henry George*: 196.
148. Draft reply from John Stuart Mill to Henry George, 23 October 1869, M.T.C., file 1, no. 333.
149. *National Standard*, 30 July 1870, and Alexander Saxton, 1971, *The Indispensable Enemy: Labour and the Anti-Chinese Movement in California*: 100-103.
150. George jnr: 361.
151. Jenny Wyse Power, 1909.
152. *Freeman's Journal*, 3 November 1881.
153. *Liverpool Mercury*, 14 November 1881.
154. Ibid.
155. Ibid.
156. Helen Taylor to Mrs Annie George, 20 December 1881, M.T.C., file 20, no. 265.
157. Helen Taylor to Mrs Annie George, 20 December, 1881, H.G.G.C.
158. Henry George to Mr Shaw, 11 February 1882, H.G.G.C. Malthus (1766-1834) in his *Essay on Population* argued that the world's population was inevitably growing faster than man's ability to provide food and resources for all. This overpopulation inevitably caused war, poverty and famine by which means the population was controlled. He advocated moral restraint to reduce the number of births. Malthusianism - Oxford Reference His ideas were taken up by those who advocated contraception. A materialist believes that only matter exists and denies spirituality. Helen, we have seen was greatly moved spiritually by nature, music and religious services.
159. Anna George to Helen Taylor, 17 December 1895, M.T.C., file 20, no. 265.
160. Anna George de Mille, 1944, 'Henry George: The Fight for Irish Freedom,' in *American Journal of Economics and Sociology, vol. 3 issue 2*: 260.

161. *The Nation*, 24 December 1881.
162. *United Ireland*, 31 December 1881.
163. *United Ireland*, 7 January 1882.
164. Letters between the Georges during early 1882 reveal Mrs George to have been at the South Kensington flat.
165. *Irish Times*, 18 January 1882.
166. Ibid.
167. Michael Davitt in his 'The Story of the Land War,' in *The Nation*, 9 September 1882.
168. *Eastern Morning News,* 10 November, 1886.
169. Anna Parnell: 123.
170. See reports of their meetings in *The Nation*.
171. *The Nation*, 14 January 1882.
172. *South London Press*, 11 March 1882.
173. *Irish Times*, 17 January 1882. See next section.
174. E. P. Lawrence, 1957, *Henry George in the British Isles*: 24.
175. Henry George to Annie George, 28 May 1882, H.G.G.C. Annie was looking forward to the trip.
176. Helen Taylor to Henry George, 7 January 1883, H.G.G.C. 'I am ashamed to have letters from you unanswered, and one from Mrs George,'
177. Helen Taylor to Henry George, 12 October 1886, H.G.G.C.
178. Henry George to Helen Taylor, October 1882, M.T.C., file 17, no. 81.
179. Helen Taylor to Mrs Annie George, 7 June, 1883, H.G.G.C.
180. Anna Angela George to Helen Taylor, 17 December 1895, M.T.C., file 20, no. 265.
181. B. O'Hara, 2009, *Davitt: Irish patriot and father of the land league.*
182. Henry George jnr., *The Life of Henry George*: 371.
183. *The Nation*, 12 August 1882.
184. Henry George to Mrs George, 3 May 1882, H.G.G.C.
185. Anna Parnell, 1986: 154-8.
186. Ibid: 164.
187. Henry George to Patrick Ford, 21 May 1882. Quoted in George, *The Life of Henry* George: 377.
188. Ibid: 349.
189. Letter from Henry George, published in *The Irish World* and reprinted in *The Nation*, 14 October 1882.
190. Ibid.
191. George jnr., *The Life of Henry George*: 371.

192. Henry George to Helen Taylor, 1 October 1882, M.T.C., file 17, no. 81. The letter is addressed to Helen in Avignon.
193. Smith, 2016.
194. Jessie Craigen to Helen Taylor, M.T.C., file 18, no. 71.
195. Priscilla McLaren to Helen Taylor, 21 September 1882, M.T.C., file 13, no. 237.
196. Sandra Stanley Holton, 1996, 'Silk dresses and lavender kid gloves: the wayward career of Jessie Craigen, working suffragist,' in *Women's History Review, vol. 5, no. 6*: 139. '*(Jessie)* was soon reporting to Helen Taylor her disillusion with Charles Parnell, and her conviction that he was about to sell out the Land League in return for a post in Gladstone's government. Helen Taylor chose to regard such independence of thought as a sign of personal disloyalty, and she deliberately distanced herself from Jessie Craigen's outraged, and no doubt outrageous, stand in Ireland. She refused any further contact with her ardent admirer, but mutual friends recorded how nonetheless Jessie Craigen continued to love Helen Taylor 'with all the fervour of her passionate nature' and how she 'was dazed with anguish' at the breach.'
197. Davitt, 1904: 362.
198. A.J. Kettle & L.J. Kettle, 1958, *The Material for Victory: being the memoirs of Andrew J Kettle*: 48.
199. Ethel Leach to Helen Taylor, 6 December 1890, M.T.C., file 18, no. 49.
200. Anna Priestman to Priscilla McLaren, 14 August, 1882, box 21, Millfield Papers.
201. Jessie Craigen, 1882, *Report on a Visit to Ireland in the Summer of 1881*: 6.
202. Ibid.
203. Adrian N Mulligan's assessment of the membership of the Ladies' Land League, in A. N. Mulligan 'By a Thousand Ingenious Feminine Devices. The Ladies' Land League and the Development of Irish Nationalism,' in *Historical Geography, vol 37, 2009:* 159.
204. Katherine Tynan, 1913: 83.
205. See Coté, 1991.
206. Sandra Stanley Holton, 1996. See Holton for an examination of Jessie's eccentricities.
207. *Englishwoman's Review*, January 1899.
208. *School Board Chronicle*, 25 February 1882.
209. *London School Board Minutes*, 4 May 1882.

210. Ibid, 20 April 1882.
211. *South London Press,* 11 March 1882.
212. Ibid.
213. *School Board Chronicle*, 1 July 1882.
214. *The Times*, 28 June 1882.
215. *School Board Chronicle*, 1 July 1882.
216. This would be worth approximately £121,000 today.
217. *Eastern Evening News*, 1 July 1882.
218. Ibid.
219. Henry George writing in *The Irish World*, 5 August 1882.
220. Priscilla McLaren to Helen Taylor, 1 July 1882, M.T.C., file 13, no. 231.
221. Helen Taylor to Henry George, 4 January 1883, H.G.G.C.
222. *Sevenoaks Chronicle and Kentish Advertiser*, 13 October 1882. This syndicated report appeared under the heading 'London Correspondence' in the regional papers throughout Great Britain and Ireland.
223. Editorial, *School Board Chronicle*, 21 October 1882.
224. *School Board Chronicle,* 4 November 1882.
225. *Southwark and Bermondsey Recorder*, 18 November 1882.
226. Ibid, 2 June 1883.
227. *School Board Minutes*, 28 June 1883.
228. *School Board Chronicle*, 10 October 1885.
229. *Report of the Endowment Committee to the London School Board,* 11 February 1884.
230. *School Board Chronicle*, 27 October 1884.
231. Ibid, 2 April 1883.
232. Ibid, 30 June 1883.
233. Charles Booth, 1892, *Life and Labour of the People in London, vol. 2*: 29.
234. A. Mearns, 1883, *The Bitter Cry of Outcast London*: 7.
235. *London School Board Minutes*, 20 April 1882.
236. See J. Lloyd, 1910, *London Municipal Government: History of a Great Reform 1880-1888*.
237. Ibid.
238. Ibid.
239. *School Board Chronicle*, 20 October 1883.
240. *School Board Minutes*, 16 July 1884.
241. *School Board Chronicle*, 21 June 1883.
242. Ibid, 16 June 1883.

243. Charles Booth, *Life and Labour of the People of London,* 1892, quoted Victorian London - Education - Education for the poor - School Board Visitors
244. *School Board Chronicle,* 2 June 1883.
245. Ibid, 24 February 1883.
246. Ibid, 17 October 1885.
247. Ibid, 28 March 1885.
248. *London School Board Minutes*, 5 March 1885.
249. Ibid, 9 July 1885.
250. Gautrey, 1936: 86.
251. *School Board Chronicle*, 2 July 1883.
252. *School Board Chronicle*, 13 December 1883.
253. Gautrey, 1936: 139–41.
254. *The Women's Time Line*, http://www.mmu.ac.uk/humanresources/equalities/doc/gender-equality-timeline.pdf
255. Information regarding land nationalisation taken from Janet Smith, 2017, 'Helen Taylor's work for land nationalisation in Great Britain and Ireland, 1879–1907.'
256. Henry George to T.E. Walker of the Land Nationalisation Society, 1 October 1882, H.G.G.C.
257. Henry George, 1881, *Progress and Poverty* (reprinted New York, 2006): 242.
258. This analysis of George's theory is indebted to Ursula Vogel, 'The Land Question: A Liberal Theory of Communal Property:' in *History Workshop Journal*, *vol 27,* 1989: 106-135: 122.
259. Davitt's speech in Liverpool, *The Nation,* 10 June 1882.
260. Henry George to Mr Shaw, 30 May 1882, H.G.G.C.
261. A.C. Swinton to Helen Taylor, 14 June 1882, M.T.C., file 17 no. 119.
262. *Bristol Mercury*, 15 May 1883.
263. *Huddersfield Chronicle*, 3 November 1883.
264. *The Irish Times*, 28 November 1883.
265. E. P. Lawrence, 1957: 34.
266. *Land and Labour,* November 1889.
267. Draft letter to Scottish Land Restoration Union, 11 Nov 1895, M.T.C., file 17, no. 146.
268. J.S. Mill, 1873, *Autobiography*: 130.
269. H. W. Lee writing in the 1912 introduction to H. Hyndman & W. Morris, 1884, *A Summary of the Principles of Socialism*: 3.

270. Figure quoted by Martin Crick, 1994, *The History of the Democratic Federation*: 61.
271. P.A. Watmough, 1977, 'Membership of the Social Democratic Federation 1885-1902,' in *Bulletin - Labour History*, vol. 34, 1977:345-40: 38.
272. The newspaper of the Democratic Federation.
273. Letter from Eleanor Marx to her sister Laura, 21 July 1884, published in Olga Meier and Faith Evans (eds), 1982, *The Daughters of Karl Marx: Family Correspondence – 1866-1898*: 179.
274. Henry Hyndman to Helen Taylor, 25 July, 1881, M.T.C., file 18, no. 32.
275. Only three women were on the executive of the SDF in 1884: Eleanor Marx, Mrs Hyndman and Mrs Hicks. See Yvonne Knapp, 1976, *Eleanor Marx: The Crowded Years*, vol. 2: 12.
276. Herbert Burrows to Henry Hyndman, 11 August 1884, L.S.E., Coll Misc. 522 Democratic Federation.
277. *Birmingham Daily Post*, 14 August 1884.
278. Mira Matikkala, 2011, *Empire and Imperial Ambition: Liberty, Englishness and Anti-imperialism in late Victorian Britain*. Vron Ware, 1992. Discussed in Janet Smith, 2016 & 2020.
279. Henry Hyndman to Helen Taylor, 25 July 1884, M.T.C., file 18, no. 25.
280. Helen Taylor to Henry Hyndman, undated draft, M.T.C., file 18, no. 27.
281. Ibid.
282. Eleanor Marx to Laura Lafargue, 31 December 1884, cited in Meier and Evans: 179.
283. *Freeman's Journal*, 2 June 1882.
284. George Bernard Shaw to Andreas Scheu, *A. Scheu Papers*, Institute of Social History, Amsterdam.
285. *The Democrat*, founded by Henry George, Michael Davitt and Helen Taylor, on 22 November 1884.
286. See Karen Hunt, 1996, *Equivocal Feminists: The Social Democratic Federation and the Women Question 1884- 1911*: 40.
287. Janet Smith, 2022.
288. Marilyn J. Boxer, 1978, 'Socialism Faces Feminism. The failure of Synthesis in France 1879-1919,' in Marilyn J. Boxer & Jean H. Quataert, eds., 1978, *Socialist Women: European Socialist Feminism in the Nineteenth and early Twentieth Centuries*: Chapter 4: 77.
289. Sheila Rowbotham, and others, have evidenced that women in socialist politics at this time usually had no family demands. 'The nationally

known figures tended to be middle class educated women, and they were invariably single, or, most significantly childless.' (Rowbotham's introduction to Olga Meier and Faith Evans,1982: xvii).

290. *Justice*, 15 March 1884.
291. E. Sylvia Pankhurst, 1932, *The Suffragette Movement*: 111.
292. Draft letter from Helen Taylor to Henry Hyndman, undated, M.T.C., file 18, no.33.
293. Olive Schreiner to William Philip Schreiner, 21 April 1912, which dates the event as 1884. BC16/Box5/Fold1/1912/14, *Olive Schreiner Letters*, Online, http://www.oliveschreiner.org.
294. *Justice,* 12 April 1884.
295. Ibid.
296. Henry Hyndman to Helen Taylor, 9 June 1883, M.T.C., file 18, no. 54.
297. Andreas Scheu, *Umsturzkeime*. 'Es wird Hyndman schemer fallen, ihr ''Freund'' zu bleiben…Mann konnte namlich deutlich sehen, wie sehr die Dame dem Vorxitzeer unbequem war, der sie van Stund on als bedenkliche Opponentin seiner Zwecke betrachtete und behondelte:' Quoted in Wilkins, 1958: 204.
298. Henry Hyndman, 1881, *England for All. The Text Book for Democracy*: 116.
299. E. Belfort Bax, 1913, *The Fraud of Feminism*: 31 & 51.
300. Ibid: 65.
301. E. Belfort Bax, 1918, *Reminiscences and Reflections of a Mid and Late Victorian*: 110.
302. Ibid.
303. Ewen A. Cameron, '"Setting the Heather on Fire" The Land Question in Scotland 1850–1914,' in M. Cragoe & P. Readman (eds), 2010, *The Land Question in Britain 1750–1950*: Chapter 6: 109.
304. *Birmingham Daily Post*, 23 January 1884 & 23 January 1884.
305. *The Democrat,* 22 November 1884.
306. *Freeman's Journal*, 20 November 1884.
307. See D.W. Crowley, 1956, 'The Crofter's Party 1885 – 1892: The First British Independent Common People's Party,' in *Scottish Historical Review, 1956*, *vol 35*.
308. Crowley, 1956: 116 & 119.
309. *The Times*, 9 December 1886.
310. *The Lancashire Evening Post,* 19 October 1886.
311. *North Wales Chronicle,* 13 February 1886.

312. I am indebted to Cragoe for all the background to the Welsh land question. M. Cragoe, 2010, '"A Contemptible Mimic of the Irish." The Land Question in Victorian Wales,' in M. Cragoe & P. Readman, (eds.) *The Land Question in Britain 1750* -1950: Chapter 5.
313. Douglas, 1976.
314. See Janet Smith 2018 & 2020.
315. Henry Hyndman to Helen Taylor, 9 June 1883, M.T.C., file 18, no. 31.
316. *School Board Chronicle,* 1 August 1885.
317. Martin, 1995, quoting Florence in *The Woman's Penny Post,* 24 November 1888: 288.
318. Information taken from Janet Smith, 2019 & 2020.
319. *The Saturday Review*, 17 August 1878 and *Pall Mall Gazette*, 9 August 1878.
320. Parry, 1993: 221 quoted in Smith, 2020.
321. Henry Hyndman to Helen Taylor, 12 October 1881, M.T.C, file 18, no. 28.
322. See Parry, 2006: 346-9 for public reaction to the death of Gordon. Besieged for a year in Khartoum, many people in Britain blamed the Liberal Government for organising a rescue too late to save him. He had been sent there to rescue British soldiers and many regarded him, on his death in the besieged city, as a Christian martyr.
323. J. Owen, 2008: 221-229.
324. Pelling, 1967: 51.
325. Soutter, 1923: 92.
326. See Smith, 2019, for the legal arguments as to the validity of Helen's candidature. Section 4 of Lord Brougham's Act of 1850, The Interpretation Act, had declared that 'persons' did include women unless it was directly indicated that only men were being referred to. In 1867 a number of women had attempted to register to vote, quoting Brougham's Act, though an ensuing court case, Chorlton v Lings, ruled that 'persons' did not include women. Upper-class women, including Georgina, Duchess of Devonshire, had long controlled seats through patronage. They had voted by proxy through the influence they wielded over their men and by canvassing for their relatives (Chalus, 2005). There were instances of women voting by clerical area. Once their names were included on the electoral register, they could not be denied their vote if they presented themselves. The most well-known is Lily Maxwell who voted in the 1867 general election

in Manchester for the Liberal candidate, Jacob Bright. Bright and the suffragist, Lydia Becker, discovered that Maxwell's name had been put, in error, on the electoral roll and accompanied her to cast her vote as a rate paying shopkeeper (Rendall, 2000).

327. Ethel Leach to Helen Taylor, 6 December, 1890, M.T.C, file 18, no. 49.
328. Philippa Levine, 1990: 63.
329. A. Taylor, 1892, *Memories of a Student*: 175. The Tetsworth School Board was set up in 1877 and its first members, which included Algernon, were elected unopposed. *Oxford Chronicle and Reading Gazette*, 29 December, 1877.
330. Election handbill, M.T.C. box 7.
331. This information is taken from Smith, 2020.
332. Windscheffel, 2007: 48. Quoted in Smith, 2020: 15.
333. *South London Press*, 21 November 1885. Quoted in Smith, 2000: 16.
334. Election handbill, M.T.C., box 7.
335. *South London Press*, 29 August 1885.
336. 'Notes from the Ladies' Cage' in *The Celtic Monthly, May 1880* reprinted in Beverly Schneller, 2005, *Anna Parnell's Political Journalism: Contexts and Texts*: 17.
337. *Leeds Mercury,* 11 November 1885.
338. *Yorkshire Gazette,* 29 October 1885.
339. *Leeds Mercury,* 21 November 1885.
340. *Sheffield Independent*, 24 October 1885.
341. *Liverpool Mercury*, 30 May 1885.
342. *Lloyds Weekly Paper*, 1 November 1885.
343. Soutter, 1923: 94, quoted in Smith, 2020.
344. A.A.W. to Helen Taylor, 14 June 1885, M.T.C., file 13, no. 361, quoted in Smith, 2020: 22.
345. *Englishwoman's Review,* June 1885.
346. So wrote the Pankhursts' suffragette daughter, Silvia, in S.E. Pankhurst, 1932, *The Suffragette Movement*: 71.
347. *Cuttings and leaflets connected with the election of 1885*, M.T.C., box 7 quoted in Smith, 2020: 24.
348. See next section.
349. *Cuttings and leaflets connected with the election of 1885*, M.T.C., box 7 quoted in Smith, 2020: 25.
350. Henry George to Helen Taylor, 25 September 1885, M.T.C., file 17, no. 23.

351. John Burns to Helen Taylor, 9 October 1885, M.T.C., file 22, no. 34.
352. *Pall Mall Gazette*, 21 November 1885, quoted in Smith:2020: 18.
353. *Huddersfield Daily Chronicle*, 1 June 1885.
354. *Dublin Weekly Nation*, 28 November 1885.
355. Anna Parnell to Helen Taylor, 5 November 1885, M.T.C., file 18, no. 98.
356. *Freeman's Journal*, 24 November 1885.
357. Roy Foster, 1976, *Charles Stewart Parnell, The Man and His Family*: 283.
358. Ethel Leach wrote to Helen that she had received a letter from Anna, 'written on your new typewriter,' 7 August 1888, M.T.C., file 18, no. 42.
359. Anna Parnell to Helen Taylor, 20 April 1887, M.T.C., file 18 no. 83.
360. 1885 General Election (parliament.uk)
361. Smith, 2020: 29 quoting Longford, 1979: 221. See also, Smith, 2019.
362. John Chapman to Helen Taylor, 5 December 1885, M.T.C., file 4, no. 55.
363. *The Times*, 27 November, 1885. See Smith, 2020.

Part 3: The Twilight Years, 1889-1904

1. See letters between Algernon and Helen, M.T.C., file 24.
2. Algernon Taylor to Helen Taylor, 12-15 March 1889, M.T.C., file 24, no. 122.
3. Algernon Taylor to Helen Taylor, 22 May 1889, M.T.C., file 24, no.131.
4. Algernon Taylor to Helen Taylor, 29 July 1889, M.T.C., file 24, no. 135.
5. Algernon Taylor to Helen Taylor, 21 August 1889, M.T.C., file 24, no 136.
6. Algernon Taylor to Helen Taylor, 1 May 1890, M.T.C., file 24, no. 164.
7. Helen Taylor to Henry George, 12 April 1889, H.G.G.C.
8. Algernon Taylor to Helen Taylor, 1 March 1888, M.T.C., file 24, no. 114.
9. *Hull Daily Mail,* 29 September 1887.
10. Draft letter from Helen Taylor to Algernon Taylor, marked '1888 not sent', M.T.C., file 24, no. 109.
11. Letter from Helen Taylor to Wild and Wild Solicitors, asking them to act on her behalf and dated 8 July 1895, M.T.C., file 26, no.104.
12. Herbert Taylor to Algernon Taylor, 5 March 1894, M.T.C., file 29, no. 256.
13. Herbert Taylor to Mary Stuart, 6 April 1897, M.T.C., file 29, no. 290.
14. Herbert Taylor, jnr, to Helen Taylor, 10 November 1893, M.T.C., file 25, no. 860.

15. Ethel Taylor to Helen Taylor, 27 August - no year but dated in archive '1900?', M.T.C., file 25, no. 849.
16. Helen Taylor to Henry George, 12 October 1882, H.G.G.C.
17. Helen Taylor to Elizabeth Surr, 1 October 1883, M.T.C., file 23, no. 678.
18. Elizabeth Surr to Helen Taylor, 2 February 1891, M.T.C., file 23, no. 680.
19. Florence Fenwick Miller, *An Uncommon Girlhood:* 96.
20. Ibid: 453.
21. Helen Taylor to Elizabeth Surr, 1 October, 1883, M.T.C., file 23, no. 678.
22. Margaret Wright, 2011, *Elizabeth Wolstenholme Elmy and the Victorian Feminist Movement*: 210-11.
23. Ibid: 143.
24. Ibid: 143.
25. Elizabeth Surr to Helen Taylor, 17 November 1888, M.T.C., file 23, no. 675.
26. Elizabeth Surr to Helen Taylor, 7 December 1892, M.T.C., file 23, no. 684.
27. Elizabeth Surr to Helen Taylor, 26 May 1898, M.T.C., file 23, no. 688.
28. Ibid.
29. Elizabeth Surr, *Stories about Cats*.
30. WikiTree, Elizabeth (Grabham) Surr (1825-1901) | WikiTree FREE Family Tree.
31. Ethel Leach to Helen Taylor, 17 April 1887 M.T.C., file 18, no. 37.
32. Ethel Leach to Helen Taylor, 1 July 1888, M.T.C., file 18, no. 40.
33. Ethel Leach to Helen Taylor, 7 August 1888, M.T.C., file 18, no. 42.
34. Ethel Leach to Helen Taylor, 3 March 1890, M.T.C., file 18, no. 46.
35. Ethel Leach to Helen Taylor, 6 December 1890, M.T.C., file 18, no. 49.
36. Ethel Leach to Helen Taylor, 6 October 1888, M.T.C., file 18, no. 43.
37. Ethel Leach to Helen Taylor, 7 July 1888, file 18, no. 41.
38. Ethel Leach (1850-1936) | Humanist Heritage – Exploring the rich history and influence of humanism in the UK (humanists.uk)
39. See Coté's account of Anna's last years.
40. I am indebted for this information to Dana Hearne's introduction to Anna Parnell *The Tale of a Great Sham*: 9.
41. Helen Taylor, 1888, *Nationalisation of the Land,* Land Nationalisation Tracts – No. XIX, Bristol Selected Pamphlets 1888, University of Bristol Library, URL:http://www.jstor.org/stable/60249652, referred to in Smith, 2016.
42. Ibid.

43. *The Standard*, 30 May 1885.
44. *Lancashire Evening Post*, press cutting, 21 October 1886, M.T.C., box 7.
45. Helen Taylor, *The Restoration of their Homes to the People. An Appeal to Women,* 1890, English Land Restoration League Tracts – No. 17, LSE Selected Pamphlets, 1890, L.S.E. Library, URL:http://www.jstor.org/stable/60214923.
46. Ibid: 2 & 3.
47. Helen Taylor to Mr Moberley, December 1893, M.T.C., file 17, no. 11.
48. Mr Moberley to Helen Taylor, 8 May 1894, M.T.C., file 17, no. 112 & Helen Taylor to Mr Moberley, 17 May 1894, M.T.C., file 17, no. 113.
49. Helen Taylor to Mr Moberley, 17 May 1894, M.T.C., file 17, no. 113.
50. Mr Walker to Helen Taylor, 15 December 1897, M.T.C., file 17, no.143.
51. J. Hyder to Helen Taylor, 7 October 1893, M.T.C., file 17, no. 93.
52. Helen Taylor to Mr and Mrs Hyder, August 1898, M.T.C., file 17, no. 97.
53. Mr Moberley to Helen Taylor, 8 May 1894, M.T.C. file 17, no.112 & 113.
54. Mr Walker to Helen Taylor, 15 December 1897, M.T.C., file 17, no.143.
55. *Huddersfield Daily Chronicle,* 30 December 1887.
56. *Derby Daily Telegraph*, 29 May 1885 & *Hampshire Telegraph*, 16 April 1887.
57. Hatcham Liberal Club to Helen Taylor, 15 November 1888, M.T.C. file 15, no. 85.
58. Ethel Leach to Helen Taylor, M.T.C., file 18, no. 44.
59. *Essex Standard*, 20 November 1886.
60. Mr Talbot to Helen Taylor, 7 January 1890, M.T.C., file 18, no. 66.
61. Helen Taylor to Mr Talbot, 21 January 1890, M.T.C., file 18, no. 67.
62. Helen Taylor to A. Day, 11 January 1890, M.T..C, file 18, no. 15.
63. Stanningley Liberal Club had done so in 1884, as reported in *The Democrat*, the paper founded by Henry George, Michael Davitt and Helen Taylor, on 22 November 1884.
64. *Englishwoman's Review*, July 1887.
65. *South and East London Press*, 14 January 1888, press cutting, M.T.C., box 7.
66. F.H. Herrick, 1945, 'The Origins of the National Liberal Federation,' in *The Journal of Modern History*, vol. 17, no. 2, 2 June 1945: 116-129.
67. June Hannam, 'Women and Politics,' in June Purvis (ed.), 2000, *Women's History: Britain 1850-1945*: Chapter 9.
68. Herrick, 1945: 20.

69. *Women's Liberal Union, Annual Report 1890.*
70. Ibid.
71. Herrick: 20.
72. Eva McLaren to Helen Taylor, 29 November 1888, M.T.C., file 18, no. 120.
73. Ethel Leach to Helen Taylor, 16 February 1889, M.T.C., file 18, no. 36.
74. Ethel Leach to Helen Taylor, 6 October 1888, M.T.C., file 18, no. 33.
75. *Englishwoman's Review*, January 1889.
76. *Manchester Times*, 29 May 1891.
77. *Englishwoman's Review*, September 1888.
78. *Englishwoman's Review*, May 1890.
79. *Moral Reform Union, First Annual Report*, April 1882.
80. Ibid.
81. S. Rowbotham, 2008, *Edward Carpenter: A Life of Liberty and Love*: 91.
82. Mrs Leigh Browne to Helen Taylor, 11 February 1890, M.T.C., file 10, no. 88.
83. Copy of speech is held in M.T.C., file 20, May 1890.
84. Lucy Bland, 1995, *Banishing the Beast*: 154.
85. *7th Annual Report,* 26 June 1889.
86. Roy Jenkins, 2004, *Sir Charles Wentworth Dilke, 1843-1911*, https://doi.org/10.1093/ref:odnb/32824
87. *6th Annual Report,* May 1888.
88. Ibid.
89. E. L. Miers to Helen Taylor, 22 November 1890, M.T.C., file 10, no. 21.
90. Draft letter, Helen Taylor to Fanny Albert, 5 January, 1895, M.T.C., file 10, no. 34.
91. Draft letter Helen Taylor to Mrs Tremehere, 22 April 1895, M.T.C., file 11, no. 215.
92. Moral Reform Union | Orlando (cambridge.org).
93. Bland: 144.
94. *Leeds Mercury,* 28 June 1890.
95. Mary Taylor to Mrs Browne (of the Moral Reform Union), 17 February 1906. M.T.C., file 58, no. 6.
96. Joseph Hyder to Helen Taylor, 5 October 1900, M.T.C., file 17, no. 96.
97. Christina A Bremner to Helen Taylor, 4 February 1900, M.T.C., file 4, no. 49.
98. Helen Taylor to Alfred Dyer, January 1898, M.T.C, file 10, no. 100.
99. Ibid.

100. Colin Holmes, 1979, *Anti-Semitism in British Society 1876–1939*: 13 & 63.
101. M.T.C., file 15.
102. B. M. Dallimore to Helen Taylor, 23 September 1888, M.T.C., file 15, no. 51.
103. B.M. Dallimore to Helen Taylor, 8 July 1888, M.T.C., file 15, no. 18.
104. B.M. Dallimore to Helen Taylor, 1 August 1888, M.T.C., file 15, no. 49.
105. Philippa Levine, 1990, 'Love, Friendship and Feminism in the later Nineteenth Century,' in *Women Studies International Forum, vol 13, numbers 1/2, 1990*: 63-78:72.
106. Ibid: 63.
107. Mary Taylor to Helen Taylor, 10 October 1890 & 14 November 1897, M.T.C., file 25, nos. 172 & 244.
108. *Bucks Herald,* 24 November 1894.
109. *Torquay Times and South Devon Advertiser*, 1 February 1895.
110. Algernon Taylor to Helen Taylor, M.T.C., 27 February 1900, file 24, no. 782.
111. Mary Taylor to Helen Taylor, 21 October 1889, M.T.C. file 25, no. 902.
112. Mary Taylor to Helen Taylor, 30 September 1897, file 25, no. 965.
113. Mary Taylor to Helen Taylor, 22 July 1899, M.T.C., file 25, no. 971.
114. Algernon Taylor to Helen Taylor, 11 May 1900, M.T.C. file 24, no. 191.
115. Mary Taylor to Helen Taylor, 28 July 1899, M.T.C, file 25, no. 258.
116. *Labour Leader*, 15 November 1902.
117. Mary Taylor to Helen Taylor, 18 February1900, M.T.C., file 25, no. 972.
118. Mary Taylor to Helen Taylor, 10 July 1900, M.T.C., file 25, no. 980.
119. Mary Taylor to Helen Taylor, 13 September 1900, M.T.C., file 25 no. 981.
120. Mary Taylor to Helen Taylor, 10 March 1900, M.T.C., file 25, no. 973.
121. *Evening Standard*, 18 November 1903.
122. *East and South Devon Advertiser,* 21 November 1903.
123. The will of Algernon Taylor, file 58, M.T.C.
124. *Morning Post*, 19 November 1903.
125. 1901 UK Census.
126. Diary of Mary Taylor, 9 August 1904, M.T.C. file 58.
127. See part 1 footnote 30.
128. Josephine Kamm, 1977: 229.
129. Nelly Taylor to Mary Taylor, 30 January 1907, M.T.C. file 29, no. 313.
130. *Torquay Times and South Devon Advertiser,* 1 February 1907.

131. Lydia S Whitfield to Mary Taylor, 5 July 1916, M.T.C., file 58, no. 7.
132. *Birmingham Mail,* 19 November 1910.
133. Lost Hospitals of London, Ezitis.myzen.co.uk.
134. *Labour Leader*, 18 September 1908.
135. Ibid, 30 November 1906.
136. Joseph Hyder to Mary Taylor, M.T.C., file 29, no. 297.
137. *Labour Leader,* 1 February 1907.
138. Olive Schreiner to Rev. J.T. Lloyd, 29 October 1892 in E.R. Rive, 1988, *Olive Schreiner Letters 1871-99, Vol. 1*: 212.
139. See conclusion to J. Smith, 2014, *The Feminism and Political Radicalism of Helen Taylor in Victorian Britain and Ireland* on which this summing up is based.
140. Thomas Gautrey, 1936: 78.
141. Emily Hill to Helen Taylor, 5 November 1895, M.T.C. file 10, no. 43.
142. Letter Helen Taylor to Kate Amberley, 24 October 1864, Bertrand Russell Archive, Ontario, Canada.
143. Soutter, 1925: 86.
144. Press cutting of Emily Hill's obituary of Helen Taylor taken from *Women and Progress,* 8 February 1907, M.T.C., box 7.
145. *Justice*, 2 February 1907.
146. Soutter, 1923.

BIBLIOGRAPHY

Archives

A Scheu Papers, Institute of Social History, Amsterdam.

Annual Reports of the Moral Reform Union, British Library.

Annual Reports of the Women's Liberal Union, British Library.

Eleanor Marx Papers, Institute of Social History, Amsterdam.

England and Wales Merchant Navy Crew Lists 1861-1913, The National Archives.

Helen Taylor's papers and letters, Mill Taylor Collection, London School of Economics.

Henry George General Correspondence 1852 – 1897, (H.G.G.C.) microfilm, New York Public Library.

Letters of Anna Maria Priestman, Millfield Papers, The Clark Archive, Street, Somerset.

Letters of Barbara Bodichon, Autograph Letters, Women's Library @LSE.

Letters of Elizabeth Garrett Anderson, Autograph Letters, Women's Library @LSE.

Letters of Lady Amberley, Bertrand Russell Archive, McMaster University, Canada.

Letters of Olive Schreiner, www.oliveschreiner.org.

London School Board Minutes, London Metropolitan Archives.

Mill-Taylor Collection, L.S.E.

Papers of the Democratic Federation, Coll. Misc. 522, London School of Economics.

Report of the Educational Endowment Committee on City Parochial Charities, 19 July 1879, London Metropolitan Archives.
The Educational Endowments Committee of the London School Board Reports, 1876, 1879, 1883 and *1884*, London Metropolitan Archives.
The Minutes of evidence taken before a Special Committee re Upton House Industrial School 21 May 1879, London Metropolitan Archives.

British Newspaper Library

Bermondsey and Rotherhithe Advertiser
Birmingham Daily News
Birmingham Daily Post
Birmingham Mail
Bristol Mercury
Bucks Herald
Cork Examiner
Daily News
Daily Post
Derby Daily Telegraph
Dublin Weekly News
Dundee Courier and Argus
East and South Devon Advertiser
Eastern Evening News
Eastern Morning News
Essex Standard
Freeman's Journal
Glasgow Herald
Globe
Gloucester Citizen
Hampshire Telegraph
Huddersfield Chronicle and West Yorkshire Advertiser
Huddersfield Daily Chronicle
Hull Daily Mail
Ipswich Chronicle
Irish Times
Irish World
Justice

Labour Leader
Lancashire Evening Post
Lancaster Gazette and General Advertiser
Land and Labour
Leeds Mercury
Lincolnshire Chronicle
Liverpool Mercury
Lloyds Weekly Newspaper
London Standard
Manchester Evening News
Manchester Times
Morning Herald
National Standard
Norfolk News
Northern Echo
North Wales Chronicle
Northern Whig
Pall Mall Gazette
Press (London)
Punch
Reynold's News
School Board Chronicle
Sevenoaks Chronicle and Kentish Advertiser
Sheffield Daily Telegraph
Sheffield Independent
Sinn Fein Weekly
South and East London Press
South London Chronicle and Southwark and Lambeth Ensign
South London Press
Southwark and Bermondsey Recorder
Southwark Recorder and Advertiser
Suffolk Herald
The Bury and Norwich Post
The Democrat
The Echo
The Hull Packet and East Riding Times
The Morning Post
The Nation

The Saturday Review
The School Master
The Scotsman
The Standard
The Times
The Western Daily Press
Torquay Times and South Devon Advertiser
United Ireland
Western Mail
Western Morning News
West London Advertiser
West Yorkshire Advertiser
Yorkshire Gazette
York Herald
Waterford Standard

Women's Library, L.S.E.

Englishwoman's Review

Online Resources/Websites

Blackheath Village | Case Studies | Ideal Homes (ideal-homes.org.uk)
Encyclopedia.com, Henry Thomas Buckle | Encyclopedia.com
Ethel Leach (1850-1936) | Humanist Heritage - Exploring the rich history and influence of humanism in the UK (humanists.uk)
Greenwich Industrial History: Blackheath Station 150 years
House of Commons - Hansard - UK Parliament
Labour World | National Library of Ireland (nli.ie)
Lost Hospitals of London, Ezitis.myzen.co.uk.
Moral Reform Union | Orlando (cambridge.org)
Oxford Reference, Malthusianism - Oxford Reference
Risborough~Oxford Railway – Aston Rowant & Chilterns Spring Line Villages (wordpress.com)
UK Census, Historic census data - Office for National Statistics (ons.gov.uk)
Victorian London - Education - Education for the poor - School Board Visitors

The Women's Time Line, http://www.mmu.ac.uk/humanresources/equalities/doc/gender-equality-timeline.pdf

William George Ward | Victorian Era, Anglican Church, Theology | Britannica

Will of John Stuart Mill, The Online Library of Liberty, oll.libertyfund.org

WikiTree, Elizabeth (Grabham) Surr (1825-1901) | WikiTree FREE Family Tree

1885 General Election (parliament.uk)

Primary

Bax, Ernest Belfort, 1918, *Reminiscences and Reflection of a Mid and Late Victorian,* London, G. Allen.

Bax, Ernest Belfort, 1913, *The Fraud of Feminism*, London, Grant Richards Ltd.

Booth, Charles, 1892, *Life and Labour of the People of London, Vol i & Vol ii: Streets and Population Classified*, London, Macmillan.

Craigen, Jessie, 1882, 'Report on a Visit to Ireland in the Summer of 1881,' Dublin, Webb & Son. #4 - Report on a visit to Ireland in the summer of 1881: / by Jessie ... - Full View | HathiTrust Digital Library.

Davitt, Michael, 1904, *The Fall of Feudalism in Ireland,* London, Harper and Brothers.

Edwards, Joseph (ed.), 1909, *Land and real tariff reform: being The Land Reformers' Handbook for 1909*, London, J. Edwards.

Elliot, Hugh, S. R. (ed.), 1910, *The Letters of John Stuart Mill*, London, Longmans, Green and Co.

Fawcett, Millicent, 1924, *What I Remember*, London, F. Unwin.

Fenwick Miller, Florence, *An Uncommon Girlhood,* unpublished memoir, Welcome Institute, London.

Gautrey, Thomas, 1936, *Lux Mihi Laus. School Board Memories,* London, Link House Publications.

George, Henry, 1881, *Progress and Poverty*, London, D. Appleton & Co.

George Henry, (jnr.), 1904, *The Life of Henry George*, London, Doubleday, Page & Co.

Gladstone, Herbert, '*Diary*' reprinted in *Irish Historical Studies, vol. 17*, 1970/71: 521 – 548.

Holmes, F.M., 1881, *History of the Irish Land League, Impartially Reviewed,* London, F. E. Longley.

Hyndman, Henry M., & Morris, William, 1884, *A Summary of the Principles of Socialism*, London, Modern Press.

Hyndman, Henry M., 1881, *England for all: The Text Book for Democracy*, London, E. W. Allen.

Hyndman, Henry M., 1911, *Record of An Adventurous Life*, London, Macmillan.

Kettle A. J. & Kettle L. J., 1958, *The Material for Victory: being the memoirs of Andrew J Kettle*, Dublin, Fallon.

Lloyd, John, 1910, *London Municipal Government: History of a Great Reform 1880-8*, London, P.S. King.

Lobb, John, 1889, *Extravagance and Mismanagement of the London School Board*, London, 'Christian Age' Offices.

London Library, 1846, *Laws and regulations of the London Library: established MDCCCXLI, (at no. 49, Pall Mall, and now removed to) no. 12, St. James's Square. With a list of the subscribers to the 1st of June, 1846, inclusive London*: London, London Library.

Mill, John Stuart, (1873), 2018, *Autobiography*, Oxford, Oxford University Press.

Mill, John Stuart, (1859), 2016, *On Liberty*, CreateSpace Independent Publishing Platform.

Mill, John Stuart, 'Report of Commissioners on Education in Schools in England 1867-8,' *The Collected Works of John Stuart Mill, vol. xxi*, www.oll.libertyfund.org

Mill, John Stuart, 'The Admission of Women to the Electoral Suffrage,' in Robson, Ann & Robson, John M. (eds.), 1994, *Sexual Equality, Writings by John Stuart Mill, Harriet Taylor Mill and Helen Taylor*, Toronto: 234-246.

Mill, John Stuart, 'The Contagious Diseases Act 1871,' *The Collected Works of John Stuart Mill*, vol XX1, www.oll/libertyfund.org.

Mill John Stuart. [1869] 1994. 'The Subjection of Women' in Robson, Ann & Robson, John M. (eds.), 1994, *Sexual Equality, Writings by John Stuart Mill, Harriet Taylor Mill and Helen Taylor*, Toronto: 305-400.

Mill, John Stuart, *vol xiv & xv & xxxii* : 114, fn. 1, *The Collected Works of John Stuart Mill, Volume XIV - The Later Letters 1849-1873 Part I* | Online Library of Liberty (libertyfund.org).

Mitchel, John, (1882), 2020, *The Last Conquest of Ireland (perhaps),* Alpha Editions, Milton Keynes.

O'Shea, Katherine, 1914, *Charles Stewart Parnell: His Love Story and Political Life, vols 1 & 2,* London, Cassell.

Pankhurst, E. Sylvia, 1932, *The Suffragette Movement*, London, Longmans, Green & Co.

Parnell, Anna, 1986, *The Tale of a Great Sham,* Hearne, Dana (ed.), Dublin, Arlen House.

Power Cobbe, Frances, 1904, *Frances Power Cobbe: As told by herself*, London, S. Sonnenschein & Co.

Rey, Louis, 'Le Roman de John Stuart Mill,' *The Nineteenth Century and After*, 7.4.1913, 14: 502-526.

Rey, Louis, 'Le Souvenir de John Stuart Mill en Avignon,' *Revue des Deux Mondes* (*1829-1971 Huitième Période*), 1 Septembre 1937, *vol. 41, no.1*: 211-222.

Rive, E. (ed.), 1988, *Olive Schreiner Letters 1871-99, vol 1,* Oxford, Oxford University Press.

Robson, Ann & Robson, John M. (eds.),1994, *Sexual Equality, Writings by John Stuart Mill, Harriet Taylor Mill and Helen Taylor*, Toronto, Toronto University Press.

Russell, Bertrand & Russell, Patricia (eds.), 1937, *The Amberley Papers, vols 1 & 2*, New York, W.W. Norton & Co.

Schneller, Beverley (ed.), 2005, *Anna Parnell's Political Journalism: Contents and Texts,* Dublin: Maunsell & Co.

Soutter, F. W., 1925, *Fights For Freedom*, London, Fisher Unwin.

Soutter, F. W., 1923, *Recollections of a Labour Pioneer*, London, Fisher Unwin.

Surr, Elizabeth, 1901, *Stories about Cats*, Edinburgh, T. Nelson and Sons.

Taylor, Algernon, 1862, *Convent Life in Italy*, London, C.J. Skeet.

Taylor, Algernon, 1879, *Guienne, Notes of an Autumn Tour*, London, C.K. Paul.

Taylor, Algernon, 1895, *Memories of a Student*, London, Simpkin, Marshall, Hamilton.

Taylor, Algernon, 1866, *Scenes in French Monasteries*, London, C.J. Skeet.

Taylor, Harriet, 'Enfranchisement of Women' (1851), in Robson A. & Robson John M. (eds), 1994, *Sexual Equality, Writings by John Stuart Mill, Harriet Taylor Mill and Helen Taylor*, Toronto, Toronto University Press: 178-203.

Taylor, Harriet & Mill, John Stuart, 'Remarks on Mr Fitzroy's Bill for the More Effectual Prevention of Assaults on Women and Children,' in Robson, Ann & Robson, John M. (eds.*)*, 1994, *Sexual Equality, Writings by John Stuart Mill, Harriet Taylor Mill and Helen Taylor*, Toronto, Toronto University Press: 91 –98.

Taylor, Harriet & Mill, John Stuart, 'The Suicide of Sarah Brown,' 'The Case of Anne Bird,' 'The Case of Susan Moir' and 'Wife Murder,' in

Robson, Ann & Robson, John M. (eds.), 1994, *Sexual Equality, Writings by John Stuart Mill, Harriet Taylor Mill and Helen Taylor*, Toronto, Toronto University Press: 53-91.

Taylor, Helen, *Nationalisation of the Land,* Land Nationalisation Tracts – No XIX, London, 1888, Bristol Selected Pamphlets 1888, University of Bristol Library, accessed at: www.jstor.org/stable/60249652.

Taylor Helen, *The Claim of Englishwomen to the Suffrage Constitutionally Considered*, 1867, www.indiana.edu/letrs.vwwp/taylor/suffrage.

Taylor, Helen, *The Ladies' Petition,* in Robson, Ann & Robson, John M. (eds.*)*, 1994, *Sexual Equality, Writings by John Stuart Mill, Harriet Taylor Mill and Helen Taylor*, Toronto, Toronto University Press: 216-233.

Taylor, Helen, *The Restoration of their Homes to the People: An Appeal to Women*, English Land Restoration League Tracts – No 17, London, 1890, L.S.E. Selected Pamphlets 1890, www.jstor.org/stable/60214923.

Taylor, Helen, *Women and Criticism,* in Robson, Ann & Robson, John M. (eds.), 1994, *Sexual Equality, Writings by John Stuart Mill, Harriet Taylor Mill and Helen Taylor*, Toronto, Toronto University Press: 103-111.

Tynan, Katherine, 1913, *Twenty-Five Year Reminiscences*, London, Smith Elder & Co.

Webb, Sydney, 'Socialism in England,' *American Economic Association, vol. 4, no. 2, April 1889*: 7-73.

Wilson, Mary, 1987, *A European Journal*, Simpson Jennifer (ed.), London, Bloomsbury.

Winkworth, Catherine & Winkworth Susanna, 1908, *Memorials of Two Sisters*, Shaen, Margaret J. (ed.), London: Longmans, Green & Co.

Wollstonecraft, Mary, (1792), 2008, *A Vindication of the Rights of Woman.* Oxford, Oxford University Press.

Secondary

Arsdel, Rosemary T. Van, 2004, 'Miller, Florence Fenwick,' *Oxford Dictionary of National Biography*, https://doi.org/10.1093/ref:odnb/37764.

Bevir, Mark, 'The British Social Democratic Federation 1880-85; from O'Brienism to Marxism,' *International Review of Social History, vol. xxxv, no. 11, 1992*: 207- 229.

Bland, Lucy, 1995, *Banishing the Beast*, London, Penguin.

Bloomfield, Andrea L., 1997, 'Walking a Narrow Line: Helen Taylor's Literary Contribution to the British Women's Rights Movement,' *Women's Studies, 1997, vol. 26, issue 3-4:* 259-83.

Boxer, Marilyn J., 'Socialism Faces Feminism. The failure of Synthesis in France 1879-1919,' in Marilyn J. Boxer & Jean H. Quataert (eds.), 1978, *Socialist Women: European Socialist Feminism in the Nineteenth and early Twentieth Centuries*, New York, Elsevier North-Holland: chapter 4.

Bull, Philip, 1996, *Land, Politics and Nationalism: A Study of the Irish Land Question,* Dublin, Gill & Macmillan.

Burton, Antoinette, 1994, *Burdens of History, British feminists, Indian women, and imperial culture, 1865-1915*, Chapel Hill, University of North Carolina Press.

Caine, Barbara, 1996, *Victorian Feminists*, Oxford, Oxford University Press.

Cameron, E.A., '"Setting the Heather on Fire." The Land Question in Scotland 1850 – 1914,' in Cragoe, M. & Readman, P. (eds.), 2010, *The Land Question in Britain 1750* – 1950, Basingstoke, Palgrave Macmillan: chapter 6.

Capaldi, Nicholas, 2004, *John Stuart Mill, A Biography*, Cambridge, Cambridge University Press.

Chamberlain, Kathy, 2017, *Jane Welsh Carlyle and Her Victorian World*, London, Duckworth.

Conway, Moncure D., 1882, *Travels in South Kensington*, New York, Harper.

Coté, Jane, McL., 1991, *Fanny and Anna Parnell: Ireland's Patriot Sisters,* London, Palgrave Macmillan.

Cragoe, Michael, '"A Contemptible Mimic of the Irish." The Land Question in Victorian Wales,' in Cragoe, M. & Readman, P. (eds.)., 2010, *The Land Question in Britain 1750-1950, Basingstoke*, Palgrave Macmillan: chapter 5.

Crick, Martin, *The History of the Democratic Federation*, Keele, 1994.

Crowley, D.W., 'The Crofter's Party 1885–1892: The First British Independent Common People's Party,' *Scottish Historical Review, vol 35, 1956.*

Curtis, Liz, 1996, *Nothing But the Same Old Story: The Roots of Anti-Irish Racism*, Belfast, Sasta.

Davis, J., 1989, 'Radical Clubs and London Politics 1870–1900,' Feldman, D. and Stedman Jones, G. (eds.), 1989, *Metropolis: Histories and Representations of London Since 1800*, London, Routledge: Chapter 5.

Davis, Tracy C., 1991, *Actresses as Working Women: Their social identity in Victorian culture*, London, Routledge.

Douglas, Roy, 1976, *Land, People and Politics: A History of the Land Question in the United Kingdom 1875* – 1952, London, Allison and Busby.

Dyhouse, Carol, 1981, *Girls growing up in late Victorian and Edwardian England*, London, Routledge & K. Paul.

Fishman, J. J., 2005, *Charitable Accountability and Reform in Nineteenth Century England. The Case of the Charity Commission,* Pace University, DigitalCommons@Pace, http://digitalcommons.pace.edu/lawfaculty/108.

Flaherty, Seamus, 2019, 'H M Hyndman and the Intellectual Origins of the Remaking of Socialism in Britain, 1878-1881,' *English Historical Review, vol 34, no. 569*: 855-880.

Flint, Kate, 2000, 'The Victorian Novel and its Readers,' in David, Deirdre (ed.), *The Cambridge Companion to the Victorian Novel*, Cambridge, Cambridge University Press: 13-35.

Flint, Kate, 1993, *The Woman Reader 1837-1914*, Oxford, Oxford University Press.

Foster, Roy, 1976, *Charles Stewart Parnell: the man and his family,* Harvester Press, Hassocks.

George, de Mille, Anna, 1944, 'Henry George: The Fight for Irish Freedom,' *The American Journal of Economics and Sociology, vol. 3, no. 2*, Jan. 1944: 251-272, URL: https://www.jstor.org/stable/3483649

Gleadle, Kathryn, 1995, *The Early Feminists: Radical Unitarians and the Emergence of the Women's Rights Movement*, Basingstoke, Macmillan.

Hall, Catherine, 1992, *White, Male and Middle Class*, Cambridge, Polity Press.

Hannam, June, 'Women and Politics,' in Purvis, June (ed.), 2000, *Women's History: Britain 1850*-1945, London, Routledge: Chapter 9.

Hayek, F. A., 1951, *John Stuart Mill and Harriet Taylor: their friendship and subsequent marriage*, London, Routledge & Kegan Paul.

Herrick, F. H., 'The Origins of the National Liberal Federation,' *The Journal of Modern History, vol. 17, no. 2, June 1945:* 116-129.

Hollis, Patricia, 1989, *Ladies Elect: Women in English Local Government*, Oxford, Clarendon Press.

Holmes, Colin, 1979, *Anti-Semitism in British Society 1876-1939*, London, Routledge.

Holton, Sandra, 'Silk dresses and lavender kid gloves: the wayward career of Jessie Craigen, working suffragist,' *Women's History Review, vol. 5, no. 6, 1996.*

Holton, Sandra, 'Women and the Vote,' in June Purvis (ed.), 2000, *Women's History: Britain, 1850-1945*, London, Routledge: Chapter 11.

Howkins, Alan, 'From Diggers to Dongas, the Land in English Radicalism,' *History Workshop Journal, vol. 54,* 2002: 1-23.

Hunt, Felicity (ed.), 1987, *Lessons for Life, The Schooling of Girls and Women 1850- 1950*, Oxford, B. Blackwell.

Hunt, Karen, 1996, *Equivocal Feminists: The Social Democratic Federation and the Woman Question 1884- 1911*, Cambridge, Cambridge University Press.

Jacobs, Jo Ellen, 1994, '"The Lot of Gifted Ladies is Hard:" A Study of Harriet Taylor Mill Criticism,' *Hypatia, Summer 1994, vol. 9, no. 3*: 132-162.

Jacobs, Jo Ellen, 2002, *The Voice of Harriet Taylor Mill*, Bloomington, Indiana University Press.

Jenkins, Roy, 2004, 'Sir Charles Wentworth Dilke, *Oxford Dictionary of National Biography*, https://doi.org/10.1093/ref:odnb/32824.

Kamm, Josephine, 1977, *John Stuart Mill in Love*, London, Gordon & Cremonesi.

Kent, Christopher, 'Image and Reality: The Actress in Society,' in Vicinus, Martha (ed.), *A Widening Sphere: Changing Roles of Victorian Women*, 1977, Bloomington, Indiana University Press: Chapter 5.

Kinzer, Bruce L., 'The 1870 Education Bill and the Method of J.S. Mill's Later Politics,' *Albion: A Quarterly Journal Concerned with British Studies, Summer 1997, vol. 29, no. 2*: 223-245.

Knapp, Yvonne, 1976, *Eleanor Marx: The Crowded Years, vol 2*, London, Virago.

Lawrence, E.P., 1957, *Henry George in the British Isles,* Lansing, Michigan State University Press.

Levine, Philippa 1990, 'Love, Friendship and Feminism in the later Nineteenth Century,' *Women Studies International Forum, vol. 13, nos. 1/2, 1990*: 63-78.

Longford, Elizabeth A., 1979, *A Pilgrimage of Passion. The Life of Wilfrid Scawen Blunt*, London, Weidenfeld & Nicolson.

McCabe, Helen, 2023, *Harriet Taylor Mill. (Elements on Women in the History of* Philosophy), Cambridge, Cambridge University Press.

McCabe, Helen, 'John Stuart Mill: market socialist?' *Review of Social Economy, 79:3, 2021*: 506-527, DOI: 10.1080/00346764.2020.1781923.

Martin, Jane, 'Fighting down the idea that the only place for women was home? Gender and Policy in Elementary Education,' *History of Education, vol. 24, no. 4, 1995:* 277-292.

Martin, Jane, 2004, 'Surr (nee Grabham) Elizabeth,' *Oxford Dictionary of National Biography*, https://doi.org/10.1093/ref:odnb/48591.

Martin, Jane, 'To "Blaise a Trail for Women to Follow Along": Sex, gender and politics of education on the London School Board (1870-1904),' *Gender and Education, vol. 12, no. 2, 2000:* 165-181.

Martin, Jane, 1999, *Women and the Politics of Schooling in Victorian and Edwardian England,* London, Leicester University Press.

Matikkala, Mira, 2011, *Empire and Imperial Ambition: Liberty, Englishness and Anti-imperialism in late Victorian Britain*, London, I. B. Tauris.

Mazlich, Bruce, 1975, *James and John Stuart Mill: Father and son in the nineteenth century*, New York, Basic Books.

Mearns, Andrew & Preston William C., 1883, *The Bitter Cry of Outcast London*, Boston, Mass, Cupples Upham and Co.

Meier, Olga & Evans, Faith (eds.), 1982, *The Daughters of Karl Marx: Family Correspondence – 1866-1898*, New York, Harcourt Brace Jovanovich.

Miller, Dale E., 'Harriet Taylor Mill,' Zalta, Edward N. & Nodelman Uri (eds.), *The Stanford Encyclopedia of Philosophy, Fall 2022 Edition*, URL = <https://plato.stanford.edu/archives/fall2022/entries/harriet-mill/>.

Mulligan, A. N., 2009, 'By a Thousand Ingenious Feminine Devices. The Ladies' Land League and the Development of Irish Nationalism,' *Historical Geography, vol. 37, 2009.*

O'Hara, Bernard, 2009, *Davitt: Irish Patriot and Father of the Land League*, Woodford Green, Tudor Gate Press.

Mitchell, Rosemary, 'Alice Westlake' in 'Andrews, Marian (nee Hare; pseud. Christopher Hare, 1839-1929,' *Oxford Dictionary of National Biography*, doi-https://doi.org/10.1093/odnb/9780198614128.013.59077.

Owen, J., 2008, 'Triangular Contests and the Caucus Rhetoric at the 1885 General Election,' *Parliamentary History, 27 (2)*: 215–235, doi: https://doi.org/10.1111/ j.1750-0206.2008.00037.x.

Packe, M. S., 1954, *The Life of John Stuart* Mill, London, Secker and Warburg.

Parry, J. P., 2006, *The Politics of Patriotism: English Liberalism, National Identity and Europe, 1830–1886.* Cambridge: Cambridge University Press. DOI: https://doi. org/10.1017/CBO9780511495984.

Pelling, H., 1967, *Social Geography of British Elections 1885–1910*, London: Macmillan.

Persky, J., 2016, *The Political Economy of Progress: John Stuart Mill and Modern Radicalism*, New York: Oxford University Press.

Pugh, Martin, 'The Liberal Party and Women's Suffrage 1866-1918,' *Journal of Liberal History, no 67, Spring* 2009: 17-22.

Purvis, June, 1991, *A History of Women's Education in England (Gender and Education Series)*, Milton Keynes, Open University Press.

Rendall, Jane, 'Who was Lily Maxwell,' in Purvis, June & Holton, Sandra (eds.), *Votes for Women*, London, 2000: Chapter 3.

Robson, Ann, 'Helen Taylor and John Stuart Mill: Travels with a Donkey,' *Queen's Quarterly, 101, no* 2, *1994*: 319–343

Rowbotham, Sheila, 2009, *Edward Carpenter, A Life of Liberty and Love*, London, Verso.

Ryan, Alan, 2011, 'J.S. Mill on Education,' *Oxford Review of Education*, 2011, 37:5: 653- 667.

Sanders, Lisa Sapiro, 2015, '"Equal Laws based upon an Equal Standard": The Garrett Sisters, the Contagious Diseases Acts, and the Sexual Politics of Victorian and Edwardian Feminism Revisited,' *Women's History Review* 24, no. 3, 2015: 389-409.

Saxton, Alexander, 1971, *The Indispensable Enemy: Labour and the Anti-Chinese Movement in California*, Berkeley, University of California Press.

Smith, Janet., 2020, 'Crossing the Border of Citizenship: Helen Taylor, the Independent Radical Democrat Candidate for Camberwell North, 1885,' *Open Library of Humanities, 6(2): 19*: 1–38. DOI: https://doi. org/10.16995/olh.540.

Smith, Janet, 2023, 'Feminism and Women's Rights in Great Britain and Ireland: Tracking Developments and Debates through the Case of Helen Taylor,' Moland, Lydia, Stone, Alison Laura (eds), *The Oxford Handbook of American and British Women Philosophers in the Nineteenth Century,* Oxford, Oxford University Press (online edn., Oxford Academic, 18 July 2023), https://doi.org/10.1093/ oxfordhb/9780197558898.013.42.

Smith, Janet, (forthcoming) '§25: Feminism and the Rights of Women UK,' in Jensen, Kipton & Keefe, Jenny (eds.), *Grundriss der Geschichte der Philosophie: Nineteenth Century British and American Philosophy* (Schwabe Verlag)

Smith, Janet, 2019, 'First Woman Parliamentary Candidate, Helen Taylor 1885,' in Rackley, E. & Auchmuty, R. (eds.), *Women's Legal Landmarks*, Oxford, Hart: Chapter 9.

Smith, Janet, 2016, 'Helen Taylor's anti-imperialist feminism: Ireland and the Land League Question.' *Women's History*, 2 (4): 19–24.

Smith, Janet & Morris Stern, Claire, 2017, Helen Taylor becomes Miss Trevor, actress, *Theatre Notebook, vol 71, no. 1*: 21-43.

Smith, Janet, 2017, 'Helen Taylor's work for land nationalisation in Great Britain and Ireland, 1879–1907.' *Women's History Review*, 25 (5): 778–798. DOI: https://doi. org/10.1080/09612025.2017.1366968.

Smith, Janet, 2018, '"She fought for the people," Helen Taylor's work for the advancement of socialism and feminism on the London School Board, 1876–85.' *The Independent Scholar*, 4: 4–20.

Smith, Janet, 2014, *The Feminism and Political Radicalism of Helen Taylor in Victorian Britain and Ireland*, unpublished PhD, London Metropolitan University.

Solow, Barbara, 1971, *The Land Question and the Irish Economy 1870-1903*, Cambridge, Harvard University Press.

Stone, Alison, 2022, *Frances Power Cobbe*, Cambridge, Cambridge University Press.

Turnbull, A. M., 'Learning her womanly work. The Elementary School Curriculum 1870 –1914,' in Hunt, F. (ed.), 1987, *Lessons For Life, The Schooling of Girls and Women 1850*- 1950, Oxford, Wiley-Blackwell: 83-100.

Vogel, Ursula, 'The Land Question: A Liberal Theory of Communal Property,' *History Workshop Journal, vol 27, 1989*: 106-135.

Ward, Margaret, 'Gendering the Union: Imperial Feminism and the Ladies' Land League,' *Women's History Review, vol 10, no 1, 2001*: 71 – 92.

Ware, Vron, 1992, *Beyond the Pale, White Women, Racism and History*, London, Verso.

Watmough, P. A., 'Membership of the Social Democratic Federation 1885-1902,' *Bulletin - Labour History, vol 34,* 1977: 345-40

Wilkins, M. S., 'The Non-Socialist Origins of England's First Important Socialist Organisation,' *International Review of Social History, vol 4, 1959*: 199-207.

Windscheffel, A, 2007, *Popular Conservatism in Imperial London, 1868–1906*, London: Royal Historical Society.

Wolfe, Willard, 1975, *From Radicalism to Socialism: men and ideas in the formation of Fabian Socialist doctrines, 1881 – 1889*, New Haven, Yale University Press.

Worzala, Diane, 1974, *The Langham Place Circle*, Wisconsin, University of Wisconsin-Madison Press.

Wright, Margaret, 2011, *Elizabeth Wolstenholme Elmy and the Victorian Feminist Movement*, Manchester, Manchester University Press.

INDEX